The Struggle of Hungarian Lutherans
under Communism

Eugenia and Hugh M. Stewart '26 Series on Eastern Europe
Stjepan Meštrović, General Editor
Series Editorial Board
Norman Cigar
Bronislaw Misztal
Sabrina P. Ramet
Vladimir Shlapentokh
Keith Tester

The Struggle of Hungarian Lutherans under Communism

H. David Baer
Foreword by László G. Terray

Texas A&M University Press
College Station

To my father
To my grandfather

"Therefore, since we are surrounded by so great a cloud of witnesses,
let us also lay aside every weight, and sin which clings so closely,
and let us run with perseverance the race that is set before us"
—HEBREWS 12:1

Copyright © 2006 by Helmut David Baer
Manufactured in the United States of America
All rights reserved
Second Printing, 2013
The paper used in this book meets the minimum requirements
of the American National Standard for Permanence
of Paper for Printed Library Materials, Z39.48-1984.
Binding materials have been chosen for durability.
∞

Library of Congress Cataloging-in-Publication Data

Baer, H. David (Helmut David), 1968–
    The struggle of Hungarian Lutherans under communism / H. David Baer ;
    foreword by László G. Terray.— 1st ed.
        p. cm. — (Eugenia and Hugh M. Stewart '26 series on Eastern Europe)
    Includes bibliographical references (p.   ) and index.

    1. Lutheran Church—Hungary—History—20th century. 2. Lutherans—Hungary—History—20th century. 3. Church and state—Hungary—History—20th century. 4. Communism and Christianity—Hungary—History—20th century. 5. Hungary—Church history—20th century. I. Title. II. Series.
    BX8025.3.B34   2006
    284.1′43909045—dc22
                                                                    2005025901

ISBN 13: 978-1-58544-480-9 (cloth)
ISBN 13: 978-1-60344-990-8 (paper)
ISBN 13: 978-1-60344-560-3 (ebook)

Contents

ix	*Foreword*, by László G. Terray
3	*Preface*
9	*Chapter One.* Dealing with Dictators: Fundamental Choices in the Lutheran Church in Hungary, 1945–49
27	*Theological Excursus One.* The Compromise Type: In Search of a Modus Vivendi, *Ahogy Lehet*
39	*Chapter Two.* Working with Dictators: Totalitarianism and the Choices of Desperation, 1949–56
46	*Theological Excursus Two.* The Collaboration Type: Removing Choices and Affirming Socialism (or *Ahogy Lehet* Gone Bad)
62	*Chapter Three.* An Understanding with Dictators: Hopes for a New Beginning, 1956–58
76	*Theological Excursus Three.* The Witness Type: A Readiness for Martyrdom, a Challenge to *Ahogy Lehet*
91	*Chapter Four.* Service to Dictators: The Church for the Building of Socialism, 1958–87
110	*Theological Excursus Four.* The Diaconia Type: Between Service and Subordination (or *Ahogy Lehet* Revisited)
123	*Conclusion:* The End of an Unresolved Argument
134	*Notes*
151	*Bibliographic Essay*
159	*Index*

Foreword
László G. Terray

Few studies exist that examine the smaller "minority churches" of Eastern Europe. Yet these churches have, throughout the centuries and under changing conditions, nobly represented basic Christian values in thought, belief, and way of living. Among those churches, some have roots in Martin Luther's sixteenth century Reformation. Lajos Ordass, bishop of the Evangelical-Lutheran Church in Hungary, became known throughout the Christian world when in 1948 Hungary's communists sentenced him to prison on trumped-up charges of foreign currency manipulation. Although he was rehabilitated eight years later and allowed to return to his office, he was removed again by the communists in 1958. After bravely resisting both Nazism and communism, Bishop Ordass was forced to live out the remaining twenty years of his life in isolation and loneliness.

The ways of arranging one's relationship to the totalitarian system of Marxist-Soviet socialism varied in Eastern European churches from country to country and period to period. The attitudes of the communist parties toward the churches also moved along a broad spectrum, ranging from brutal oppression to aggressive persuasion, when parties would swarm around the churches and offer advantages in exchange for cooperation in "building socialism." From among a conglomerate of attitudes, beliefs, and theologies, the author of this book investigates the different ways the Evangelical-Lutheran Church in Hungary related to the communist state.

Helmut David Baer learned the very difficult Hungarian language and stayed long enough in Hungary to make use of the language in interviews with contemporary witnesses and to conduct research in Budapest archives. He succeeded in finding documents of great value and relevance that had been unknown and that were a surprise even to Hungarian researchers. By analyzing these materials and working also with published Hungarian sources, Baer has been able to identify the main types of Lutheran response to, and ways of thinking about, the power-wielding communist party. At the same time, when writing about these various attitudes and theological positions, Baer manages to portray historical figures as living personalities struggling to find a way to live in communism that is compatible with their Christian belief and ethical standards.

It is a pleasure for me to recommend this book as a substantial contribution to the consideration of the complex problems that arise whenever a Christian church is forced to confront dictatorship.

The Struggle of Hungarian Lutherans
under Communism

Preface

The memory of communism may be fading for some, but its legacy remains hard and real in Eastern Europe. The shadow of that era, receding but slowly, extends over still the many spheres of life, both public and private, that define a culture and make a people. Communism denied whole nations political liberty and economic prosperity. It also distorted the soul. It summoned each person to collaborate in the building of socialism and thus threatened individual integrity. Not only did the people of Eastern Europe have to live under communism, they had to come to terms with it, too. Their successes and failures in doing that are part of communism's moral bequest. They are also the subject of this book.

The moral challenge of living in communism was perhaps nowhere more poignant than in the churches. Communist doctrine declared that religion would someday disappear, and communist practice worked to bring it about. Far worse than official atheism for the churches was communism's totalitarian claim on society, its vision of an all-embracing socialism that allowed no place for independent institutions and associations. At no point during the roughly forty-five years of communist rule in Eastern Europe did the regimes abandon the long-term goal of eliminating religion. This was true even in later decades, when most communist states worked out a mode of peaceful coexistence with the churches. The terms of that peace dictated social space for the churches so narrowly restricted that, had communism endured another century, organized religion in Eastern Europe might well have ceased to be. The attitude of the state was inherently adversarial; thus, people in the churches, when seeking to come to terms with communism, confronted situations with choices that cut at their deepest commitments.

The story of the Lutheran Church in Hungary during communism is about such difficult choices. Disagreement over the character of those choices is the source of a profound division within that church today. On the one hand are those who say the church betrayed its divine commission by collaborating with the communists in the stifling of religion; on the other hand are those who say that, given the limits of totalitarian dictatorship, the church struck necessary compromises with the regime in order to survive until communism collapsed. This sharp disagreement among Hungarian Lutherans reflects their effort to appropriate the moral legacy of the past. Although painful and difficult, such work needs to be done, because the place the church fills in Hungary today will be shaped by the parts of the past it chooses to carry into the future.

Nevertheless, appropriation depends on interpretation, and sometimes the best way to interpret an era is by first listening carefully to the contour of arguments that define it. The pattern of those arguments may give expression to historical forces larger than the individual protagonists. No one in the history we are considering brought communism to Hungary, and yet communism was the intractable reality that determined each of their choices. The shape of those choices and the differences between them reveal something about the possibilities for living as a Christian in communism. I would like to describe those possibilities. The reader can liken my task to that of a cartographer seeking to mark out roads and obstacles in Hungary between 1945 and 1989, so that future travelers, arriving to this lost world, will see it correctly. If I do the job well, then I will have placed each position that appeared in the Lutheran Church in Hungary during communism on the right spot on the map, and those who come after me, even when disagreeing with my evaluation of particular characters and arguments, will have to acknowledge that I got the landscape right, that the possibilities and positions were as I describe them.

My central concern with the contour of argument means, also, that this book should not be considered first as a work of history. It is a study of moral argument and the way moral argument emerges from, and is related to, historical location. In embarking on this study I took my bearings from a tradition of academic inquiry represented in its prime by H. Richard Niebuhr, in books such as *Christ and Culture*, *The Social Sources of Denominationalism*, and *The Kingdom of God in America*. Niebuhr was a theologian, but one who understood that religious faith was socially embodied and that, therefore, the choices made by Christian churches in particular times and places could be understood fully only within the context of the interaction between faith and history. This holds true for the present work. My primary concern is with the theological arguments developed in Hungary's Lutheran Church in response to communist dictatorship. Those arguments, while theological, were tied to concrete choices and were determined in important ways by the historical possibilities. Thus, as a study in moral argument, this book is defined by history in a special way. It wrestles with issues that arise from a specific social and historical situation. It focuses on a complex of questions and answers that emerge from the nexus of faith and history.

In my effort to identify the different Hungarian Lutheran responses to communism, I was led to compose what might be called "ideal-types." These ideal-types are synthetic constructs intended to group together common patterns of thought. Many arguments advanced by the protagonists had an occasional character about them; they were put forth in response to particular occasions and then lost in the flow of events. To make moral sense of the story, I needed to piece those arguments together, identifying their common threads and integrating them into synthetic wholes, or ideal-types. That, of course, required a degree of abstraction; it meant discerning connections and evaluating them in ways not necessarily apparent to the historical actors themselves. In treating the subjects of the story this way, however, I have endeavored to be faithful to their experience by working inductively from the narrative. I have tried to allow my Hungarian protagonists to determine the questions and categories relevant to a moral analysis of their own history, and the types I construct are intended as distilled but still accurate descriptions of the actual strategies used by Hungarian Lutherans in responding to communist dictatorship.

My inductive typological approach has shaped, also, the way I have chosen to present the material. The book alternates between chapters and theological excursuses, which together are intended to illustrate the interplay between history and moral argument. Each chapter relates part of the story of the Lutheran Church in Hungary during communism, pointing to issues as they arise, thereby allowing the relevant complex of questions and answers to emerge as patterns in the history. Once enough of the story has been told to identify the contours of a distinct strategy, I step out of the narrative to consider that strategy individually in a theological excursus. Each excursus presents an ideal-type, describing and evaluating it in light of the theological and historical factors that shaped it. After discussion of the type is complete, I return to the narrative, picking up where I left off in the earlier chapter. This alternating sequence of chapter and excursus continues until the entire history is told and each type considered. Then, in the concluding chapter, I review the history and offer a complete moral interpretation of the history of the Lutheran Church in Hungary during communism.

In that history four ideal-typical strategies appeared for dealing with communism, which I call compromise, collaboration, witness, and *diaconia* (or service). Each of these strategies, although distinct, was a response to the same underlying historical problematic. The Lutheran Church in Hungary confronted a hostile political regime that threatened its long-term existence. Confronted with this threat, Hungarian Lutherans asked themselves two central questions, "how can we survive?" and "how can we be church?" The tension and interplay between these two questions defined the moral contours of the Lutheran experience in Hungarian communism and shaped the response of the Lutheran Church to the communist state. Many Hungarian Lutherans, drawing inspiration from their theological heritage as well as from distinctive themes in Hungarian history, argued that the church could do whatever was necessary to survive so long as it did not compromise the essence of its ministry. Other Hungarian Lutherans, however, appealing to the witness of Bishop Lajos Ordass, rejected survival as a legitimate focus of the church's concern, and argued that the church must uncompromisingly witness to the truth even if that meant ecclesiological extinction. The story of the Lutheran Church in Hungary, therefore, is the story of an argument about how much responsibility Christians have for the survival and well-being of the church, as well as an argument about the proper Christian attitude toward an oppressive state. Each type articulates a strategy for dealing with political oppression, but the shape of each typical strategy grows out of deeper judgments concerning the question of survival.

Naturally, the texture of the argument will become fuller by telling the history. Perhaps, then, the time has come to tell it. The story is a true one; the questions posed were posed by history itself, and the answers given determined the fates of real people. To understand the history truly, one must understand the experience of those who lived through it and struggled with its challenges. Unfortunately, the realness of that experience can get lost in the examination of it. Let me appeal, therefore, to the reader's imagination and empathy as I try to tell how it was to be a Lutheran in Hungary under communism.

The debts I have accumulated in the course of researching and writing this book are huge. I wish to acknowledge receipt of a Fulbright Fellowship and a Kellogg Institute for International Studies Dissertation Fellowship from the University of Notre Dame, both of which enabled me to carry out my research over the extended period of time that proved necessary. Additionally, I am grateful to the National Lutheran Archives in Hungary (Evangélikus Országos Levéltár) and the National Hungarian Archives (Magyar Országos Levéltár) for allowing me access to documents that constituted an integral part of my research. More personally, I wish to thank Jean Porter, the director of what was originally my doctoral dissertation, for granting me the freedom to plunge into what by most accounts was an unorthodox project and for consistently believing in and defending that freedom. I wish to express my indebtedness to the late John Howard Yoder for first introducing me to Ernst Troeltsch and for helping to conceptualize this project. I wish to thank Gilbert Meilaender for a single suggestion, of singular importance, at a critical moment in the composition of the manuscript. I wish to thank the people of the Lutheran Theological University in Budapest, particularly the dean, András Reuss, for kindly receiving me and generously providing me with my own office in which I conducted the bulk of my research. I wish to thank Enikő Böröcz of the National Lutheran Archives for energetically digging up the documents I requested and for helping in countless other ways. I wish to thank László Terray for providing me with documents from the Ordass Archives in Oslo and for reading numerous drafts of this manuscript and taking the time to make detailed and constructive comments on each of them. Lastly, I wish to thank my wife, not only for being my wife, but for helping me to learn Hungarian and for introducing me to Hungary.

CHAPTER ONE

Dealing with Dictators

*Fundamental Choices
in the Lutheran Church in Hungary, 1945–49*

> Oh my people, your leaders mislead you,
> and confuse the course of your paths.
> —ISAIAH 3:12

World War II ended for Hungary early in April 1945, when Russian troops drove out the last of the occupying German army. For the second time in the twentieth century, as so many times in its history, this small nation-state, roughly the size of Indiana, had become a theater for greater powers to resolve their greater interests. Approximately 115,000 Hungarian soldiers died in service of those greater interests—but, considering the numbers, Hungarian civilians may not have been better off. Within the borders of present-day Hungary, approximately 80,000 civilians died. Somewhere between 400,000 to 600,000 Jews and 50,000 gypsies had been deported, then killed in Nazi concentration camps. From Sub-Carpathia (Ukraine), 80,000 Hungarians were deported, and 20,000 of them were killed. In the southern Bachka region (now part of Yugoslavia), 40,000 Hungarians were killed. In Transylvania, although there are no official figures, certainly thousands of civilians died. Another 200,000 Hungarian prisoners of war, not all of them soldiers, died in Soviet prison camps. Totaled, more than 900,000 Hungarians died in the Second World War, which, counting roughly, was about 8 percent of all Hungarians living in Europe.

The war also caused tremendous material damage. As a consequence of battles and looting, Hungary's national income in 1945 shrunk 40 percent. Between 45 and 60 percent of Hungarian livestock was decimated, 90 percent of factories were seriously damaged, and 40 percent of railway lines and 70 percent of railway cars were destroyed. In Budapest 30,000 apartments were destroyed or rendered uninhabitable, and another 48,000 were seriously damaged. The city, including its famous bridges, the hotels along the Danube, and the Buda Castle, was in ruins.[1]

Standing among the rubble after the war, Hungarians must have been uncertain about the future. "Old Hungary"—the thousand-year monarchy, the centuries of Habsburg rule, the semifeudal and aristocratic society—lay in ruins together with the buildings and had been lost like the dead. Certainly many realized that Hungary was standing on the threshold of tremendous changes, changes so great as to be properly compared only with a handful of major turning points in Hungarian history. To appreciate the changes to come, however, one must know a little bit about the "Old Hungary."

"Old Hungary" and the Lutheran Church

For Hungarians, the period in history which lies between the two world wars is known as the Horthy era. It takes its name from Miklós Horthy, who had distinguished himself as an admiral in the Austro-Hungarian navy during World War I. Indeed it was Horthy's prestige as a war hero, rather than any sort of political acumen, that secured for him the position of Hungary's head of state. Horthy's official title was regent. Historically the regent had exercised the powers of the king in the king's absence until his return. Thus, Horthy was regent for the king—only Hungary had no king. Neither did Austria for that matter; it had become a republic in 1918. The Habsburg monarchy, which had ruled in Austria and Hungary for centuries, no longer existed. Horthy's title was an attempt to express continuity with Hungary's thousand-year monarchy, and Hungary in the Horthy period was technically a monarchy. It was a monarchy without a king, governed by a temporary regent whose position was permanent.

Sometimes Horthy and the political system over which he presided have been portrayed as fascist. That portrayal is inaccurate.[2] Horthy, who had spent a good portion of his life in the court of the Austro-Hungarian Emperor Franz Joseph, had the predilections of a constitutional monarch. Given the peculiarities of interwar Hungary, however, those predilections could manifest themselves in strange ways. Rather than fascist, the Horthy regime should be understood as oddly authoritarian.

Horthy assumed the post of regent after a period of extended political instability in Hungary. At the end of World War I, as the Austro-Hungarian monarchy crumbled, Hungarians were left to search for a new form of government. In March 1919, after a desperate attempt to introduce liberal democracy in Hungary had failed, a communist named Béla Kun seized power. Kun had close ties with the Soviet Union, and he managed to establish the first communist dictatorship in Europe outside Russia. The Republic of Councils, as it was called, both embarked on hopeless military campaigns and employed brutal force at home against the Hungarians. After 131 days, it collapsed and was replaced by Horthy's regency. This brief experience of communist rule was so traumatic for Hungarians that in the Horthy era almost every proposal for social reform was viewed with suspicion and conflated with communism. The Horthy regime was fiercely anticommunist, antiliberal, and antireform. Thus, rather than implementing much-needed policies of modernization, Horthy and his supporters clung stubbornly to their vision of "Old Hungary"—a semifeudal, authoritarian, neo-baroque society.

Hungary's historical churches, however, flourished in the Horthy period. Horthy turned to the churches for legitimation, and, responding, the churches filled a role in Hungary's political and civil spheres more significant than that of the preceding era.[3] Their importance was reflected in part by the regime's self-description as *Christian* and *national*, two words intended to designate the governing ideals of Hungarian society. What these words meant precisely was not altogether clear. They meant different things at different times, but basically, they idealized a conservative social and political order. *Christian* designated the responsibility of the ruling classes before God but also connoted the special social and political privileges that usually accompany such responsibility. *National* evoked the authority of distinctive Hungarian traditions but did not necessarily distinguish between the bad and the good, the archaic and the living. *Christian-national* could, on more ugly occasions, be contrasted with *Jewish-foreign*. This was especially so when defining the Horthy regime's fierce opposition to communism. In Hungary as in many places, communism was portrayed occasionally as some kind of Jewish conspiracy.

Many churches in Horthy's Hungary enjoyed social and political privileges that might be characterized with the term *establishment*. Legally established (in Hungarian, *bevett* or "accepted") churches received substantial state subsidy. Their highest officeholders (for example, bishops) held seats in the upper house of parliament, and middle-level church representatives often held important positions in local government.[4] Membership in established churches was recognized by the state and determined at birth, so that a child legally belonged to the religious denomination of his or her parents and was required to attend religious education class in school. Adult church members were required to pay a church tax, levied by the churches and, if necessary, collected by the state.

Most, but not all, of Hungary's churches were legally "accepted." These were the Roman Catholic Church (constituting 65 percent of the population) and the Greek-Catholic Church (2 percent of the population), the Reformed Church (21 percent of the population), the Lutheran Church (6 percent of the population), the Orthodox Church (.5 percent of the population), the Unitarian Church (.1 percent of the population), and until 1941 the Israelite Denomination (the legal name for the Jewish religious community—5 percent of the population).[5] The Lutheran Church, although significantly smaller than the Roman Catholic and Reformed churches, was the third largest church in Hungary and possessed a proud and distinguished heritage.

A particularly important dimension of church life in the Horthy period was parochial education. In the interwar years, somewhere between

60 to 70 percent of schools were operated by the churches. Furthermore, 75 to 80 percent of teacher-training institutions were operated by the churches, which meant that the overwhelming percentage of Hungarian teachers were trained in religious institutions.[6] Parochial schools had been an integral part of Hungarian Protestantism since the beginning days of the Reformation. Virtually every village parish had an elementary school, while parochial high schools were located in cities. Many of the church schools were highly distinguished. The prestigious Lutheran Fasor Gymnasium, for example, educated a number of future Nobel Prize winners.

In the Lutheran Church during the Horthy period, religious life stretched out along two identifiable currents. One might be called "evangelist" or "pietist," the other "churchly" or, perhaps, "confessional." The evangelization wing was centered in the northwestern Hungarian town of Győr, where the greatest Lutheran evangelists originated or worked. The churchly trend was strongest in Budapest — perhaps because Budapest was where the general church was seated, and in Budapest the institutional characteristics of the church were most prominent.

The Hungarian connection with pietism was wide and deep, extending back to pietism's beginnings in the seventeenth century.[7] One striking expression of the way that pietism had taken hold in Hungary by the Horthy period were well-institutionalized "home mission" programs. Frequently home mission was carried out by means of "evangelization weeks." For Americans, these "evangelization weeks" should perhaps be understood as revivals, although as revivals they had distinctive features. First, they were evangelizations within already established congregations. Since everyone in Hungary belonged by law to a particular denomination, and since conversion from one denomination to another was a legally cumbersome endeavor, home mission meant mission to those who were already Christian and, indeed, to those who already belonged to one's own denomination. Thus, the purpose of evangelization weeks was not to win new converts but to deepen the faith of those who were already, at least nominally, Christian — or more precisely in this case, Lutheran. A second distinctive feature of these Hungarian evangelizations was the way they were sponsored by the ecclesiastical church. Dioceses had their own "mission pastors" who were commissioned to travel through the country and, collaborating with parish pastors, would visit congregations to hold evangelization weeks.

Evangelization weeks, however, were only part of a much broader evangelical or pietist movement that shaped Hungarian Protestantism in the early twentieth century. By the time of Horthy's regency, evangelical movements had produced hosts of voluntary associations dedicated both to deepening the faith and to social work. There was, for example, a Protestant hospital and a National Protestant Orphans Association. Another notable association was the Phoebe Lutheran Diaconess Association, a women's monastic order, which at its peak had more than one hundred members. Members took vows of poverty and chastity, and dedicated themselves to various kinds of charity work. Numerous student associations were founded as well. A Hungarian branch of the YMCA was established in 1883. Soon there were similar, native Hungarian student organizations, such as the Hungarian Evangelical Christian Student Federation and the National Hungarian Protestant Student Federation.[8]

All of these organizations—and the list is hardly exhaustive—had a genuine ecumenical character about them. Indeed the student organizations were explicitly ecumenical in their mission. Even diaconical institutions like the Phoebe association were denominationally flexible and focused on the inner life of faith rather than confessional differences. Moreover, these institutions enjoyed a fair degree of autonomy from the institutional church. For the most part they were not subordinated to, and in fact they often had no official connection with, the ecclesiastical churches.

Alongside and sometimes intertwined with evangelical life in the Lutheran Church was the churchly trend. It expressed itself partly through renewed interest in Luther and the Lutheran tradition. Various organizations, such as the Luther Association and the National Luther Federation, committed themselves to strengthening Lutheran identity. Efforts were made to translate the works of Luther into Hungarian. Interestingly, however, this churchly trend does not appear to have existed in tension with the evangelical movement. Hungarian Lutherans in the Horthy period were interested in their confessional identity, and many were loyal to their churches, but there does not appear to have been a Lutheran confessional movement self-consciously delineating itself in opposition to other theological movements or trends. Certainly the confessional movement did not exist in opposition to the evangelization movement. Sometimes, even, a Hungarian pietist was also a passionate "churchman."

In 1945 the Lutheran Church in Hungary was comprised of four dioceses, called the Dunántúl, the Dunáninnen, the Tisza, and the Bánya. Each diocese had its own bishop as well as a nonclerical "inspector." The place of nonclerical officeholders in the Lutheran Church in Hungary is one of the distinctive features of its polity. Authority and administration in the church rests in the hands not only of ordained clergy but also of non-ordained "inspectors," who are elected from the congregations. Historically these inspectors were members of the nobility, and their purpose was to protect the church from government persecution. As a consequence, in 1945 the highest authority in the Lutheran Church rested not in a bishop but in the secular office of General Inspector of Church and School. Second to the general inspector in authority was the senior ranking bishop, the bishop who had held office longest. In 1945 the General Inspector of the Church and School was Baron Albert Radvánsky. The senior bishop was Béla Kapi of Dunántúl. Zoltán Túróczy was bishop of the Tisza diocese, and in the Bánya diocese was Lajos Ordass. These last two bishops are of particular importance to the history that follows.

Zoltán Túróczy was born in 1893 in Árnot, a town located in the northern part of present-day Hungary. His father was a pastor, and his grandfather had been bishop. Growing up, the young Túróczy attended the Lutheran parochial schools near his birthplace, then traveled to the Lutheran seminary in Pozsony (today Bratislava, Slovakia) and was ordained in 1915. He was a pious man with a rigorist disposition and a strong affinity for evangelism. Once he traveled to Finland, where he was affected by his encounter with Finnish revivalism. As a young man he belonged to the Hungarian Evangelical Christian Student Association, an evangelically and ecumenically minded organization. Not long after his ordination, Túróczy was given a pastorate in the city of Győr, a location congenial to him because it was a thriving center for Lutheran evangelism. Over time a special relationship developed between the man and the city. Pastor Túróczy distinguished himself as a preacher. In fact many considered him the greatest preacher of his generation. Túróczy rose to prominence. Indeed, few men in the Lutheran Church in Hungary have been more revered and loved than Zoltán Túróczy. In 1939 he was elected bishop.[9]

Lajos Ordass was born in 1901 in the village of Torzsa, which lay in the southern part of the Hungarian Kingdom that was transferred to Yugoslavia at the end of the First World War.[10] Ordass is an archaic Hungarian word for wolf, and Wolf was the name of his parents, who were ethnic Germans. When the Nazis occupied Hungary in 1944 Lajos changed his name to Ordass, but when he was a child he had spoken German at home. In Torzsa, Ordass's father worked as teacher and organist for the Lutheran congregation. As befits the son of a schoolmaster, young Lajos was a diligent student—so much so that at the age of eleven he was offered a scholarship to attend a gymnasium in Hermannstadt, which was a "Saxon" city in Transylvania (today it is called Sibiu and can be found in Romania; its Hungarian name is Nagyszeben). Centuries earlier, ethnic Germans had migrated from Saxony to Transylvania, where they established prosperous cities. The Transylvanian Saxons were unique, fiercely independent, and protective of their cultural identity. When Ordass's father learned of the offer from Hermannstadt, he told his son, "Ich lass' aus dir keinen Pangerman machen, mein Kind—I will not have them make a pan-German out of you, my child," and that was the end of it.[11] Ordass went instead to a church school in central Hungary. When World War I ended and Torzsa and the surrounding area became Yugoslavian, Ordass was still studying in

Hungary. He could not return home, nor were letters or packages permitted across the border. For the next five years Ordass had no contact with his family. Alone in Hungary, one kind of war's many orphans, he found a second home and a foster parent in the church. In 1920 Ordass went to Budapest to study at seminary, and in 1924 he was ordained.

Unlike Bishop Túróczy, Ordass was not a prominent personality in the church when he became bishop. In fact he had attracted broad public notice only a short time before his election. Ordass worked as a pastor in Budapest during the Second World War, which placed him near the church's central administration and gave him greater exposure to the issues then confronting the church leadership. One of these was the so-called German question. Within the Lutheran Church in Hungary, some ethnic Germans were clamoring for the creation of an independent German diocese, which in turn would have close connections with the Volksbund, a pan-German cultural organization that connected Germans throughout Europe to the Third Reich. The Hungarian German Lutherans made their demands public by publishing a "Memorandum on the Solution of Burning Questions for the German Congregations." The church leadership preferred to avoid the issue and delay any decision, knowing that the outcome of the war would effect a solution. This approach dissatisfied Pastor Ordass—still known then as Pastor Wolf—who wanted direct confrontation with the pan-Germans, believing this would expose them as having little popular support. On his own initiative, therefore, Ordass wrote a lengthy refutation of the demands set out in the "Memorandum" and, out of his own pocket, had it published and distributed in the church.[12]

Through this and other bold demonstrations of his anti-German convictions, Ordass began to attract attention in the church. Consequently when the sick and elderly Bishop Sándor Raffay announced his retirement at war's end, there may have been a shared perception that Lajos Ordass was particularly suited to represent Hungary's Lutheran Church abroad and before Western ecumenical leaders. Credible representation would be important for a church in a small, defeated country that had been allied with Hitler. Moreover, Ordass knew some seven foreign languages and had close contacts in the Scandinavian churches.[13] In September 1945 he was installed as bishop of the Bánya diocese, which was seated in Budapest.

In crucial respects Bishop Túróczy and Bishop Ordass represented the two currents, evangelical and churchly, that comprised Hungarian Lutheran church life. Túróczy was a great evangelizer, shaped by years of experience in the evangelizing city of Győr. Ordass was from Budapest and a man of the church in a near-literal sense—the church had reared him when he was separated from his family. Photographs of Bishop Túróczy show a balding, elderly man with round steel-rimmed glasses and a thin, tight little mustache. He is Túróczy the well-established evangelizer, who may or may not understand the self-righteousness which is the temptation of every great preacher and pietist. Photographs of Bishop Ordass show a face, stern and drawn, with Germanic discipline and the clear, purposeful eyes of a man of conviction. In fact, Ordass is unique among persons in this history in that even his pictures are striking. He must have been charismatic, hinting at, perhaps, a kind of greatness. Only among the early generation of reformers in Hungary can one find a figure who stamped his church as much as Ordass was to.

The Rise of Dictatorship: The Lutheran Church Confronts Salami Tactics

Although the Soviets occupied Hungary in 1945, they did not immediately introduce themselves as totalitarian dictators. Dictatorship appeared unambiguously only in 1947—known to Hungarian historians as the "year of the turn." In that year Hungary turned from "bourgeoisie democracy" to "people's democracy." The turn itself, of course, was not too democratic. It was the achievement of what Hungary's Stalinist dictator, Mátyás Rákosi, called "salami tactics." Salami tactics expressed the principle of "divide and conquer" in the colorful imagery of Rákosi's imagination. The communists sliced up their enemies like pieces of salami and disposed of them.

In the first years after the war, however, the course on which Hungary was set was yet contested, and political leaders and public personages were vying to define it. From early on there were battles to be fought, even for Hungary's little Lutheran Church. In May 1945, Bishop Túróczy was arrested and tried before a so-called "people's court." Such trials were a common feature of postwar Hungarian life. The provisional government had erected special people's courts to prosecute individuals guilty of nefarious political activity in the Horthy period. Putatively, the people's courts worked to weed out undesirable elements from public life, such as war criminals and fascists; in truth, they were little more than a tool for the realization of political interests, particularly those of the communists. Between 1945 and 1950 close to 60,000 people were tried by these special courts, 27,000 convicted, and 189 sentenced to death.[14]

Why Bishop Túróczy caught the attention of the people's court in Nyíregyháza, the seat of his diocese, is not known. He probably had conservative political dispositions, although he was not a figure prominent for his political views. In the past he had expressed anticommunist and anti-Soviet sentiments, and, although this was no special distinction in Horthy's time, perhaps it was why he was convicted by a people's court on charges of inciting to war against the Soviet Union and subsequently sentenced to ten years in prison.[15]

The Lutheran Church was stunned by Túróczy's conviction; the church leadership petitioned to have it overturned. Their efforts met with little success, however, and in failure they encountered a quandary. The government approached Túróczy early in his imprisonment to present him with an option: he could resign and be freed immediately, or he could stay in prison and stay a bishop. This was a difficult choice: ten years is a long time; the church certainly knew of men capable of succeeding Túróczy; and, moreover, Túróczy was in poor health. On the other hand, could a leader of the church resign under duress? Túróczy was uncertain and sent word to the bishops, who took up the matter at a meeting on October 29, 1945. Béla Kapi, the senior ranking bishop, reasoned that in light of his poor health and the long prison sentence, Túróczy should resign. Everyone agreed except Bishop Ordass, who, speaking to the matter last, argued that if Túróczy resigned he would implicitly admit the truth of the charges against him. "God might have need, in the interests of the church, for Túróczy to die in prison," Ordass argued; "Do we have the freedom to advise him to ask to be released when the price is his resignation?"[16] The impact of Ordass's words was so great that the bishops reversed themselves. They sent a message to Túróczy advising against resignation, although they placed the final decision in Túróczy's hands.[17]

Túróczy did not resign, and, as it happened, he did not have to spend ten years in prison either. Through its intercessions with the government, the church leadership obtained his release in February 1946. However, Ordass's stern stance at the 1945 bishops conference later extended into the common consciousness of the Lutheran Church, helping to define a fundamental moral argument about how the church should respond to dictatorship. That moral argument sharpened considerably in the "year of the turn."

In 1948 the Lutheran Church elected a new bishop, József Szabó. Szabó was another figure steeped in the tradition of Hungarian evangelism. He had served for a while as an assistant pastor in Győr, where he came into contact and worked with Zoltán Túróczy and where the two men became friends. Szabó's installation ceremony took place on March 18, 1948. Besides church members, a representative of the government named Ernő Mihályfi also attended. In an unplanned event, Mihályfi delivered a speech in which he accused the church of harboring "political reaction," a blanket charge used by the communists to eliminate their enemies. In the events leading up to the turn, the communists diligently ferreted out of public life all "reactionaries," thereby ensuring Hungary's move to "people's democracy." Thus Mihályfi's speech was a rude political attack that marked the beginning of the government's assault on the Lutheran Church.[18]

The day after Szabó's installation, the bishops were visited by a man named Iván Reök, who introduced himself as a "semi-official emissary" from the government to the church.[19] Iván Reök was a surgeon by profession but also a member of the Lutheran Church and, most importantly, a deeply committed Christian. Reök had experienced personal conversion through his encounter with Hungary's evangelization movement, and he had devoted a good portion of his life to converting or deepening the faith of others. An educated man, Reök was especially committed to spreading the Gospel among intellectuals, and he took part actively in the weekly "intellectual evangelizations" at the Lutheran church at Budapest's Deák tér (Deák Square). His participation in the evangelization movement brought him into contact with some its leading figures, men such as Zoltán Túróczy. In fact, Reök and Túróczy knew each other well enough that, with a few other leading "evangelists," they compiled a book of their lectures and devotions directed toward the evangelization of intellectuals and published it in the early 1940s. After the war, Reök became active in politics. He joined a political party and even became a representative in Parliament. His political involvement brought him into contact with the communist party's general secretary, Mátyás Rákosi, with whom Reök boasted of having a good relationship. Thus, it was as Rákosi's "friend," as a parliamentary representative, and as an active church member that Reök took upon himself the self-designated assignment of mediating between the government and the Lutheran Church.[20]

Reök first visited Bishop Ordass and urged that the bishops issue a public statement expressing the church's goodwill toward the state and a willingness to enter into church-state negotiations. In fact, Reök had already troubled to prepare such a statement, which he pulled out of his pocket and showed to the bishop. Ordass refused, saying the statement was excessive in confessing the church's past sins and obsequious in its praise of Hungary's current political leadership. Not to be rebuffed, Reök went to Béla Kapi, the senior ranking bishop, whom he did persuade, and a statement was issued—although not the one drafted by Reök. Kapi's statement was signed by all four bishops and distributed in the form of a circular letter.

This statement, issued immediately after Mihályfi's attack, represented the bishops' attempt to position the church vis-à-vis a government that had clearly become antagonistic. The bishops started with a mild confession of the church's past sins, acknowledged the legitimacy of the newly formed Hungarian Republic, and expressed a desire to enter into church-state negotiations. Significantly, however, the bishops also established conditions for arranging the church's relationship with the state. The church needed to be free to conduct its full ministry, which consisted of the clear preaching of the Gospel, the unimpeded administration of the sacraments, the baptism of children, the unhindered conduct of social and charity work, and, most importantly in light of later developments, the education of children in the church's schools.²¹

After the statement was issued, contact between Lutheran leaders and high-level government officials grew frequent in preparation for the negotiations that the government had requested. As would become clear, the government's purpose in these negotiations was to secure the church's consent to the nationalization of its schools. In order to do this, the communists needed first to divide the church leadership.

On April 21, 1948, at a meeting of the church's presidium, Bishop Kapi announced his intention to retire and immediately relinquished his position as senior ranking bishop. Under normal conditions, Bishop Túróczy would have succeeded Kapi, but Túróczy was still under conviction of the people's court. In 1946 he had been released from prison, and in February 1948 he received permission to exercise his bishop's office under certain restrictions. Túróczy, therefore, could not exercise the duties of senior bishop, and those duties were assigned to Bishop Ordass, who would also head up the negotiations with the state. After the presidium adjourned, Ordass was called to an informal discussion taking place between Iván Reök and bishops Túróczy and Szabó. Reök was pressing the church to issue another statement and calling attention to the bloody costs of resisting the state. Having convinced Túróczy and Szabó, Reök was anxious to persuade Ordass. But Ordass, with the authority of senior bishop, rebuffed Reök, and no statement was issued.²²

The next day Iván Reök and Bishop Túróczy visited Mátyás Rákosi, reportedly to discuss the matter of Túróczy's amnesty. At the meeting Rákosi said he wanted Ordass removed from the church-state negotiations. Afterward, Túróczy met with Ordass. Relating Rákosi's demands, Túróczy suggested Ordass remove himself from the church delegation. Ordass responded emphatically, saying the government could not dictate which persons would represent the church.²³

A month later, on May 21, negotiations between the Lutheran Church and the government got underway. The minister of culture, Gyula Ortutay, opened the meeting, expressing his hope that the two sides would come to an agreement quickly in light of the preliminary discussions with church representatives that had already taken place. Ordass asked what Ortutay meant by preliminary discussions. Ortutay said he was referring to discussions held the previous day among Bishop Túróczy, Bishop Szabó, Iván Reök, Ernő Mihályfi, and Rákosi. Ortutay then read out a proposed text for the church-state agreement in which the church agreed to the nationalization of its schools. Ordass defended the church's right to its schools, generating a storm. Members of the government delegation accused Ordass of representing "clerical reaction," and the first round of negotiations ended in upheaval.[24]

A few days later the church leadership met informally with Mihályfi to discuss the proposed agreement. Things were progressing as before when suddenly Mihályfi announced that the church leadership was divided. At a meeting with Rákosi on May 20, Mihályfi said, Túróczy and Szabó had stated their willingness to accept school nationalization and had found the proposed agreement acceptable. Ordass was thrown off guard. Túróczy and Szabó did not deny Mihályfi's assertions. The meeting ended. The church delegation left. Walking back to the church office, Túróczy, turning to Ordass apologetically, said, "One's relationship to these people is like that to highway robbers. They force a man to undress and he needs to beg them to at least leave him his underwear!" Ordass answered, "You know Zoltán that there's no need to beg for underwear! Let everyone see openly that we've been dealing with highway robbers!"[25]

In a clean execution of the divide and conquer principle behind Rákosi's salami tactics, the church leadership was split. Unfortunately, little is known about the two meetings that took place between Túróczy, Reök, and Rákosi on April 22 and May 20. No known records for those meetings exist. However, the fact that Reök was present at them raises uncomfortable questions about Reök's influence on Túróczy.

Bishop Ordass, clear about the division in the leadership and about the state's intentions, modified his negotiating strategy. In the next round of negotiations on May 27, the church leadership put forth the following position: the bishops were not authorized to make binding legal agreements, and certainly they were not empowered to relinquish the church schools. Such changes could only be approved by a general church synod, the highest legislative organ in the Lutheran Church in Hungary, comprised of representatives from the church's congregations. The church delegation asked for a written text of the proposed church-state agreement so that its responsible ecclesiastical organs could discuss the agreement concretely.[26]

Over the next few weeks the government's position became clear. Parliament was going to nationalize the church schools regardless of what the church did. Either the church could consent to this nationalization through a church-state agreement and in so doing obtain certain concessions from the state, most notably the continuation of state financial support, or the church could refuse to sign the agreement, lose the schools anyway, and also lose the concessions the government was presently willing to make.

The prospect of school nationalization created a crisis in the Lutheran Church, driving people behind either the "Túróczy line" or the "Ordass line." The "Túróczy line" argued that the church should relinquish its schools. To resist school nationalization would be to disobey the decrees of a legitimate government, and, more importantly, it would be costly and hopeless. The church only had the right, and duty, to oppose the state if the state intervened into the church's essential ministry. Parochial schools, however, did not belong to the church's essential ministry, and, therefore, the church had to give them up if the state asked for them.

The Túróczy position broke abruptly from the position of the church as defined in the earlier bishops' statement in March. True, Túróczy was not alone among the leadership. Bishop Szabó also supported relinquishing the schools. Curiously, however, the primary theoretical architect of the Túróczy line was not Túróczy himself, nor Bishop Szabó, but their mutual friend, the pastor Imre Veöreös.

Imre Veöreös was from Győr. He was born in Győr and later, although Lutheran, he went to high school at the Benedictine school in Győr. In 1937 Veöreös was ordained, and sometime after that he began working in the office of Bishop Béla Kapi, whose diocese was seated in Győr. In Győr Veöreös got to know both Túróczy and Szabó, and considered them his friends. As a pastor for the bishop in Győr, Veöreös prepared evangelization programs for the diocese and also traveled through the diocese to preach at evangelization weeks; that is, Veöreös was a mission pastor and evangelizer. However, Veöreös the evangelizer was also an intellectual. He had a thin, usually expressionless face and an unflinching look, which conveyed both a sense of self and a reserve of intelligence. Imre Veöreös was smart, and knowing he was smart, he was strong willed and independently minded, too.[27] In 1948 Veöreös published a series of articles in which he mounted commanding arguments in favor of relinquishing the church schools, thereby giving theological integrity to the Túróczy position.

The reasoning behind the "Ordass line" was somewhat more difficult to discern. On the one hand, because the church had previously asserted an integral connection between parochial education and its ministry, Ordass was only affirming the church's traditional position. He believed the church possessed the right to maintain schools and should not give up that right voluntarily. On the other hand, even if one granted that the church possessed this right, that alone provided little guidance for responding to the concrete threat facing the church in 1948. The state was going to nationalize the schools anyway. It had issued an ultimatum to the church: either go along with us and obtain a few concessions, or go against us and lose everything. This was not much of a choice. If the church leadership accepted its terms, then why would they refuse an agreement? Yet, apparently, Ordass did accept these terms, and he was unwilling, nevertheless, to consent to school nationalization.

To understand this, one needs a sense of how the schools were incorporated into the structure of the church. The church schools were maintained and operated mostly by individual congregations. In fact, schools constituted an integral part of the life of most parishes. Several generations of families might attend and maintain the same school. Thus, if in one sense the schools belonged to the general church, in another sense they belonged to the congregations. Probably Ordass reasoned that the school question would be decided locally, and, as a bishop, he believed his duty was to support the local congregations, especially if those congregations wanted to fight for their schools. The bishops, Ordass may have reasoned, should not give up the schools over the heads of the congregations.

Secondarily, Ordass may have thought that if the Lutheran congregations stood by their schools doggedly, then the state, forced to take note of this, would be unable to seize all of them. The Lutheran Church, after all, was not the only church with parochial schools. The leader of the Roman Catholic Church in Hungary, Cardinal József Mindszenty, was at this time organizing stiff opposition to school nationalization.[28] If Mindszenty managed to force the state to back away from nationalizing Catholic schools, Ordass may have thought, then perhaps some Lutheran schools could also be saved. However, these sorts of considerations were only secondary in Ordass's thinking. He clearly reckoned with the possibility that his stance could lead to the loss of the schools, even the loss of state subsidy, and perhaps worse. Thus Ordass's position seemed grounded finally only in the conviction that nationalizing the schools was a wrong against the church with which he was unwilling to cooperate.

As the date set for nationalization, June 16, drew near, forces within the government increased pressure on the church. On June 12, Iván Reök convened an assembly of the National Luther Alliance, of which he was president. Reök arrived at the meeting in the company of a few men from the government and said, "I will have anyone who opposes me arrested!" Then Reök read a statement in which the National Luther Alliance expressed its support for the government and its approval of nationalizing the schools. Reök announced that the assembly had approved the statement, and then he adjourned the meeting.[29]

On June 14, two days before the vote in Parliament, the Lutheran Church had scheduled a meeting of its presbytery and the general assembly. Early that morning the government announced that Túróczy had received amnesty. The amnesty removed the obstacles which prevented Túróczy from holding the position of senior bishop. Thus, when the general assembly met later that day, it transferred the powers of senior bishop from Ordass to Túróczy. Simultaneously, it passed a resolution expressing the desire that, if at all possible, the church should keep its schools. Meanwhile, the Association of Hungarian Lutheran Pastors also passed a resolution that day urging the church leadership not to consent to the nationalization of the schools.

The minutes from this pastors' meeting also attest to Ordass's remarkable adherence to principle. The transfer of the senior bishop's post from Ordass to Túróczy meant that Túróczy would head the church delegation in its negotiations with the state. Everyone knew this, and everyone knew, also, that Túróczy's position was fundamentally different from Ordass's. With this in the background, a pastor named András Keken submitted a proposal to the pastors association urging that Ordass remain as senior bishop. Ordass certainly understood that should Túróczy replace him in the church-state negotiations, it would seriously, if not decisively, undermine Ordass's own position. Considering the stakes, Ordass might have attempted to prevent Túróczy from returning to the church presidency. However, Ordass also knew that, in light of Túróczy's amnesty, this would be a deviation from church law. The minutes of the June 14 pastors meeting report that "András Keken's proposal was withdrawn at the request of D. Bishop Ordass."[30]

Protests notwithstanding, Hungary's Parliament nationalized the country's parochial schools on June 16, 1948.

Disposing of Bishop Ordass

After the nationalization of church schools, no large-scale struggle ensued in the Lutheran Church. Ordass never tried to organize political opposition. The state began the process of taking over the schools, but it also wanted the church to sanction the nationalization of its schools by approving the proposed church-state agreement. Since only a synod had the authority to approve such an agreement, the government wanted to eliminate any church leaders (potential synod members) who were unwilling to cooperate. On August 24 the police arrested General Inspector Albert Radvánsky and another churchman, Sándor Vargha. The next day they arrested Bishop Ordass.

Bishop Ordass, however, had become internationally known. Between February and July 1947 he had traveled abroad extensively, in Scandinavia, Switzerland, and even the United States, representing his church. During those travels Ordass had met and forged friendships with many leading figures in world Lutheranism. Ordass also attended the constituting assembly of the Lutheran World Federation in Lund, Sweden, where he was elected LWF vice president. Later, at the constituting session of the World Council of Churches in Amsterdam, Ordass was elected to the body's Central Committee.[31] Thus, Bishop Ordass's arrest attracted attention and elicited protest from international church bodies, and within a day he was released. Radvánsky and Vargha were not released, however, and in prison they both resigned their church offices.[32]

The Hungarian government, aware now of Ordass's international stature, moved against him more cautiously. On August 30 the government delivered an ultimatum to the church's central office demanding that Bishop Ordass resign by September 8. If he refused, he would be arrested for misappropriating foreign donations to the Lutheran Church in Hungary. The punishment for such a crime varied from a few years' imprisonment to death. At the same time, the government promised to release Radvánsky and Vargha in exchange for Ordass's resignation.

Once again Ordass was forced to consider the resignation of a bishop under duress, this time his own. His position was the same as it had been in Túróczy's case. Ordass believed that to resign would be to flee from the responsibilities of the bishop's office, which had been entrusted to him by the church. To flee in the face of personal danger would be a betrayal of his office. Ordass's sense of duty overrode considerations of personal risk, and he refused to resign.[33]

He was arrested on the evening of September 8 and charged with failing to register financial donations to his church with the Hungarian National Bank. On October 1 he was sentenced to two years in prison. In the meantime, the church's inspectors, compelled by threats, began resigning. By the end of September most of the higher offices in the Lutheran Church were empty. Túróczy and Szabó were leading the church alone. By December the atmosphere was right for convoking a synod. The synod met for a day and empowered Bishop Túróczy to sign the church-state agreement, which he did on December 14, 1948. It would remain legally in effect until 1989.

If one disregarded the section treating the nationalized schools, "the agreement," as it was called, actually looked good on paper. It guaranteed the church freedom of religious practice, defining that broadly to include worship, bible study, evangelization, charity work, and autonomous church administration. For a time it guaranteed the church a state subsidy, prescribing that this financial assistance be eliminated only gradually over the next twenty years. Particularly generous, given the circumstances, was a provision allowing the church to retain two of its Budapest high schools (gymnasia). Also exempted from nationalization were all educational institutions with an exclusively ecclesial function, that is, the church's one seminary. The agreement even provided for the continuation of obligatory religious education in the public schools. In return, the church recognized the legitimacy of the state and promised to intercede for it with prayer, to commemorate state holidays, and to endeavor to raise conscientious citizens. Thus, on paper the agreement provided for the gradual separation of church and state and guaranteed the church's institutional freedom, even while doing away with the parochial schools. In practice, however, the state violated virtually every provision in the agreement over the years.

The communists had executed their intentions easily. The nationalization of the schools, the signing of the agreement, and the removal of Bishop Ordass had posed no serious difficulties. However, the power of Ordass's personal witness would haunt the Lutheran Church in Hungary throughout the entire communist period. The moral disagreement embodied in the conflict between Ordass and Túróczy would remain unresolved. Meaningfully, the climax to that conflict took place while Ordass was in prison. In January 1949, Túróczy visited Ordass in prison and asked him to resign his bishopric. The encounter, described by Ordass, was dramatic:

> On January 8, 1949, Zoltán Túróczy came to me in Szeged's Csillag prison with a ready proposal.... The government was pressuring the church to have my case reviewed by a church court. He—Túróczy—had told the people in the government that there was no court in the Lutheran Church in Hungary which would deliver a guilty verdict in the case. Then Zoltán Túróczy told me that he had brought up the possibility with Rákosi of having me and my family travel abroad—as had come up once before, prior to the trial. Rákosi now firmly ruled this solution out. However, the government was willing to offer the following: They would release me from prison immediately upon my resignation of the Bánya diocesan bishop's office. They would even guarantee a state pension so that I wouldn't have to worry about supporting my family. I needed to pass away the time in quiet isolation for a short while, and then, if there were no new confrontations between myself and the government, I could take up pastoral work in some congregation.
>
> After informing me of this, Túróczy went through the arguments by which he hoped to persuade me to accept this as a solution. He told me that the situation in the Lutheran Church today was altogether different from when I had seen him last. My wife, whom he had visited in the hospital, had also expressed the opinion that she could count on the fingers of one hand those pastors who were loyally standing by my case....
>
> After listening to Zoltán Túróczy, I expressed myself briefly. I had asked for a review of my case. I needed justice, not amnesty. I was sorry that he had raised the possibility of my going abroad without my having asked for it, because I could only imagine going abroad once I had received justice. As for resigning my bishop's office, my position was unalterably the same as it was in the past. I cannot be removed from my bishop's office at the government's insistence, because it was not the government which placed me into that office. If I should became convinced that I had lost the confidence of the diocese's congregations, at that moment, without hesitation, I would step down. But I have no way to be convinced of this, because, although today I have heard that the pastors have left me, I have also heard that no court in the Lutheran

Church today would render a guilty verdict against me. Therefore, I cannot determine how I actually stand in the matter of confidence.

Zoltán Túróczy's answer was very sharp. I can't quote him word for word, of course. But the essence of what he said was as follows: I was assessing the situation only from my selfish viewpoint. I was not hearing the loud, compelling words about the church's need to live. I was led only by the ambition to place a halo around my head (This final expression I quote word for word!) That is why I am left coldly unmoved by the fact that the Lutheran Church in Hungary will be slandered more now than ever in its history.

After this Zoltán Túróczy spoke with the warden, and after that he proposed to me that they go out to lunch. . . . He asked that in that time I consider everything we had discussed and then give him a final answer. The warden permitted Zoltán Túróczy to give me a Bible.

I was placed in a special cell for the hour and a half deliberation time. I did not pass this time in agitation, nor in spite. I read the Bible and prayed. . . . I read the thirteenth chapter of Romans, which had been quoted so often recently, and I read the famous words written in the fifth chapter of the Acts of the Apostles, "We must obey God, rather than men." Then I consciously searched through the New Testament for places where some disciple of Christ was in a situation similar to mine. In this way I came to the sixteenth chapter of the Acts of the Apostles. This chapter relates the history of Paul and Silas' unjust imprisonment. I had the feeling that the end of this history was a biblical message speaking directly to me; "And when it was day, the magistrates sent the bailiffs, saying: Let those people go. And the prison keeper reported these words to Paul: the magistrates have sent me here that I may let you go. Now therefore departing, go in peace! And Paul said: They have beaten us openly, without sentence, although we are Roman people, and have thrown us into prison. And now they want to send us out in hiding? No indeed! Let them come themselves and take us out!"

When Túróczy . . . returned I informed [him] of my decision with a few words: I'm staying here in prison!

I added only that I considered Túróczy's words about the halo around my head to be unjust, unbrotherly and uncharitable. Túróczy didn't withdraw the statement. He didn't even soften it. And so, with a fair amount of tension, our visit ended.[34]

Underneath this exchange was a profound moral disagreement about how to respond to dictatorship. Playing out that disagreement would take forty-five years.

THEOLOGICAL EXCURSUS ONE

The Compromise Type

In Search of a Modus Vivendi, Ahogy Lehet

> Behold, I send you out as sheep in the midst of wolves;
> so be wise as serpents and innocent as doves.
> —MATTHEW 10:16

Compromise as a moral strategy for coping with the regime occupies a central place in the history of the Lutheran Church in Hungary in socialism. It defines the structural framework of the compromise, collaboration, and diaconia types. Thus, also, compromise is a fundamental dynamic in this history. As an ideal-typical response, however, compromise appears only at the beginning of our story, later to be eclipsed by collaboration and diaconia. This is a puzzle, and, in fact, the dissonance between the centrality of compromise to this history, on the one hand, and its almost complete invisibility in the history, on the other, conveys the emotion and meaning of the moral experience which comprises three-fourths of the history this study seeks to understand.

The two most important representatives of the compromise type were Bishop Zoltán Túróczy and Pastor Imre Veöreös. Of course, the strategy encompassed many more people, but Bishop Túróczy was the one who put compromise into practice at the level of church politics, and Imre Veöreös was the strategy's primary theological exponent. The compromise type under consideration here emerged from the fusing of key theological premises, distinctively Lutheran, with a mode of dogged persistence dating in Hungarian history back to the Turkish invasion. Fundamentally, Túróczy and his followers advocated a pragmatic, compromising response to the regime. Their reasoning is expressed in the Hungarian phrase *ahogy lehet* (AH-hodz LE-het), which means "in the way that is possible." Times were difficult; Hungary rested firmly within the Soviet sphere of influence, and a ruthless proletariat dictatorship was in power bent on the destruction of religion. The church needed to find a modus vivendi, a way to save what was savable, *ahogy lehet*, so that its ministry would continue in the midst of powerful enemies.

This did not mean the Túróczy group was unprincipled. To the contrary, their framework was theologically informed. Compromise for them implied both concession to the regime and resistance. The limits of each were determined by the essential ministry of the church. Thus the Túróczy group established a theological frame for compromise consisting of two elements: (1) a willingness to accept losses and relinquish activities and possessions of the church that were not part of its essential ministry, and (2) a commitment to engage the future creatively to find new ways to carry out the church's ministry within the limits established by the new regime. Each of these will be considered in turn.

The Theological Dimensions of Compromise: Conceding the Nonessential Elements of the Church

The crisis for the Lutheran Church in 1948 was the nationalization of the schools, and in response to this crisis the Túróczy group began to articulate a comprehensive vision for the church in socialism.[1] Imre Veöreös set out clearly the theological underpinnings of the Túróczy position in a lead article published on the front page of the church paper *Új Harangszó* in June 1948 entitled "What Do We Say to the Nationalization of the Schools?" Veöreös wrote:

> The schools do not belong to the essence of the church. The words of Jesus, "Go so that you may make disciples of every people . . . teaching them . . . " (Mt. 28:19–20) is not a cultural command, but a command for preaching, religious instruction, and mission. God gave the church its school work through the course of history, and in the same way through the course of history he can take them away. The church remains even without the church schools.
>
> Nevertheless, there are things without which the church cannot live. There are indispensable elements of its essence. The church cannot live without preaching, it cannot live without charity work, it cannot live without education in church teaching, it cannot live without baptism and the Lord's Supper.
>
> From this it follows that martyr's blood cannot flow for the schools. The time may come when martyr's blood must flow. If the state would say some day, you cannot preach—even in the catacombs we would preach. If the state would say, you cannot through charity work give a piece of bread to the starving—even under the weight of punishment we would give out bread. If the state would say, you cannot distribute the body and blood of Christ—crawling on our stomachs we would carry the sacraments. But everyone can rest assured; we will not establish schools in secret, and we will not teach geography if it is forbidden us.[2]

This argument not only set out a position on the impending school nationalization but also introduced a distinction intended as a moral guide for the church in its journey through socialism. The argument was as follows: The church must distinguish between that which belongs to its true mission and essence and that which is merely adventitious cultural accretion. It may and must defend those things integral to its ministry, but when confronted with social or political claims on nonessential items, the church must concede. The schools are nonessential.

The larger distinction behind the particular question, therefore, was between the essence and form of the church's ministry or, stated differently, between the ministry of the church and the means by which it is carried out. If the church could conduct its essential ministry, Veöreös was saying, then it was free to relinquish historical forms of the Hungarian church, which are only particular arrangements through which the ministry of the Gospel has been carried out in Hungary. Veöreös approached the school question by applying this distinction. He reasoned that the schools were a cultural arrangement of the churches in Hungary. As such, they did not comprise an essential element of the church but a gift of God given through history that could also be taken away through history. Of course the loss of particular historical arrangements meant that the church needed to find new forms of ministry, but this did not warrant a conclusion that the historically factitious was essential.

Lest anyone think that Veöreös's position on the schools was itself a factitious innovation for the moment, let it be noted that Veöreös had used the same distinction a year earlier, in April 1947, before school nationalization was a serious issue, in response to a government proposal to abolish obligatory religious education. In an article entitled "Our Position on the Question of Optional Religious Education," Veöreös objected vigorously to the abolition of obligatory religious education on the grounds that the church has both a right and a duty, derived from the sacrament of baptism, to raise every baptized child. Religious education, Veöreös argued, as an activity derived from baptism, was part of the essential mission of the church, something the church could never surrender. After asserting this, however, Veöreös went on to draw a distinction between the essential work of the church and the particular historical arrangement by which that work is carried out. Although he objected to the abolition of obligatory religious education, he did not recommend political resistance in the event the government plan were realized. Instead he suggested a series of measures all within the boundaries of the law: The church should take strong disciplinary action against parents who withdrew their children from religious instruction, or the church should only agree to baptize children after receiving written assurance from the parents that they would enroll their child in religious instruction. The church still needed to educate its children members, but it did not need to do this through obligatory religious education. That is to say, although religious education was an essential task of the church, the form in which this task was carried out was not essential.[3]

However, an argument built on a distinction between essence and form needs to define the essential ministry of the church clearly, and doing that is tricky. In March 1948 the Lutheran bishops had issued a statement defining the church's ministry in robust terms, consisting of preaching, administration of the sacraments, charity work, and education—both religious and secular. In his June 1948 article "What Do We Say to the Nationalization of the Schools?," Veöreös also described the church's true ministry robustly, except that he narrowed the work of education to education in church teaching. This minor redefinition shaved off a considerable portion of the actual ministry of the Lutheran Church in Hungary before June 1948. Did the Túróczy group have a principle for sifting out the true from the adventitious?

The answer to the question is, sort of. Writing in 1990, Imre Veöreös identified the roots of his and Túróczy's framework in Article VII of the Augsburg Confession, which reads:

> The church is the assembly of saints in which the Gospel is taught purely and the sacraments are administered rightly. For the true unity of the church it is enough to agree concerning the teaching of the Gospel and the administration of the sacraments. It is not necessary that human traditions or rites and ceremonies, instituted by men, should be alike everywhere.[4]

Augsburg defines the church as Word and Sacrament while appearing indifferent to questions of external order—such as rites and ceremonies, feast days, and ecclesiastical structure. So long as the Gospel is rightly taught and the sacraments rightly administered, Augsburg seems to say, the form of the church is no matter, and, in fact, Lutheran polity has varied historically from country to country. Thus, in denying the indispensability of Hungary's parochial schools and, indeed, of the historical shape of the Hungarian church in its every aspect, Veöreös and Túróczy were reasserting the Lutheran viewpoint that church order is *adiaphora*, morally neutral or indifferent.

Nevertheless, despite its Lutheran credentials, the distinction between essence and form was problematic for at least two reasons. First, the formula "Word and Sacrament" is a fairly abstract definition of the church's ministry open to broad interpretation. Are acts of charity part of the ministry of the Word? Is education? Because Veöreös and Túróczy's definition of the church's essence was fairly loose, it was also prone to countless redefinitions and progressive reductions. Second, by separating completely essence from form, the Túróczy group risked conceptualizing the church's essential ministry as reified and ahistorical. To say the Gospel makes use of many historical forms means one thing; to say the Gospel has no need for any historical form means another. Clearly the ministry of the Gospel depends upon the church, and the church as a historical institution must have some kind of sociological form. Thus the actual ministry of the Word is dependent upon actual historical forms. Might not some church forms be more amenable to pure teaching and right administration of sacraments than others? If so, then church order and ecclesiastical structure cannot be wholly indifferent, and at some point questions of form will impinge upon questions of ministry.

The Theological Dimensions of Compromise: Searching for New Forms of Ministry

The Túróczy position was not only about how to make concessions with integrity. It coupled a readiness to let go of the church's current historical arrangements with a commitment to find new forms for the Word's ministry in Hungarian socialism. Rather than pine for the past, Túróczy supporters said, the church ought to find new ways to fulfill its ministry in the ways that were possible. Thus, the Túróczy group determined to view socialism in Hungary not merely as a communist dictatorship that hated Christianity but also as a historical transformation bringing with it new possibilities for the church.

As Túróczy and his followers saw it, the most significant consequence for the church effected by socialism was an end to the form of "people's church" (*népegyház*). The term "people's church" designates a sociological relationship between the community of faith and general society. Strictly speaking, it refers to the nature of church membership: membership comes automatically at birth rather than by deliberate choice, and the boundaries of the religious community usually coincide with those of the dominant society. More broadly, however, as it was used by Hungarian Lutherans, "people's church" denoted the entire "established" character of the Lutheran Church in Hungary during the Horthy period. The end of "establishment" was not all bad, the supporters of Túróczy said. A "people's church" has to wrestle with its own set of serious problems. It makes Christianity easy, a social given rather than a conscious decision. That kind of Christianity, although comfortable, is objectionable because it makes for superficial faith. It does not require commitment.

The end of "establishment" in Hungary, said the Túróczy group, contained the possibility of new, hidden blessings. Precisely because the regime was hostile, the church had to draw upon the commitment of its true members in order to survive. Imre Veöreös, in an article entitled "We Must Become a Missionary Church!" described the new situation as follows:

> The present path of the church . . . can only be a path of mission, and in this simple respect: to win people over for Jesus Christ. . . . We need to adapt our ministry to mission. This means that today certain

occasions in congregational life need to take on a missionary character: preaching, religious instruction, family visits. The time is over when the "pastoral visit" can pass away in conversations about the weather.... That pastor is right who always carries a Bible under his arm at family visits, and when he sits down immediately places it on the kitchen table. Two or three sentences follow, and at once the message of the Gospel is mentioned in the given conversation, from the opened Bible or without it. It should be possible to use other occasions in the same way. The religion class becomes a missionary hour with the quality of a child's bible study group.... The church service becomes evangelization. Not only to "preach the Word" (oh, if we would do this truly our sermons would acquire an evangelizing character on their own), but to struggle so that in the course of the sermon something happens within the heart through the Holy Spirit. There is no other path.[5]

The church envisioned here is smaller, lay oriented, and more vital. The church will be smaller in socialism because believing comes with a cost, but the church will be vital in socialism because its members are those, only, who believe. The daily life and spiritual vigor of Christians will be nourished by pastors who practice the art and have the gift of evangelization. Not by the comforts of privilege, but by the power of the Spirit, the church will live in socialism.

Thus to become a "missionary church" entailed turning away from the institutional church and toward the laity. Pastors and parishioners must now shoulder the greater burdens of church life. In the hostile social environment determined by communist dictatorship, the church's survival hinged on the commitment of its lay people and their willingness to sacrifice. If the state outlawed religious instruction in the schools, then parents and pastors would teach children about Jesus at home. If the state forbid people to worship in church, then families and pastors would meet together at home to sing hymns and read the Bible. Of course this was not a comfortable Christianity. It was not the pleasant thruway of other periods in Hungarian history, but it was a road on which the faithful could travel — even in socialism.

Indisputably, this theological vision drew inspiration from Hungarian evangelism. Indeed its major exponents and supporters, Veöreös and Túróczy, and also Túróczy's close ally, József Szabó, were rooted in the evangelization tradition, and all came from the evangelical city of Győr. The evangelicals were already lay oriented. They were more ecumenical and less "confessional." They focused on personal faith and piety rather than issues of church. Thus evangelicals were less likely to view attacks on church institutions as equivalent to attacks on the Gospel. The true church lived in people's hearts.

Evangelical skepticism about church institutions must have been reinforced by the fact that religious life was flourishing in the first years after the war, right when the communists were trying hardest to suppress it. In Hungary many Lutherans refer to the 1940s as the "Decade of Revival."[6] Lutheran press accounts report a dramatic increase in congregational evangelization weeks in the late 1940s. In 1937–38 approximately six congregational evangelizations were held, and in 1938–39, there were ten.[7] By 1947 there may have been as many as 129, and in 1948 there were 164 evangelizations.[8] Thus while communists pontificated on the science of atheism, people were flocking to church. Túróczy, Veöreös, and others must have seen this as testimony to the wiliness of the Gospel. They believed in the power of the Word alone to outwit the communists, and they were strengthened in their confidence that the living church could survive the state's hostility.

The Historical Framework for Compromise: *Ahogy Lehet*

The theological reasoning just considered established the boundaries for compromise; it delimited the borders of the field within which the church might both yield to and defy the regime. However, the framework of compromise itself, that is, the field on which theology marked off limits, was the repetition of a central pattern in Hungarian history. Reflecting on his life in 1990, Imre Veöreös described his strategy for living as a pastor in socialism with reference to the poem "Ahogy lehet."[9] The phrase means "in the way that is possible." It crops up often in the reminiscences of churchmen who lived through communism, as if somehow it captures an essential aspect of their experience. Following them, therefore, and with Veöreös's assistance, the overarching structure of the compromise type might be termed *ahogy lehet*.

As a phrase and a concept, *ahogy lehet* was captured for posterity by the Hungarian poet Sándor Reményik. Reményik was a Transylvanian who lived in the first half of the twentieth century. In the mid-twentieth century, after Hungary lost the First World War, Transylvania was transferred to Romania. As a result, Transylvanian Hungarians, who had been citizens of Hungary and part of the dominant national group, found themselves a minority in a new country hostile to them. After World War I, Transylvanian Hungarians were in a radically different political environment, surrounded by enemies, struggling to preserve their cultural identity. That was the context for the poem "Ahogy lehet," written in 1935, two stanzas of which read as follows:

> Singing the collaborator's psalter
> We go in unending slave procession.
> We have no weapons.

The rebellion of our spirit is unarmed,
Although every drop of our blood deeply
Desires that wild movement of Peter
When, in defense of God,
Unexpectedly he cut off the ear of Malchus.
Who are we?
Oh not the Humble one,
But the sons of humiliation.
Between the proud bridge-heads of generations
We are a rounded arch, a hunched connection.
Brethren, truly our lives are not good,
Not worthy of our forefathers.
But he who in our place could do otherwise
Let him cast on us the first stone!
Our every minute a tortuous compromise,
The way that is possible (*ahogy lehet*).

Brother, you mongrel hero, hero of compromises,
Does your sentence falter, change?
Perhaps a cinder still sparks, reverberating
from the maelstrom of flames that churns within you.
Overflowing forces swell up within you,
Niagaran falls would fall—
Satisfy yourself if they fill
with crystal clear water a glass.
They push us back, and back,
And what they leave, less and less—
So cast your foot down where you can
And save the little bit of earth you stand on,
The spark from the flame, the drop from the river,
The remnant from your broken sentence;
Everything remains in small amounts,
The way that is possible (*ahogy lehet*).[10]

The poem describes not only the inner turmoil but also the vulnerable, dogged persistence of a people who face a much greater enemy. They live not in the great age of great ancestors, and they do not perform heroic acts, but like a rickety rope bridge over a ravine, they span time and endure. From the outside they appear as collaborators, and indeed they are compromised, because they confront their oppressors silently and without weapons. But the exterior hides an inward rebellion, which fights to hold on to what common values it can.

In short, the poem articulates for a weak and conquered people a strategy of survival. As strategy, *ahogy lehet* concedes when necessary and fights back silently. The beaten party is prepared to cooperate with the oppressor, because it is weaker, but it also fights back with trickery and stubbornness, so that in giving up something it gets something back. *Ahogy lehet* means survival through compromise. It means a dogged struggle through a never-ending chain of unequal compromises. The compromises are unequal because between disparate parties, but so unrelenting is the weaker side that, nevertheless, it preserves something for the future.

As in the poem, the struggle for survival is a central motif in the history of the Lutheran Church in Hungary in socialism. Preoccupation with survival was a natural response to fear. Believers were frightened, both as persons and as Christians, by the party's consistent but indiscriminate brutality. Deportation or police interrogation or court conviction or torture or execution could happen to anyone. Lutherans, especially, feared that their church, among the smallest in Hungary, was vanishing slowly. In 1910 Lutherans in Hungary had numbered approximately 1.3 million people.[11] In 1930, after the territorial revisions of the First World War, Lutherans in Hungary numbered less than half that, 530,000. In 1949, after the Hungarian government expelled ethnic Germans, many of whom were Lutheran, the Lutheran Church numbered 480,000 people.[12] In the communist period, Hungary's Lutheran Church feared obliteration.

If one wants to understand the experience at root of this history, one should not underestimate the existential immediacy produced by the prospect of extinction. More than most anything, the Túróczy group feared for the survival of the church, and that fear far outweighed anxieties about state intervention into church life or even concern for the parochial schools. The willingness to compromise, at root, was a response to the fear of extinction. It was a strategy premised on ad hoc bargains with the regime, made not because one liked or trusted the communists, but so that the church would remain. In this respect, compromise entailed cooperation with the party, and so at times it appeared like unprincipled collaboration. However, those compromises were struck with an inner commitment to resist in the ways that were possible, with a commitment to search for new ways to outsmart the party and continue the work of the church. Thus each agreement was tentative, reached only because there was no better option, and valid only as long as no better option came along. Compromise was the strategy of a scrapper, like the Jacob in Genesis.

The mongrel spirit expressed in the verse "Ahogy lehet" extends back into Hungarian history at least half a millennium. The struggle for survival is a central theme for the peoples of Eastern Europe, arising from the experience of small nations whose histories contain the memory of a never-ending sequence of foreign conquest. Hungary was once, in the middle ages, a major European power. Then in 1526 its heirless king, the upper nobility, and not a few archbishops and clerics met a superior Turkish army on a field called Mohács and were massacred. The next 160 years, from a Hungarian point of view, tell the story of a double-fronted battle to regain independence. Shortly after Mohács, Hungary was divided into three parts; the middle region of the country—the area coinciding with much of contemporary Hungary—was annexed to the Ottoman Empire. In the north, over the region that comprises present-day Slovakia, the German Habsburgs ruled what was called Royal Hungary. To the east was the Principality of Transylvania, a distinct region today belonging to Romania that in Turkish times was a Turkish suzerainty, ruled by Hungarian princes who nevertheless managed to exhibit a remarkable degree of independence from their overlords.

Thus greater Hungary was ruled by two alien powers, the Turk and the German, and Hungarians developed two different techniques for trying to remove them. The first strategy came from Transylvania. It was radical and uncompromising, and strove to regain independence quickly through military conquest. The history of Transylvania is built on story after story of brilliant military campaigns by brilliant Hungarian princes who almost reunited Hungary but were defeated in the end, exiled, and killed. Hungary's great heroes are all losers. Eventually the Transylvanian armies that fought those freedom fights were called *kuruc* armies. *Kuruc* derives from the Latin word for cross.[13] It connotes the suffering that comes with an uncompromising commitment to Hungarian freedom.

The second strategy came out of Royal Hungary. It was cautious and patient, and advocated by upper Hungarian nobility, who naturally had close ties to the Habsburgs. The Habsburg-friendly nobles reasoned that the Turks were too strong for the Hungarians to drive out and that they should work with the Habsburgs to remove the Eastern scourge. In time northern Hungarian armies, which were allied with the Habsburgs, were called *labanc* armies. *Labanc* soldiers were often mercenaries, and the word perhaps evokes thoughts of the remuneration which in Hungarian history accompanies cooperation with occupying powers. Indeed much about *labanc* smacks of collaboration and treason, but, to be sure, they were *labanc* troops that drove the Turks out finally.

Ahogy lehet is a reprise of the *labanc* theme that is integrally a part of Hungarian history. It is a particular articulation of one distinctive Hungarian strategy for coping with oppression. The strategy, also, is deeply ambiguous. It can attain good things, if the compromisers are shrewd and not easily manipulated, but it can also slip into collaboration, because the compromisers risk helping the enemy by cooperating with him. Their success depends on their ability to assess gains, losses, and hidden dangers each time they strike a bargain. That is no easy task.

Therefore, the *ahogy lehet* strategy adopted by the Túróczy group tottered always on the edge of a slippery slope. It made survival the center of moral concern and only secondarily limited what one could do for the sake of surviving. That there be limits was crucial, however, because without them anything could be justified in the name of survival. The question to ask of the *ahogy lehet* framework time and again is, what were the limits? To be sure, Veöreös and Túróczy did enunciate limits. They said the church could not compromise on its essential ministry. However, because this essence could be abstracted from concrete practices and institutions, it could be redefined endlessly. That made the borders around compromise hazy.

Besides the theoretical framework, one should also consider how *ahogy lehet* would work as a psychological framework. In a proletariat dictatorship, to set clear limits on cooperation with the regime was dangerous. It could mean imprisonment, torture, or death. In a setting where refusing to compromise entails great personal risk, and where the line drawn around compromise is hazy, sharpening the line becomes difficult and improbable. One can imagine a pastor or bishop thinking like this: "The state says we cannot do x, and if I keep on doing x, I could get killed, and only the church's essential ministry matters; if everyone gets killed just because of x, the church will disappear, and the church needs to survive; so no false heroics for me—I will put the interests of the church first and give up x." The point is this: a line drawn in the sand that is hard to see is easy to cross. As both a moral and psychological framework *ahogy lehet* was premised on a calculation of self-interest that was only vaguely restricted. How can a person assess the limits when the limits mean martyrdom?

In fact Bishop Túróczy illustrated the problem in an intriguing reflection on martyrdom. In a speech delivered in 1948, a few days before the church-state agreement was ratified, Túróczy explained why he supported it. At one point he said:

> In these times my thoughts have been occupied a lot with the behavior of Jesus and Paul before the state. I was shocked to see how many times Jesus had occasion to die for the world before Good Friday, and he didn't do it.... [Jesus] explains this behavior at John 7:6–8 with these words, "My time is not yet here, my time is not yet filled." As long as the time determined by God had not come he avoided martyrdom. When, however, the time arrived, then the plea, indeed rebuke, of his disciples could not—according to Matthew 16:21—deter him from going to Jerusalem.

> Jesus did not permit the first Christians to seek martyrdom for themselves. Matthew 24:15–18 speaks about what Christians should do when they see the desolating sacrilege standing there in the holy place. Is it possible to imagine a situation where God would command more clearly to his people that they should allow the desolating sacrilege into the holy place only over their dead bodies? Nevertheless, Jesus commands that they should flee to the mountains.
>
> No one can say about Paul that he was a cowardly person. Nevertheless, in a basket lowered through a brick wall his disciples rescued him from Damascus. He did not consider it cowardly, and he did not object to it.... When, however, the Spirit made it clear to him that the time of captivity, torture, and death had arrived in his life, then, in the 20th chapter of Acts, in vain do the Ephesian elders cry and embrace him. He didn't consider it any account, nor was his life dear to him, but he went on the road of martyrdom.
>
> Woe to us if we seek martyrdom when God still wants to use us for his service. Of course, woe to us as well if we cravenly compromise when He commands us and expects of us a hero's death.[14]

Túróczy here does not reject out of hand the possibility of martyrdom. One might say, however, that he has established a strong a priori presumption against it. The big question raised by the speech is, how does one know when the time for martyrdom has arrived? Túróczy neither asks nor answers this, but the *ahogy lehet* framework implies the approach to the problem. *Ahogy lehet* gives order of privilege to survival and then allows for exceptions to the rule—the exception being martyrdom—in poorly specified instances where the church's essential ministry has been encroached upon. Hence the presumption against martyrdom. No prohibition or injury can in itself encroach upon the essential ministry, because as many forms of ministry exist as there are ways of imagining. Consequently every harm against the church must be weighed against the still remaining possibilities of the future and also against the additional harm—martyrdom or even collective extinction—that will result from identifying the present case as the limit to compromise.

In short it was difficult to establish clear limits within the moral framework provided by Veöreös and Túróczy. Theirs was a dangerous strategy, best suited for brave and clever people. That compromisers were not always brave and clever is a lesson of the next phase in this history.

CHAPTER TWO

Working with Dictators
Totalitarianism and the Choices of Desperation, 1949–56

LORD, where is thy steadfast love of old, which by thy faithfulness thou didst swear to David?
—PSALM 89:49

After the "year of the turn," political power in Hungary was wielded by what is often called a "party-state." The term indicates the way that, in a "people's democracy," party and state were inseparable. The apparatus of the state (for example, Parliament and government ministries) was preserved; however, because all political parties but one had been eliminated, the one party controlled all branches and organs of government, and it wielded complete political power. In principle, the party's highest organ was the Party Congress, but power was in fact exercised by the Central Committee, even more so by the Politburo, and ultimately by four "Muscovites" (communists who had received their training in Moscow), Mátyás Rákosi, Ernő Gerő, Mihály Farkas, and József Révai. From among these, the short, chubby, bald-headed Rákosi became Hungary's dictator. In fact, Rákosi was more than a dictator; he was Hungary's "leader," cloaked in a cult of personality, "divinized," and portrayed as uniquely qualified to lead the Hungarian people.[1]

The party's monopoly on political power did not lead to a reduction in political brutality but to its increase, and it inaugurated a kind of totalitarianism unexampled in Hungary's history. The party-state aimed not only at a monopoly of political power but also at complete supervision of all spheres of life. Thus, even after eliminating meaningful political opposition, the party insisted on the lurking presence of reactionaries and imperialists. *Vigilance* became a key word in Hungarian politics; Mátyás Rákosi exhorted party members to "take note of the smallest adversarial sound or deed, and seek out and find behind the mistakes the hand of the enemy."[2] The country lived in the terrors of Stalinism.

The period between 1949 and 1956 also brought the Lutheran Church in Hungary a new set of church leaders. Their golden day coincided with some of the worst days in Hungarian history and the history of their church. The new leaders worked closely with the party-state, and consulting with it they redefined the church's relationship to Hungarian society.

In October 1948, shortly after Ordass's imprisonment, a young Lutheran university chaplain named László Dezséry published a pamphlet entitled *Open Letter on the Matter of the Lutheran Church in Hungary*. It was an important, historic event. Dezséry's *Open Letter* provided a sweeping interpretation of Hungary's political past, present, and future, and defined for the Lutheran Church its proper place in Hungary. It also read like a piece of political propaganda. Dezséry frontally assaulted the church leadership and thoroughly affirmed party-led socialism in Hungary. Dezséry also set forth the outline of a theology of socialism that would later be espoused by the church leadership. Perhaps most importantly, Dezséry's *Open Letter* brought the attention of the church to a man who would be bishop.

Looking over photographs of László Dezséry in the period of his success, one finds nothing particularly striking about him—other than his youth. He was thirty-eight when he became bishop. Before that, he was interested in politics, and he was ambitious. In the early 1940s, before the advent of Hungarian socialism, Dezséry wrote essays for the church paper *Evangélikus Élet*, many of which dealt exclusively with political themes.[3] A number of those essays indicated sympathy for some form of socialism. In an article from June 1944, for example, Dezséry called socialism the "victorious ideal of the age and one today without rival," explaining that the ideals of socialism had emerged from the failures of liberal democracy and capitalism.[4]

However, Dezséry's political analysis tended toward the dilettantish, and moreover, it was often tainted with anti-Semitism. Jewry, in Dezséry's view, was more or less responsible for capitalism. Thus, any solution of Hungary's social and economic problems was inseparable from solving the economic dimensions of the "Jewish question." Even worse for Dezséry than Jewish capital, however, was Jewish culture. In a catechism written for young people, Dezséry exposited on the inherent antagonism between Jewry and Western culture, an antagonism rooted in the collective Jewish rejection of Christ.[5]

In the Lutheran Church in Hungary today, some have suggested that Dezséry's style as bishop can be explained by his early anti-Semitic writings. They conjecture that the communists, aware of what Dezséry had said in the Horthy period, threatened to expose and imprison him if he did not collaborate.[6] Although such a scenario is easily imagined, one need not assume that Dezséry's relationship with the communists resulted from mere compulsion. The real significance of Dezséry's pre-1945 political writings is not that they provided the communists material with which to blackmail him. Rather, the early writings reveal Dezséry's keen interest in politics, which was built on a crude regurgitation of common political perceptions of his day, and his bad moral judgment. This was an especially unfortunate combination of character traits in Hungary in 1948.

When the political climate changed in Hungary, Dezséry adjusted. His actions went beyond reluctantly cooperating with the communists to actively supporting them. He did this partly because he was ambitious and partly because he believed in some form of socialism (after the war he joined the Social Democratic Party) and perhaps partly because he had feelings of desperation. In any event, the *Open Letter on the Matter of the Lutheran Church in Hungary* was a crass piece of theological collaboration and collateral on Dezséry's loan of Rákosi's good favor.

Shortly after publishing *Open Letter*, Dezséry managed to become pastor of the Lutheran congregation in Óbuda, a northern district of Budapest. Óbuda's pastor was retiring; the congregation announced its search for a replacement; Dezséry and four other pastors applied for the position. When the congregation selected two pastors to compete for the position, Dezséry was not among them. Shortly thereafter, István Botta, one of the final candidates, received a telephone call from someone requesting pastoral care for his sick wife. Botta, upon visiting the woman, discovered that she was not sick but that her husband, the man who had called, was an employee of the government who wanted to transmit the following message: Mátyás Rákosi says that Dezséry needs to be pastor in Budapest so that in a short while he can take the place of Bishop Ordass. Would Botta withdraw himself from consideration for the Óbuda position? Botta refused, but members of Óbuda's presbytery started receiving threats from the party-state, and Botta relented. Still, Botta went to talk to Dezséry, hoping to convince him that they should both withdraw from the Óbuda competition. Botta recalls that Dezséry responded, "I can't do it. I am in their hands."[7] When the Óbuda congregation voted for a new pastor in January 1949, László Dezséry was the only one they considered.[8]

Another figure to emerge in this period was Lajos Vető. Vető replaced Béla Kapi as bishop in December 1948. At the time, Vető was relatively unknown. He came from Diósgyőr, a suburb of Miskolc, an industrial city in northeastern Hungary that had been occupied by the Russians in early 1945. Vető, who was of Slovakian origin, knew Russian, which was unusual in Hungary in 1945. Thus he ended up working for a time as an interpreter for the Russian army.[9]

Vető's election as bishop took place among a strange set of circumstances. When Bishop Kapi resigned, Kapi requested Túróczy for his replacement in the Dunántúl diocese. Because Dunántúl had its seat in Győr—the evangelization city—there was a certain plausibility to Kapi's request. Nevertheless, Túróczy was already bishop of the Tisza diocese. Thus he would need to resign the bishopric in Tisza to be elected bishop again in Dunántúl. The congregation in Győr issued a call to Bishop Túróczy on October 24, 1948, and on November 4 Túróczy announced to the general assembly of the Tisza diocese that he was resigning. Shortly thereafter Túróczy was elected bishop of Dunántúl. On December 22 Lajos Vető was installed as bishop of the Tisza diocese. He was aided in his election bid by the party-state, which persuaded the other candidate to withdraw from consideration.[10] Bishop Vető's ordination was described in *Evangélikus Élet* as bringing representation for Hungary's workers to the church.[11]

In March 1949, shortly after Vető's election, the church found a new general inspector—Iván Reök. Reök's election to the post made him the highest constitutional authority in the Lutheran Church.[12] As general inspector his most significant act was to resolve the "Ordass affair." Ordass's prison sentence was set to expire on May 30, 1950. In principle, Ordass would then be free to return to his bishop's office. Anticipating this, the party-state requested in January 1950 that General Inspector Reök initiate procedures within the church to remove Ordass from his bishopric.[13]

Contemporaneous with these happenings, József Darvas was appointed high inspector in Ordass's diocese.[14] Darvas had been a writer in the Horthy period and a prominent member of a populist movement. After the war, Darvas took up politics directly, representing the state in its negotiations with the Lutheran Church in 1948 and later serving as minister of culture and religion. By 1950, Darvas, of Lutheran origin, openly admitted his atheism.[15] In fact, at the ceremony installing him as inspector, Darvas was uncertain about how to receive communion.[16] Still, as the high inspector of Ordass's diocese, Darvas could contribute to a successful resolution of the Ordass affair.

To remove Ordass, Reök wanted a church court to convict the bishop of some disciplinary offense. That required finding a group of clergy willing to cooperate in such a trial—no easy task for Reök even in 1950. On March 3, the church leadership convened an exceptional session of the general assembly. The assembly carried out extensive personnel changes at the church's middle level and also established a special disciplinary court capable of stripping Ordass of his office. Wanting to guarantee a compliant court, Reök asked all current church judges to resign and arranged for new ones to be elected. When the new elections were held, Reök made sure the votes were by open ballot. So irregular were these proceedings that twenty-seven pastors signed and submitted a petition of protest to the church leadership. Reök swiftly summoned each petitioner to his office and told him to remove his signature from the petition. Then he had the noncompliant pastors suspended from their offices.[17]

Despite these machinations, Reök was still uncertain that the court would render a guilty verdict against Ordass. On the eve of the hearing, pastors György Kendeh and András Keken, two of Ordass's most loyal supporters, were arrested, taken to the headquarters of the secret police on

60 Andrássy Avenue, interrogated over the course of several days, and then placed in internment camps, where they remained for nearly a year. Reök, who was fond of reminding the clergy that interning 550 of them would be a mere ten minutes' police work,[18] may have instigated the arrest of Kendeh and Keken to provide himself ammunition with which to blackmail the Ordass court.[19]

On the day of the trial, Reök informed the court that if it did not deliver a guilty verdict, Ordass, Keken, and Kendeh would receive death penalties in another trial, and fifteen more pastors would be arrested.[20] The threats were effective. The court stripped Ordass of his office on the grounds that, having been convicted of a crime, he was unworthy to be bishop. Even then, however, the majority on the court voted by abstention. When the ballots were counted, eight were blank, and only four indicated a guilty verdict. The trial, moreover, was illegitimate, because church law stipulated disciplinary courts should have thirteen members and this court had only twelve. Reök, contemplating the problem, turned to one judge after the trial and said, "You see, there were thirteen present. Therefore the council was complete and there is no need for you to worry." When the judge stared blankly back, Reök explained, "Where two or three are gathered in my name, there I am as well. Christ, too, was among us."[21]

A short time later, on May 2, 1950, the presidium of the Bánya diocese met to deliberate about Ordass's successor. They recommended László Dezséry for the empty bishopric.[22] The pastors in the diocese, however, had formally expressed their support for another man, Lajos Kemény. Kemény publicly declined the candidacy.[23] Thus once again Dezséry found himself competing alone for a church office, and the party-state wanted to make sure he would get the post. On May 4, József Darvas wrote a letter to the ministry of the interior, recommending that "local administrative organs inform the congregations in an appropriate manner that the state also has an interest in Dezséry's election."[24] In the Hungarian archives, a handwritten note signed by Mátyás Rákosi reads, "Our comrades, there, where they are able, should take care that Dezséry is elected, the way that it was with the election of Darvas."[25] And so, on June 8, 1950, Dezséry was elected bishop by a comfortable majority.[26]

A week earlier, Ordass had been released from prison. For the next several years, he and his wife would support their family by growing vegetables in the garden and by sewing scarves, shawls, mittens, and pullovers to sell to the sympathetic.

In February 1952, the church convened another law-making synod. Its main objective was to centralize the church's administration. Accordingly the synod's most significant decision was to reduce the church's dioceses from four to two. This meant the church would only have two bishops. In such situations church law stipulated that the current bishops resign and that new elections be held to fill the newly created dioceses. However, shortly before the synod began, Bishop Túróczy and Bishop Szabó decided to resign, leaving the church with only two active bishops.[27] When the synod completed its work, therefore, bishops Dezséry and Vető were appointed, without elections, as heads of the newly created Southern and Northern dioceses, respectively. The seat of both dioceses was placed in Budapest, nearer to the organs of government.

For a while it appeared also that the 1952 synod would abolish the position of general inspector. In dealing with the churches, the party-state preferred to work closely with only one individual. Because the general inspector was legally the highest authority in the Lutheran church, Iván Reök would have seemed the natural choice for the party's contact. In the early Rákosi years, however, Reök and Dezséry were probably competing for the party's favor. When the proposal to eliminate the general inspector's position became known, Reök opposed it vehemently, arguing before the synod that the idea was contrary to Hungary's new democratic spirit.[28] Indeed, so deep was Reök's concern for people's democracy that, according to the collective memory of the church, he rushed to the Office of Church Affairs to show them Dezséry's anti-Semitic, "reactionary," writings—all to no avail.[29] The church, or the party-state, decided to keep the general inspector's office but to get rid of Reök. They replaced him with Ernő Mihályfi, the man who, as government representative, had initiated the attack against the Lutheran Church in 1948 at the installation of Bishop Szabó. The pretext for Mihályfi's election was his Lutheran origin. He rarely played a role in church life, however, even after becoming general inspector.

When the 1952 synod was over, the Lutheran Church was headed, in effect, by bishops László Dezséry and Lajos Vető. Vető was entrusted with the "foreign affairs" of the church, traveling often and participating in ecumenical functions. Dezséry, in turn, was entrusted with the church's "domestic affairs," thereby becoming the dominant figure in the church and its de facto head. As one of his first acts as supreme churchman, Dezséry gave the church's remaining two high schools to the state.[30] He did so on his own authority, without consulting broader church opinion, thereby completing the nationalization of the church's schools, and, incidentally, violating the church-state agreement.

By 1950 the last remaining independent religious associations in Hungary had been disbanded. Evangelization weeks and all evangelization activity came to an end. Church presses closed down; the Lutheran church was left with only two publications, *Evangélikus Élet* and *Lelkipásztor*, a weekly and monthly publication, respectively. In 1951 the party-state created the State Office of Church Affairs (Állami Egyházügyi Hivatal, or ÁEH).

The ÁEH supervised church life strictly and was, incidentally, in its establishment a violation of the church-state agreement.

The role of the church leaders in the Rákosi period changed. They were no longer accountable to the people of the church, over whom they lorded, but to the political power that had put them in office. Frequently the church leadership was compelled to act as a kind of propaganda department for the party, celebrating the accomplishments of the government. Reök and Dezséry, for example, initiated a series of annual pastors conferences that functioned putatively to further pastoral training but which in practice served the purpose of "political re-education." These paralleled propagandistic conferences and meetings in all Hungarian workplaces, and the clergy quickly nicknamed them "mind-broadeners."[31] The church leadership also issued pastoral letters urging believers to contribute to the building of socialism by purchasing peace loans, joining agricultural collectives, working overtime, and so on. Lajos Vető became a member of Parliament.

As part of these changes, the church leadership also fashioned for the church a new theology of socialism.

THEOLOGICAL EXCURSUS TWO

The Collaboration Type

*Removing Choices and Affirming Socialism
(or* Ahogy Lehet *Gone Bad)*

> And he said to me, "Son of man, can these bones live?"
> And I answered, "O Lord God, thou knowest."
> —EZEKIEL 37:3

Collaboration designates a distinct moral strategy in the Lutheran Church in Hungary for coping with socialism. Naturally collaboration presupposed complete cooperation with the political ambitions of the party-state, but more importantly, as a moral-theological response to oppression, collaboration entailed affirming Hungarian socialism as a religious truth. Collaborators could not satisfy the party by representing its interests in day-to-day political questions; they needed to provide ideological justification for communist rule as well. Thus they profoundly redefined the church's relationship to Hungarian society and crafted a theology of socialism. The theology of socialism equated the building of socialism with the realization of God's divine plans and thus made believing in socialism, as a political, moral, and religious project, a requirement of Christian faith.

The most prominent representatives of collaboration were Iván Reök, László Dezséry, and to a lesser extent—lesser because he was a second fiddler—Lajos Vető. However, although collaboration designates a distinct type with its own representatives, the origins of collaboration are to be found in the compromising strategy of Túróczy and Veöreös. This was so in two respects. First, Túróczy and Veöreös set the church on a course of compromise that was inherently unstable and that, when subjected to the pressures of totalitarianism, became distorted. Second, Túróczy and Veöreös introduced into the Lutheran Church a theological lexicon that was appropriated and manipulated by collaborators to suit their ends and the ends of the party. Collaboration was *ahogy lehet* gone amok: shrewd compromise without the shrewdness, dogged survival without the purpose, and tragic figures without the noble spirit.

Therefore, in order to understand the collaboration type, one must return briefly to Túróczy and Veöreös, backtracking in the narrative and gathering up strands of the story hitherto neglected. Only after the origins of collaboration have been identified can it be understood as a distinct theological position, that is, as a religious affirmation of socialism.

The Origins of Collaboration: *Ahogy Lehet* as False Realism

Hungarian Lutherans, trying to account for the emergence in their church of collaboration, often find the explanation in the personal ambitions of certain church leaders. To be sure, personal ambition and opportunism help account for the ability of the party-state always to find churchmen willing to cooperate with it. László Dezséry, for example, represents a clear instance where personal ambition influenced the shape of the church's public arguments. However, human motivations are usually complex, and to attribute collaborating behavior purely to personal ambition is to risk reducing a process of moral deliberation to its crassest element. Without denying the reality of unscrupulous opportunism, one will acquire a fuller sense of the quality of a collaboration as a moral choice by searching for additional patterns of deliberation.

Iván Reök was a deeply religious man of evangelical conviction. His unmistakable Christian commitment makes his later, seemingly unscrupulous collaboration somewhat of a puzzle. Some historians have conjectured that Reök had ecclesiastical ambitions, that he wanted to be general inspector, and that he concluded collaboration was the quickest way to achieve his end.[1] But Reök appears, also, to have possessed a weird sense of divine calling, a sense that God had specially chosen him to lead the Lutheran Church through Hungary's Red Sea.[2] This sense of special calling was integral to Reök's decision to collaborate. Reök believed in a special code for special times. His derangement, if it were that, was akin to the derangement of Raskolnikov in Dostoevsky's *Crime and Punishment*. Reök believed that necessity had placed him above the common morality. For ethical guidance he looked to *ahogy lehet*.

Reök's *ahogy lehet* reasoning becomes evident when one examines closely his conduct in the "year of the turn." On his own initiative, Reök took on the task of smoothing out the relationship between the Lutheran Church and the state, and as part of this special assignment, he frequently spoke with the church leadership about the need for compromise. Ordass recalls that in one conversation Reök told him the following:

> We need to accept that far reaching interventions into the life of the church are taking place; we need to be prepared to sacrifice our schools and many other "non-essential" appurtenances, because in the opposite case the consequence of our opposition would be a horrifying bloodbath. (In every conversation Reök endlessly emphasized the danger of a bloodbath). There is no point to opposition, because we need to prepare ourselves to live with the present conditions for a long time, and the church can have only one task, to ensure the right to preach.[3]

Reök's reasoning here, his understanding of the church's essential work as preaching, his willingness to relinquish the schools and accept state interference into church affairs echoes the convictions of Bishop Túróczy and Imre Veöreös. However, Reök's argument also appears to emphasize something new, namely the danger of a "horrifying bloodbath" and the necessity of avoiding it. Reök paints a picture in blunt realism and puts forth an argument as if to say, "there is no other choice."

Reök's bald realism was equally apparent in another conversation he had with Bishop Ordass. About that conversation Ordass remembered that:

> [Reök] spoke of streams of blood, and about the crucial significance of his rescue-ministry. He listed his merits at length, which were honored with recognition everywhere, except in the Lutheran Church. To my utmost horror he said that he was now trying to save what was savable.... In parting [Reök] emphasized that the thinking of a man steeped in the baptism of the Holy Spirit had shaped his position, while my position was that of a person without the Holy Spirit. He warned me that with the path on which I was traveling I was committing myself and my family to misfortune, that I was bringing a bloodbath down upon the church, and that for all this God would someday ask from me a very strict account.[4]

Reök's undisguised fatalism here—coupled with the intimations of his peculiar sense of mission—catches one's attention. It is a fatalism that Reök seems to have transformed into a distinct moral strategy. The reality of the situation in Hungary, Reök said, was that the communists were going to intervene into church affairs and the schools were going to be nationalized. Better to recognize the facts, he said, and do what was possible to save what one could. On one level, Reök had simply reformulated *ahogy lehet.*

Ahogy lehet was a strategy of survival through necessary compromises. Literally, *ahogy lehet* means "in the way that is possible," but in usage this phrase is ambiguous. On the one hand, "in the way that is possible" might mean that there is more than one way, that there are a variety of possibilities. In this meaning, *ahogy lehet* would be a challenge to creativity, a call to search out the possibilities and to find new ways to survive in a new historical setting. Here it would be a strategy of shrewd compromise coupled with internal resistance and a commitment to outsmart the oppressor. On the other hand, however, "in the way that is possible" might mean that there is only one way. In this meaning, *ahogy lehet* would denote not so much a strategy as an ordained fate. Here there would be no choices but only historical necessity. Rather than pointing to new possibilities, this second *ahogy lehet* would limit the possibilities to one.

To be sure, both senses of *ahogy lehet* surfaced in the Lutheran Church in Hungary in socialism. The second, however, was more sinister than the first. Indeed the second sense distorted *ahogy lehet* because it transformed a strategy of admirable tenacity into one of desperate opportunism. The distorted *ahogy lehet*, in turn, arose from the immediacy of the fear to which it attempted to respond. Thus to understand the distortion, one must understand the fear. That fear shapes the moral contours of this entire history.

In a famous essay entitled "The Misery of the Small States of Eastern Europe," the Hungarian political philosopher István Bibó isolates and analyzes distinctive features of East European history and the political distortions that can emerge from these. One of these features, Bibó says, is fear of national extinction:

> [All nationalities of Eastern Europe] have experienced what it means to know that the sacred places of one's national history are in danger, and to lose them; or to know that they have fallen into the hands of a foreign, enemy power and that all or part of one's people have fallen under the oppression of a foreign power. For all [Eastern European nationalities] there are geographical regions for which they are rightly anxious, or on which they have justified claims; and there is not one among them who has not stood near to partial or complete annihilation. For a Western-European it is an empty phrase when the statesman of some small East European state speaks about the "death of the nation" or the "annihilation of a nation." The Western-European can imagine extermination, subjugation, or slow assimilation. But whereas complete political annihilation occurring from one day to the next is for him only a bombastic picture, for East European nations it is a palpable reality. Here it is not necessary to liquidate or expel a nation, here it is perhaps only necessary that a nation feel threatened by a large enough force or violence to call its existence into question.[5]

This fear of extinction produces certain distortions in East European politics. One of those characteristic distortions, according to Bibó, is the emergence of a distinctive type of East European politician, what Bibó calls the "false realist." The false realist is a strongman who, playing off the existential fear of the community, uses the language of realism and historical necessity to assume the powers of a dictator. What characterizes this realism in part, and what makes it false, is the claim that political problems are such that only a strongman can solve them.

Just as national existential fear in Eastern Europe has produced a distorted kind of politician, so the fear of extinction within the Lutheran Church in Hungary produced a distorted kind of church-politician: the collaborator. Like Bibó's strongman, the collaborator was a false realist, because appealing to historical necessity, he denied the existence of choices or that his actions were restrained by moral considerations, and concentrating power in his hands while preserving the appearance of traditional legal structures, he turned against his church in the interest of preserving it.

It was in response to this fear that the Lutheran Church in Hungary produced its own false realists, among them Iván Reök. Fear for the existence of the church, and the judgment that collaboration was a historical necessity, drove Reök into the hands of Rákosi. It was a compromise, unpleasant but necessary to save the church.

Reök's strategy was related to that of Túróczy and Veöreös, if also different. For the Túróczy group *ahogy lehet* designated a framework of compromise within which one was to pursue strategies of survival. Compromise was possible so long as one did not relinquish the essence of the church. For Reök and the collaborators who followed him, compromise was not a framework but rather the means for survival. Instead of a policy of compromise within limits, Reök adopted a policy of compromise without limits in the sole interest of survival. Survival, not ministry, became the final good, and compromise was no longer subjected to moral considerations.

Túróczy and Reök, therefore, represented two kinds of *ahogy lehet*. The two were related, both theoretically and by historical proximity. Reök and Túróczy knew each other personally through their common participation in the evangelization movement. Later, in 1948, Reök exerted influence on Túróczy's decisions. Twice Reök and Túróczy met with Mátyás Rákosi, and at one meeting, apparently, Túróczy expressed willingness to accept school nationalization. Indeed at times Túróczy's thinking may have resembled Reök's version of *ahogy lehet* more closely than it did Veöreös's. Recall, for example, the exchange between Túróczy and Ordass after the latter learned that Túróczy was willing to give up the schools. As they left the negotiations, Túróczy said to Ordass, "One's relationship to these people is like that to highway robbers. They force a man to undress and he needs to beg them to at least leave him his underwear." Túróczy's metaphor intimates shades of Reök's *ahogy lehet* by suggesting the category of necessity and an absence of choices.

In any event, without determining Túróczy's inner thoughts, one can say that the border between the first and second *ahogy lehet* is murky. Whereas shrewd compromise can preserve the values of the community, wholesale collaboration only hands those values over. The difference between the two is delicate, and identifying the boundary is not easy, neither for historical actors themselves nor for later historians. One does best to understand the two senses of *ahogy lehet* as referring to two ideal types, conceptually distinct but with fluid boundaries not easily separated in the history. They are endpoints on a continuum, and somewhere between the two lies the border between compromise and collaboration.

Recognizing this, one must recognize also that collaboration, at the most basic level, emerged from a desire to help the church. Of course collaborators were ambitious, too, and they were willing to collaborate with the party-state to realize their ambitions, but collaboration was usually the end result of a series of bad choices. Everyone has aspirations. In Hungary pastors with aspirations found themselves living in a system that to all appearances was going to last the indefinite future. To succeed, they had to make compromises, and the more they wanted to succeed, the more compromises they needed to make. Then, somewhere along the line, not knowing exactly when, they were, at least some of the time, collaborating. Still, people do not become pastors without personal conviction. These pastors loved their church, they saw it was threatened, and they wanted it to live. To help it live, they had to make compromises. In making compromises, they forgot sometimes to limit their responsibility for the church—sometimes because they had ambitions, sometimes because they were truly frightened—and they did things they sometimes later regretted.

The Concept of "Reaction" and Reading History

When Túróczy and Veöreös made survival their central concern, they committed themselves to a constant battle of wits with the powerful party-state. Which bargains best served the church's interests? What were the long-term consequences for the church's survival of a particular course of action? To know these things one needs to understand the "signs of the times." Thus a moral framework of compromise depends for its success on historical discernment. Compromisers like Túróczy and Veöreös believed in their ability to discern the meaning of history, and they relied on special insights in making judgments about when to compromise. Their special insights, in turn, became part of the church's common theological lexicon, a lexicon that was quickly appropriated by collaborators and refashioned into a theology of socialism. Thus inadvertently Túróczy and Veöreös contributed to the theology of socialism. They introduced into the Lutheran Church the category of "reaction."

To be sure, the language of "reaction" pervaded public discourse in this period, but within the churches "reaction" was transformed into a moral-theological concept used to interpret contemporary events. The origins of this concept were rooted in a particular interpretation of Hungary's recent past. The end of the war had stirred in many Hungarians feelings of guilt about their country's alliance with Hitler. In the churches these feelings of guilt produced a desire for confession and spiritual renewal. In the eastern city of Nyíregyháza, a group of churchmen from Hungary's Reformed

Church started to put together a comprehensive program for reform. These reformers came out of the evangelization wing of their church, and they drew heavily upon the tradition of Hungarian evangelism in enunciating their vision for the future. Their calls for renewal resonated with many, and before long the reform campaign had expanded into a sizable grassroots movement. In the summer of 1946, leaders of the movement convened a national conference in Nyíregyháza for the purpose of discussing—in the words of the official announcement—"contemporary questions of evangelization, reformation, and the Hungarian awakening."[6] The National Hungarian Reformed Free Council, as they named the conference, introduced into Hungarian theological discourse important categories for interpreting Hungary's past, present, and future. Starting from a recognition of the sins of the past, those attending the Free Council wanted to break free from sin and renew both church and nation. Accordingly they dusted off the clarion of Jewish and Christian propheticism and sounded God's message for Hungary.

The message was one of undiscriminating wrath. All nations, said the Free Council, are accountable to God's moral order, and Hungary, in the interwar years, had repeatedly violated that order. Thus Hungary was reaping God's just judgment for its past sins. According to the Free Council, God had utterly condemned the entire Hungarian nation. The sign of this judgment was the indiscriminate destruction and suffering caused by the war. The obliteration of "old Hungary" was God's righteous punishment and part of his providential plan.[7]

The sweeping condemnation of Hungary announced by the Free Council, however, presupposed theological judgments that should have received explicit elucidation. If God intended the destruction of everything in the "old Hungary" as punishment for sin, that would seem to presuppose that everything in "old Hungary" was sinful. Such a presupposition, in turn, would seem to distribute blame for the past's sins among all Hungarians equally, thus amounting to an attribution of collective guilt. If, on the other hand, the judgment against "old Hungary" was such that one could distinguish between the good and the bad, why should everything from the "old Hungary" be destroyed instead of only that which was bad? The Free Council never addressed these kinds of questions but advanced a moral condemnation of the past without a framework for separating the wheat from the tares. The result was a sweeping, unnuanced ascription of general guilt to all of Hungary.

Moreover, the Free Council's sweeping assessment of guilt was interlocked with unexamined presuppositions about the relationship between God's providence and current happenings. The lost war, with its suffering and devastation, said the Free Council, was not merely a consequence of the ill-chosen policies of Hungary's political leaders, nor part and parcel of the misfortune historically attendant upon small Eastern European states; instead postwar suffering constituted a portion of God's divine plan for Hungary. It was his punishment. Such an interpretation of Hungary's situation seemed to infer directly from the course of events to God's will, as if what happened was the same as what God wanted to happen. That, however, was a questionable inference. Why should the fact that the war brought tremendous suffering mean that God wanted Hungarians to suffer? The Free Council would have needed to provide criteria for separating the good and the bad in what happened. They did not do that, but rather took a position which implied, at least in practice, that everything that happened was what God wanted to happen.[8]

These unexamined theological judgments soon appeared in the Lutheran Church. The Free Council had grown out of a reform movement that drew its force from the evangelization wing of the Reformed Church. Presumably the arguments of Reformed evangelicals exerted influence on evangelicals in the Lutheran Church. For example, Nyíregyháza, the city where the Free Council was held, also seated Túróczy's diocese. Túróczy surely knew of the happenings of the Free Council, and he may have been influenced by them. Additionally, documentary evidence indicates that in November 1946, shortly after the Free Council was held, a group of Lutheran pastors met in the city of Győr to discuss issues of reform. The results of this meeting were summarized in a statement written by Imre Veöreös and published a year later in *Lelkipásztor*.[9] Most of the proposals in Veöreös's statement echoed the proposals made at the Free Council, although they were neither as comprehensive nor as radical. In any case, the unexamined theological judgments advanced by the Free Council were soon at work in the Lutheran Church. They were particularly evident in the theological use given to the concept "reaction."

In the thinking of Imre Veöreös, for example, "reaction" became part of a larger theological reading of events in Hungary. In an article entitled "Our Church in 1948, the Historical Situation," Veöreös set forth an interpretation of contemporary events which followed the contours of that offered by the Free Council. According to Veöreös, "old Hungary" had been a "dark country," and the newest "turn of events" was a sign of God's "judging hand." Thus Veöreös, like the Free Council, believed he had discerned God's providential will in contemporary history. He then went one step further by merging his interpretation of history with the concept of "reaction." In everyday political discourse "reaction" meant only the desire and ambition to return to "old Hungary." Now in Veöreös's hands, "reaction" meant, also, rebellion against God, because God had condemned the "old Hungary."[10]

Veöreös even managed to fuse subtly the notion of "reaction" with traditional Lutheran teaching about the separation between religion and politics. According to Luther, God rules the world in two different ways, through two different kingdoms. The first kingdom, the Kingdom of God, comprises the spiritual estate, or the church. In the church, the law of love as expressed in the Gospel and the Sermon on the Mount applies directly. The second kingdom, the Kingdom of Earth, comprises the temporal estate, which includes secular authority, or the state. The state rules not by simple love, which Luther believes is nonviolent, but by the sword, so that sin be held in abeyance. The exact relationship between the kingdoms is a matter of some dispute, but generally the two are to be kept separate. Christians must not mix up political matters with matters of the Gospel. Churchmen are commissioned only with care of the Gospel and should stay aloof from political disputes.

This Lutheran imperative to separate theology and politics merged easily with arguments about the need to avoid "reaction." Thus Imre Veöreös could write, in an article entitled "The Political Position of Our Church," that the church must avoid politics and stay on the narrow path of theological conviction. Avoiding politics meant, on the one hand, that the church needed to avoid selling itself out to the ruling political power, but on the other hand—and here was the greater emphasis—that the church needed to avoid "political reaction." In Veöreös's words, "God has condemned the old Hungary together with its sins and social injustices in the storm of history; and this every Lutheran person must accept humbly and with repentance before God."[11]

Admonitions against "reaction" and appeals to the Lutheran abstention from politics were also frequent in arguments over school nationalization and the church-state agreement. Luther teaches that unless the state encroaches upon the proper domain of the church or commands something contrary to God's law, Christians must obey it. Even in the case of an unjust ruler, Luther says, the Christian must not rebel but choose to suffer. Accordingly, in Hungary arguments were made that, should the legitimate political authority decide to nationalize the schools, the church must accept it as a political decision. To resist would be to confuse the church's essential ministry with mere historical arrangements and to commit a profound theological error. It would be to fight for a political cause under the banner of the Gospel and to fall into "reaction."

Thus when the time came for the Lutheran Church to ratify the agreement, Bishop Túróczy couched the issue within the framework of obedience to the state and the problem of "reaction." In a speech entitled "Is Agreement Possible?" Túróczy argued that those in the church who opposed the agreement were doing so not for theological reasons but from political motivations. Such opposition offended the Lutheran theological heritage. Even worse, within the context of Hungarian history, such opposition amounted to political "reaction." According to Túroczy, "The antagonism to Hungarian democracy appearing in our church today . . . [originates] from affection for the bourgeoisie form of life." Those affections were a symptom of "reaction."[12]

"Reaction," however, was a sloppy category. It depended on a set of theological judgments that were both unexamined and simplistic: first, an ascription to Hungary of collective guilt, and second, a straightforward affirmation of whatever happened in Hungary on the grounds that God wanted it to happen that way. Moreover, the concept of "reaction" was a tool of communist propaganda. Given the political environment, the theological judgments invested in the concept inevitably fused with the propagandistic elements so that it was difficult to determine which was the stronger. That is to say, an external observer has trouble discerning whether the Túróczy group asked first what it meant to fulfill the church's ministry and then on that basis determined what constituted "reaction" or whether they asked first about "reaction" and on that basis determined what constituted the true ministry of the church. Oftentimes one cannot escape the impression that "reaction" was defining what constituted a confessional stance and not the other way around.

Finally the concept of "reaction," because it was sloppy and propagandistic, was also malleable and easily manipulated. Collaborating churchmen were able to pick up the theological judgments embedded in the concept and make them the cornerstone of a larger religious history for Hungary.

Theological Affirmations of Socialism

Between 1948 and 1956 collaborating church leaders worked to define for the church a new relationship to Hungarian society. They did this by placing socialism within a larger historical account of God's activity in Hungarian history. Essentially they crafted a special Hungarian salvation history. It consisted of two parts. Part one told the story of Hungary's recent past, relating, without nuance, the great evils of the Horthy era and condemning that past collectively and in its entirety. Part two told of how Hungary had been liberated by Soviet troops and the arrival of socialism. It related a radical moral break from Hungary's past and the coming of an ideal future. Then from within the framework of this salvation history, collaborating churchmen affirmed socialism theologically; that is, they treated socialism as an object of Christian faith, something that Christians, qua Christians, were required to believe in.

For Lutherans the first full telling of the new salvation history appeared in 1948 when László Dezséry published his *Open Letter in the Matter of the*

Lutheran Church in Hungary.[13] Dezséry's *Open Letter* set forth the outlines of a comprehensive interpretation of recent Hungarian history and provided a manifesto for the church's future in Hungarian socialism. Dezséry's historiography began with an account of the Horthy period that repeated the kinds of sweeping condemnations articulated by the Reformed Free Council and implied by the language of "reaction." Horthy's Hungary, said Dezséry, had been built on three pillars: anti-Semitism, irredentist nationalism, and anticommunism. For this reason Hungary allied itself with the Nazis. Meanwhile, the leaders of the Lutheran Church never objected to or struggled against the sins of the Horthy regime. Much to the contrary, said Dezséry, they actively supported the regime, either by participating in it politically or benefiting from its existence.

After condemning the Horthy period, Dezséry started developing the concept of "reaction." Once the Soviets had liberated Hungary, said Dezséry, those responsible for the church's past crimes should have been brought to account. Hungary's political leaders waited, but the church never acknowledged its mistakes. Instead the church leadership closed ranks, making it impossible to remove those holding higher church offices. Beyond that, the church leadership did everything it could to stop confession and renewal. As a consequence, said Dezséry, the church had become a gathering place for those harboring political grievances; that is, the church had become a center for "reaction." Thus the church was in a state of crisis emerging from the struggle between two opposing forces. On the one side were the communists, the forces of progress, who in the last war had struggled against and eventually defeated fascism. On the other side were "reactionaries," those who had allied themselves with Hitler and now wanted to return to the Hungary of the Horthy era. Sadly, Dezséry said, the current church leadership was standing on the side of "reaction." Therefore they needed to leave office.

Significantly, Dezséry's attack on the church leadership was coupled with an effort to win over the evangelization wing of the church and to appropriate its traditions. Dezséry worked to portray his position as the natural fruition of evangelical commitments. Between his litany of church sins, Dezséry managed to work in praise of the evangelization movement. Dezséry must have felt, or hoped, that what he was saying would echo in evangelical circles.

Certainly the argument of the *Open Letter* worked with theological presuppositions similar to those held unexamined by the Reformed Free Council and by the Túróczy group. The Free Council had claimed to discern God's providential action in recent Hungarian history. Relying on this claim, it ascribed guilt collectively to the Hungarian nation and proclaimed God's judgment against it. Imre Veöreös and Bishop Túróczy took these theological judgments one step further and argued that the church must eschew "reaction." László Dezséry picked up the concept of "reaction" and used it to advance an interpretation of history even more far-reaching. With Dezséry, the project of reading history entailed not only sweeping condemnations of the past but also unqualified affirmations of the present and future.

After discerning the meaning of the past in *Open Letter*, Dezséry moved effortlessly to describe the future unfolding. The unfolding future was socialist. As Dezséry explained:

> The present Hungarian state was born in the age of the advancement of socialism, and consciously and resolutely professes socialism. . . . This means that more has happened in Hungary than simply a change of government. We have been swept into the waves of the socialist revolution and it is this with which we must reckon. We are standing face to face with a world presence against which one cannot struggle with weapons. On my foreign travels I have experienced that truly amazing bewilderment and helplessness with which bourgeoisie societies struggle against the ideals and fighting tactics of Marxism.[14]

The argument appeared to affirm socialism as a historical inevitability, although Dezséry did not explain how he arrived at these historical insights. Was he himself a communist advancing arguments about the dialectical progression of history? Or was he illuminating God's present action in Hungary by building upon his theological assessment of the Horthy regime and the divine judgment he had discerned against the present Lutheran Church in Hungary? Whichever the case, Dezséry had advanced a claim about the workings of history, and on this basis he had predicted the future. His argument was that history stood on the side of socialism. Therefore, if the church was to be on the "right" side of history, it, too, needed to stand with socialism.

Dezséry divided Hungarian history into two halves, diametrically opposed: the evil, guilt-ridden Horthy past and the good, progressive, socialism-building present and future. Separating these two grand epochs was a radical event: the Soviet liberation of Hungary in 1945. The Soviet liberation freed Hungary from its bondage to sin of the past and freed Hungary for the building of a reborn, ideal future, namely, socialism. Given this historiography, Hungarian Christians had a moral obligation to support socialism. Indeed given this historiography, Hungarian Christians had an obligation to believe in socialism as the unfolding of God's providential will, to think of it as a kind of religious truth.

This simple historiography, built on the argument of Dezséry's *Open Letter*, provided the theological framework for defining the Lutheran Church's relationship to Hungarian socialism between 1948 and 1956. Looking through articles from this period in *Evangélikus Élet*, one encounters the formula and the accompanying religious affirmation of socialism more times than are worth counting. The following excerpt from an article commemorating Hungary's Soviet "liberation," written by Iván Reök, is representative:

> God led our people through a great historical change and brought them liberation from the East. The lying, but hard yoke of fascism was pulled off our shoulders by the hand of a young people, whom we, arrogant Christians, took for nothing, and whom we slandered. The Red Army of the Socialist Soviet Republic, against which our false prophets had announced a "Christian war," brought an end in Hungary to the rampage of fascism . . . and it led our people to the path of social and economic, indeed, to the path of spiritual renewal. . . . On the fifth anniversary of the liberation, with a heart heeding the historical lesson, full of self-searching, and obedient before God, our church greets the leading troop of the Hungarian people, the Hungarian Workers Party, and its leader, Mátyás Rákosi, who was not only the one to accomplish God's judgment against a sinful and corrupt Hungarian system, but who was also the instrument of God's mercy allowing us to rebuild.[15]

According to Reök, the Soviet "liberation" marked a moment of radical discontinuity in Hungary's history. Before the "liberation" Hungarians lived in bondage to fascism and sin; after the "liberation" they were living in hope and renewal. The undisputed author of this renewal was God, but God was working through his chosen agents, namely, the Red Army of the Socialist Soviet Republic, Mátyás Rákosi, and communists generally.

Clearly Reök's historiography functioned to legitimate Hungarian socialism. The larger point, however, is that Reök did not legitimate socialism through mere political partisanship; rather, he affirmed it religiously. He was not merely arguing that socialism was a most excellent social and political arrangement, one deeply compatible with Christian commitments to justice, and, therefore, Christians ought to advocate it as the best social and political arrangement existing on earth. Rather, Reök was asserting the coming of socialism to Hungary as the realization of God's divine plan; socialism's arrival was contemporaneous, indeed identical, with the spiritual renewal of Hungarian Christians. Reök made socialism a religious truth and hence an object of Christian faith. This religious affirmation is what made collaboration theological.

Theological affirmations of socialism, although always presupposing the historiographical account described above, could also appear independently of it. One of the main avenues for religiously affirming socialism in the Rákosi period was peace work. Peace work in Hungary was an activity initiated and organized by the party-state that involved church leaders and clergy. Hungarian peace work was conducted along two distinct avenues, foreign and domestic. Foreign peace work connected with the international peace movement then emerging in Europe and the world; domestic peace work was directed exclusively toward Hungarians. In both cases, Hungarian peace work had clear propagandistic objectives. Abroad, language of "peace" was used before ecumenical leaders to deflect criticism of events in Hungary; at home, language of "peace" was directed toward clergy, parishes, and the people in an effort to legitimate the regime.[16]

One of the main purposes of church participation in the international peace movement, from a Hungarian perspective, was to rebut and defuse criticisms of religious persecution in the Eastern Bloc. Hungarian clergy would issue statements on peace that placed the issue of East-West church relations in the context of a potential third world war. These statements generally suggested that Western Christians, by criticizing East European churches, were advancing relative Western interests and furthering the cause of war. The Hungarian churches would ask that those in the West not confuse their Christian faith with bourgeois democratic values, just as Eastern church leaders had been asked not to intertwine their faith with socialism. Eastern Christians were living in societies undergoing profound social transformations; yet there was a path for the churches in the East, too. What was needed was understanding and support, not misplaced criticism. The conclusion was always a call for Christians in the East and West to put aside their political differences and work together for peace.

Representative was a 1950 message from the Lutheran Church in Hungary to the Lutheran churches in the West, which included the following:

> The Lutheran Church in Hungary, in faith and on the basis of a decision of faith, trusting in God alone, has chosen and endeavors to travel on that path which it sees as the narrow path in accordance with God's will in this present world. . . . In this situation we ask for more understanding, patience, love and confidence from our Western Lutheran brethren, who, absent familiarity with our history and present situation, often look at us with prejudice and judge us with bias. We ask them to feel more responsibility toward us and to pray for us more. They should consider whether it is really helpful for the Hungarian Church of Jesus Christ if a series of statements are made that, usually grounded on false information and not in agreement with the actual facts, are nevertheless quite capable of harming the place of our church in the world.[17]

In the beginning, selling this line to Western church leaders was a difficult task, especially for the Lutheran Church, given that Bishop Ordass, vice president of the Lutheran World Federation, was sitting in prison. Nevertheless, arguments like these had a genuinely persuasive tone. These appeals for tolerance and mutual understanding had a certain plausibility, especially for those ignorant of the situation in Hungary. At the same time, for Hungarian church leaders to respond to criticisms of grotesque show trials or to queries about pastors suspended from their offices or in prison by referring to an impending world war or alleged ulterior economic and political motives was at best only a clever way of changing the subject. To be sure, Western perceptions may have been inordinately influenced by political and economic interests, but it was blatantly disingenuous for Hungarian church leaders to portray concern for the rule of law and basic human freedoms as the mere expression of relative Western interests—as if these were values alien to Hungarian history or a matter of indifference to victims of torture in Hungarian prisons.

Moreover, while the church leadership used the language of peace abroad to admonish against confusing Christianity with relative political values, at home they did not refrain from equating the struggle for peace with the building up of socialism. Whereas in the international forum appeals to peace were part of a call to rise above political partisanship, in Hungary the peace movement was used as a way to legitimate socialism. Consider, for example, Bishop Dezséry's description of peace work in the following passage:

> Hungarian Protestantism holds it a betrayal of the Christian faith if someone now thinks that Christianity should conduct a holy war against Marxists. We hold it to be a confession of Christianity if the Christian person thinks it necessary to struggle together with the communists in defense of peace. . . . The Soviet Union, upon whose attitude the matter of peace depends most of all, stands firmly on the side of peace and organizes the forces of peace throughout the world. We give thanks to God that the contemporary world's greatest power stands exactly on that side, the side of peace, demanded by God. Therefore, Western Christianity ought not marvel that Eastern Christianity supports the non-believing, but peace loving, communists. Rather it ought marvel that its own so-called Christian governments prepare for war and incite for war. They ought not perceive tension between Christian faith and life here in our hemisphere of the globe, but they should perceive it at home. We stand on the side of humanity in the defense of peace and by this, according to our conviction, we profess the purest principles of Protestantism.[18]

The language of peace used by Dezséry made Soviet-style socialism an object of Christian faith. Peace was a Christian commitment; and the

Soviet Union, a state run by communists, represented peace uniquely in the world of that day. Thus supporting the Soviet instantiation of peace was a confessional matter; it was an element of true Christian faith. The conscientious Christian must in some way commit himself religiously to the Soviet Union—to its foreign policy at least and implicitly to the entire socialist project. In this way the language of peace became one more avenue for collaborating with the communists theologically.

Such was the nature of theological collaboration. One must never forget, however, that behind all collaboration, both theological and political, the *ahogy lehet* dynamic was at work. In totalitarianism the Lutheran Church in Hungary experienced what was probably the hardest period in its four-hundred-year history. In truth the theology of socialism was only the outer cover of a hidden and raw moral experience with a corresponding set of unseen choices. Few people in the church actually believed the nonsense about socialism and "peace" spewed out by the leadership. A few, perhaps, believed it for a while and then believed that believing it was a good way to get ahead. Others never believed it but believed believing it was necessary for the church to survive. These kinds of believers, believing they had no choice, chose collaboration.

That in fact there were choices, even in socialism, was a lesson of the next phase of this history.

CHAPTER THREE

An Understanding with Dictators

Hopes for a New Beginning, 1956–58

> Behold, the days are coming, says the LORD, when I will make a new covenant with the house of Israel and the house of Judah.
> —JEREMIAH 31:31

The unprecedented social dislocation, economic mismanagement, and mass terror that accompanied the building of socialism in Hungary had sustained itself only by naked force. Older historical patterns, however, and the negative consequences of communist engineering began to assert themselves. On March 5, 1953, Joseph Stalin died, and soon after, signs of discontent began cropping up throughout Eastern Europe. Wary of crises, Soviet leaders summoned a delegation of Hungarian communists to Moscow and ordered Rákosi to hand over the prime ministership to a man named Imre Nagy. Imre Nagy, it turned out, was a genuine reformer, and he was to be the first of Eastern European communist leaders who would try, and fail, to carry through fundamental reforms of the Soviet-style system.

Nagy's effort to implement political and economic reforms evoked intense opposition from Hungary's hard-line communists, who fought to undermine the prime minister and remove him from public life. Vacillating signals from Moscow created uncertainty, and the tug-of-war between reformers and hard-liners in Hungary allowed opposition to the Rákosi clique to emerge openly. Finally mass demonstrations in Budapest turned into armed opposition, and on October 23, 1956, the Hungarian Revolution began. Freedom fighters successfully repelled Russian troops at first, but on November 4 the Soviets moved decisively against them. The Russians established a puppet government headed by a man named János Kádár, and after two weeks of freedom, Hungary returned to the building of socialism.

In 1956 the Lutheran Church in Hungary also faced crisis. The church leadership had announced a new path for the church in socialism, and Rákosi's unexampled oppression had created a receptive church. Unseen behind the docility, however, were grievances and scents of putrescence. When the party tried to reform, church leaders were caught off guard and before they knew it were confronting an angry church.

Time for Reform in the Lutheran Church

The first signs of trouble for the leadership of the Lutheran Church appeared when the government began to consider rehabilitating Bishop Ordass. The World Council of Churches had decided some years prior that its central committee would meet in Hungary in July 1956. When in 1956 Hungary entered a process of political change, Western church leaders saw an opportunity to raise questions concerning Hungarian church life, and they announced their intention to place the "Ordass question" on their agenda.

Quickly Ordass lost his status in Hungary as persona non grata. He was visited twice by the president of the State Office of Church Affairs (ÁEH), János Horváth, whose purpose in these visits was clearly to acquaint himself with Ordass's demeanor. Horváth inquired after the bishop's political attitudes, and the bishop, for his part, made clear that he expected to receive complete rehabilitation. The two men spoke frankly. At one point Horváth paid Ordass a personal compliment. Ordass remarked that he believed that he had actually met in Horváth an "honorable communist," adding, "You know, Mr. President, even among you there are quite a few worthless people."[1]

When the central committee of the World Council of Churches convened in Hungary, Ordass's case was taken up by an impressive group of ecumenical church leaders comprised of Hanns Lilje, president of the Lutheran World Federation; Carl E. Lund-Quist, general secretary of the Lutheran World Federation; Franklin Clark Fry, president of the World Council of Churches' central committee; and Willem A. Visser't Hooft, general secretary of the World Council of Churches. These men wanted Ordass to return to active service as bishop. That, however, would require a double rehabilitation for Ordass, one from the state for his criminal conviction and one from the church for the decision that removed him from office. Although the state rehabilitation posed no special problems, a church rehabilitation would entail invalidating the bishopric of Ordass's successor, László Dezséry.[2] The difficulty was overcome by a compromise agreement with the Lutheran World Federation. The LWF stated publicly its expectation that Ordass would return to his bishop's seat, and the Hungarian government promised a state rehabilitation in the near future with the understanding that Ordass would return to a bishopric at the first available opportunity. In the meantime, Ordass would resign his bishop's seat upon receiving the state rehabilitation and teach at the church's seminary until a bishopric became available.[3]

The news of Ordass's impending state rehabilitation brought forth no official comment from the Lutheran Church in Hungary. The bishops perhaps were worried about the impact Ordass's rehabilitation would have on their own positions. Indeed Ordass's pending rehabilitation became the rallying point for opposition to the church leadership, and his figure became a conduit through which the common church could voice much broader dissatisfaction. This widespread discontent came to a point in a series of pastors conferences held in the fall of 1956, only a few weeks before the start of the Hungarian Revolution.

Prior to the conferences, András Keken, one of the pastors arrested in 1950 in connection with Ordass's church trial, wrote a paper distributed secretly throughout the church in which he demonstrated the legal necessity of Ordass's rehabilitation and by implication undermined Bishop Dezséry's legitimacy. Keken's description of recent events gave the impression that the greatest obstacles to Ordass's rehabilitation came not from the party-state but from the church.[4] Thus Keken's paper tapped into a widespread feeling of repugnance toward the church leadership.

Similarly a group of pastors rooted in the evangelization tradition also met prior to the conferences in order to discuss conditions in the church. Together they wrote a statement, called "Observations," which was sent to the central church office and also distributed among pastors. "Observations" affirmed the centrality of evangelization to the life of the church and lamented its recent disappearance. The authors of the document, striking a traditional theme, called on the church to repent for the sins of the past ten years and called for far-reaching renewal in the church. This renewal was necessary, according to the statement, because the church had corrupted its ministry with false teachings; it had answered contemporary questions with a language other than the Word of God.[5]

Significantly these first open criticisms of the church leadership came from both Ordass loyalists and evangelizers—the two groups that had fragmented in 1948. So bad had been the previous eight years that the churchly and evangelization wings were rising up together against the bishops.

At the pastors conferences, the clergy confronted the church leadership with both theological and personal criticisms.[6] Many of the theological criticisms focused on the leadership's misuse of guilt as a moral and theological concept, and on the way the leadership drew simple correlations between providence and history. Simply because something happens does not mean God wants it to happen that way, the pastors said. The fact that Hungary lost the Second World War did not mean everything in its past was bad, and the fact that communists now ran the country did not mean everything in the present was good. One cannot, said the pastors, straightforwardly infer God's plan from the course of events.

The pastors also accused the church leadership of corrupting the Gospel by intermingling it with false teachings. Some pastors identified the source of this false teaching precisely in the straightforward inferences being made from history to providence. By seeing God's will in everything that happened, the argument went, the church leadership made "reality"—in other words, whatever the case may be—a standard of faith alongside the doctrine of justification. Because, according to this false teaching, "reality" claims allegiance from believers, the church was teaching that it must accommodate itself to whatever happens. The possibility that the church might need to stand against the stream, that things could happen in socialism contrary to God's will, was therefore excluded.

Finally, Lutheran pastors in 1956 articulated an alternative vision for their church in socialism, the vision of a martyr church. In the first years of socialism, the church's strategy for dealing with the regime had been pragmatic, focused on survival. In 1956, however, many pastors explicitly rejected that pragmatism, setting up in its place the ideal of a suffering church, one prepared to march unto death rather than concede an iota of its ministry, a church persecuted yet faithful. Although uttered only in fragmentary form, this call for a suffering church marked the beginning of a voice that would play counterpoint to the official church theology of later years and have an impact.

In addition to theological criticisms, the pastors also voiced personal criticisms of the bishops. As each week's conference came to an end, the pastors issued a common statement setting forth what they expected from the leadership. Reading these statements in chronological order, one senses that the tone at the conferences grew increasingly sharp. With increasing openness, the pastors expressed their dislike for the current leadership, and their lists of demands grew longer. Calls for general resignations grew plentiful, and by early October the church leadership confronted a mass of angry pastors only a hair's width away from open revolt. Even more disconcerting for the church leadership, the State Office of Church Affairs no longer seemed to support them.

As the pastors conferences wound to a close, the party-state, on October 5, rehabilitated Bishop Ordass. Ordass was informed of his rehabilitation on the morning of October 6 by János Horváth. Later that day a small circle of friends visited Ordass to celebrate. When the group began to sing hymns, Ordass broke into tears.[7] A few days later, on October 8, the Lutheran Church rehabilitated Bishop Ordass.[8] In accordance with the earlier agreement, Ordass resigned his office as bishop and prepared to start lecturing at the seminary on October 24.

But October 23 and the Hungarian Revolution changed all that.

A New Start in the Lutheran Church

On the day the Hungarian Revolution began, János Horváth telephoned Ordass and asked him to assume the duties of bishop. Ordass insisted that Dezséry resign first, which he did on October 30.[9] Thus on Reformation Day,

October 31, 1956, Bishop Ordass returned to the bishopric from which he had been illegally removed six years earlier. The following day Bishop Vető resigned, making Ordass the church's senior ranking bishop and indeed its only one. Two days later, on November 3, Bishop Ordass convened an emergency meeting of pastors and teachers.

This November 3 meeting, although unofficially assembled, initiated important changes in the church. It accepted recent resignations, those of Dezséry and Vető, as well as others by holders of high church offices. It passed a motion urging the resignations of General Inspector Ernő Mihályfi and Southern Diocesan Inspector József Darvas. It agreed that Bishop Ordass should request all the church's seniors (a mid-level clerical office) to resign so that new elections could be held. It placed new persons at the head of the church press. Finally, those at the meeting requested Zoltán Túróczy to take over temporary direction of the Northern Diocese.[10]

Interestingly many at the meeting expressed concern for János Horváth, and they commissioned Bishop Ordass to look after his safety. Ordass repeatedly telephoned the Horváth household and inquired after the ÁEH president's whereabouts, but he managed only to talk to a nervous sister-in-law, who said Horváth was not at home. Finally, growing concerned, Ordass offered to have the Horváth family stay in his apartment, in order to protect them from any angry insurgents.[11]

So began Ordass's second term as bishop and a new phase in the life of the Lutheran Church in Hungary. In fact Lutherans would experience early post-Revolution Hungary differently than the other Hungarian churches. Even after the Revolution, as the communists clamped down on the country, Ordass's close relationship with János Horváth seemed to bring special protection and freedom for the Lutheran Church. A secret government report written by Horváth in February 1957 provides evidence of this. Horváth noted in the report that the "counter-revolution" had brought the forces of "reaction" back to the Catholic and Reformed churches but that in the Lutheran Church, things were quite different. Although old leaders had been removed from office in that church, too, Horváth said, "Dezséry's position in the church had been seriously isolated for years," and the Office of Church Affairs had established a good relationship with Bishop Ordass. "Presently," Horváth concluded, "the situation with the Lutheran Church is satisfactory and developing in a good direction."[12]

In February, what Horváth considered a "good direction" did not preclude significant personnel changes. The changes decided upon at the November 3 meeting had been sanctioned by the appropriate church organs in mid-December at meetings that Horváth, contrary to custom, did not even bother to attend. Horváth taciturnly accepted the resignations of Dezséry, Vető, Mihályfi, and Darvas, and he and Ordass even discussed the possibility of returning two of the Lutheran high schools. On February 6 Zoltán Túróczy was installed as bishop of the Northern Diocese. When Ordass discussed Túróczy's return with Horváth, Horváth spoke so emphatically that Ordass wrote in his diary, "Horváth recognized past mistakes with an openness to shame many Christians, and he assured Túróczy that he could count on the state's confidence in his future activity."[13]

A new agreement, built on mutual consensus and anchored in Horváth and Ordass's mutual respect, seemed to exist between the Lutheran Church and the State Office of Church Affairs. Moreover, the party-state, battered by the upheaval of recent months, appeared to want a new relationship, too. In January 1957 the new Hungarian government issued a policy statement distancing itself from the Rákosi regime and also emphasizing the government's commitment to religious freedom.[14] This new attitude toward the churches was even reinforced by a concrete structural change: the government shut down the State Office of Church Affairs. Thus in 1957 Lutherans had reason to hope.

As the new year began, Hungarian Lutherans strove to establish a new relationship with the political power, one in which the party-state granted the church greater freedom, but in which, also, the church supported the Kádár regime in its endeavors to build socialism. The church attempted to explain this new relationship theologically by setting forth a normative vision of church-state relations for the Hungarian context. According to that vision, the proper foundation for the church's dealings with the state rested in the nature of the church as an institution concerned with salvation. The church's business was to administer the Word, which it has always done in different times in different settings. Thus the church accepted the existing political authority as ordained from God and, in obedience to the state, endeavored to raise good citizens.

Frequently Lutheran discussions of church-state relations in this period turned to the 1948 agreement. The letter, if not the spirit, of that agreement guaranteed the church internal autonomy. So in 1957 Bishop Ordass, who had earlier made enemies of the communists by opposing the agreement, was willing to say to the general assembly of the Lutheran Church, "our church carries out its life within the frame of the Hungarian People's Republic on the basis of the agreement which our church reached with the political power in the year 1948."[15] This represented a notable modification of the bishop's original stance and his acceptance of communist rule in Hungary. By affirming the agreement in 1957, however, Ordass was not only yielding to communist rule, he was also staking out a claim for the church in Hungarian socialism. The church was committed and loyal to the party-state, Ordass was saying, but it claimed, also, the free space to conduct its ministry unobstructed, in the fashion ensured by the agreement.

Alongside this official effort to define church-state relations, however, an unofficial theological conversation was also taking place within the church, one that concentrated on issues raised by the legacy of the Rákosi years. This conversation continued to work through ideas that had been introduced at the 1956 pastors conferences, specifically the vision of a suffering church. According to many pastors, the failure of the church had been its unwillingness to shoulder Christ's cross in dark times. The church had been afraid to suffer, and consequently it had betrayed its ministry. By implication the church's future lay in its willingness to take up the cross.

This call for a suffering church was given explicit moral-theological foundation in the principle of obedience to the church's ministry. The duty of the church was to remain true to its ministry, the argument went, regardless of cost or consequence. Indeed suffering, or in the imagery of the New Testament, the cross, was the destiny of a communion of believers who remained true to the Gospel. Thus suffering was made a normative category for the Lutheran Church in socialism.

That this normative vision of a suffering church existed side by side with a more conventional church-state understanding was incongruous. On the one hand, the exposition of church-state theory presupposed a context of responsibility. That is to say, it assumed that the politicians were upright people who would act as they should. On the other hand, the vision of a suffering church presupposed a context of disenfranchisement. It assumed that the important people were acting badly, and because they were acting badly, the church must suffer. Both positions purported to be prescriptive but for vastly different social contexts. That they were both present in 1957 indicates the Lutheran Church was uncertain about its place in socialism. The two visions could not remain side by side indefinitely. Eventually one of them would prove more appropriate to the Hungarian setting.

As the year progressed, signs of frustration with this little, independently minded Lutheran Church began to surface in the government office responsible for church affairs. An internal report written in July listed a host of complaints, from the absence of "progressive" clergy in important posts to the tone of the church press to the reluctance of the bishops to adopt positions on daily political questions. At the core of the complaints was a sense that the church was not being loyal enough to the regime. In the party-state's understanding, loyalty entailed more than a recognition of the legitimacy of the People's Republic of Hungary and more than cooperation with its worthwhile moral objectives. Loyalty meant positive, explicit affirmation of Hungary's social-political project. The government report ended with the following assessment: "Events taking place in the Lutheran church permit the conclusion that they have overestimated the loyalty exhibited on our part. We have conceded too much to them."[16]

Frustration was also mounting in the Lutheran Church. In late October 1957, one year after returning to office, Bishop Ordass wrote a long letter to János Horváth that touched upon virtually every issue of conflict between the church and the party-state: the meaning and obligations prescribed in the agreement, unresolved personnel questions, the church press, peace work, ecumenical connections, and arrested pastors.[17] Matters were coming to a head.

Disposing of Bishop Ordass, Again

In early November Horváth called Ordass into his office and announced that there would be church-state negotiations. When the negotiations began, Horváth charged that the church leadership was discriminating against pastors with "progressive" views and demanded comprehensive changes in the church's current officeholders. He wanted Lajos Vető to replace Bishop Túróczy in the Northern Diocese, and he also wanted specific changes in inspectors, seniors, church press officers, and other posts. Most of these changes would return churchmen from the Dezséry period back to their offices. The church delegation argued that such changes would create a crisis of confidence in the church. They protested furthermore that by dictating these changes, the party-state was encroaching upon the freedom of the church.[18]

The two parties discussed their differences in four separate rounds of negotiations, at times appearing to make headway but frequently coming close to deadlock. Horváth's demands were nonnegotiable, and Ordass could not consent to sweeping interventions into the church's organization. Thus on November 26 the negotiations deadlocked. János Horváth broke them off and announced that the government would be intervening into the life of the church, stating, "These measures are the result of the behavior of the church leadership and the current church leaders are responsible for them."[19]

In a secret report written in February 1957, János Horváth had set out his strategy for removing "reactionary" church leaders. The government would first isolate the reactionary by demonstrating that his conduct was creating unnecessary difficulties for the church. Then, having destroyed the reactionary's credibility, the party-state could remove him without antagonizing the religious masses.[20] This was to be Horváth's strategy for removing Bishop Ordass.

Ordass, however, was a formidable adversary. He seemed invulnerable to intimidation, and he enjoyed considerable domestic and international prestige. The Hungarian Revolution was still a recent event affecting Hungary's international reputation, and a few months earlier Bishop Ordass had attended the Third World Assembly of the Lutheran World Federation, where he was again elected vice president. Consequently Horváth and the government approached Ordass with circumspection. Their plan was to place him in a crafted catch-22, a situation where no matter what he did he would lose credibility with the clergy and be forced to leave his office in ignominious defeat.

The first phase of the operation was to isolate Ordass. A few days after the negotiations deadlocked, a government deputy named Károly Grnák appeared at the general church office and told Ordass and Túróczy that from this point forward he would be supervising all church activities. In response Ordass and Túróczy stated their unwillingness to cooperate and said that henceforth they were assuming a stance of complete passivity. Shortly after this, Ernő Mihályfi informed Túróczy that the government had never accepted Vető's resignation and that, therefore, neither did it accept Túróczy's appointment as the Northern Diocese bishop. Túróczy, protesting the measure, informed Mihályfi that he continued to consider himself bishop. Two weeks later, wanting to ensure that the transfer of Túróczy's bishopric to Vető would go off smoothly, Grnák asked Túróczy himself to chair the presbytery session in which the bishop's seat would be transferred. Túróczy refused, telling Grnák he had no intention of resigning. On December 19, 1957, Túróczy's noncooperation notwithstanding, the presbytery of the Northern Diocese acknowledged that the government had not approved Vető's resignation and that, therefore, the presbytery considered Vető the diocese's legal bishop.[21]

Túróczy's refusal to resign is striking. It suggests that in 1957 he assigned more importance to the church's institutional freedom than he had in 1948. In 1948, Túróczy had argued that the church could concede to the regime those things that did not belong to its essential ministry. Later he rebuked Ordass in prison for refusing to relinquish his bishopric. Now Túróczy himself was refusing to do the same.

Túróczy's decision contrasts poignantly with one made by Imre Veöreös in this same historical moment. Veöreös had been elected the church's head secretary in December 1956. In December 1957, as part of the government's move against the church, Grnák demanded that Veöreös declare his election as head secretary illegal. Veöreös refused this demand but nevertheless resigned, in effect, by writing a statement that relinquished control of his office to the church's general assembly.[22] The distinction Veöreös made with this choice, significant only in a legal sense, reflects consistency with his conviction in 1948. The question of who holds which office would not seem to impinge upon the essential ministry of the church. Thus Veöreös could in good conscience resign, but he could not in good conscience declare his election illegal. Túróczy's actions, however, do not evince the same consistency. In 1957 the actions of Túróczy and Veöreös diverged, while

Túróczy and Ordass acted together. How these two bitter opponents came to be allies in 1957 is an unanswered question in this history.[23]

In any event, after Vető and his colleagues were returned to the leadership of the Northern Diocese, the government started to focus its attack on Bishop Ordass. It might simply remove Ordass the same way it had removed Túróczy, by declaring his appointment as bishop illegal, but Horváth wanted to discredit Ordass and so began a six-month campaign to turn the pastors of the Lutheran Church against their bishop.

On December 23 Ernő Mihályfi, now acting as general inspector, convened the church's general presbytery. Mihályfi told the presbytery that he had been the general inspector all along, but in the rash of illegalities of the previous year, he had been illegally shunted aside. Now he desired to lead the church out of its present crisis. As his last official act before being pushed aside, Mihályfi said, he had approved Ordass's return to the bishopric. This, of course, did not preclude the need for government approval, which unfortunately was still missing.[24]

As it turned out, the government's failure to approve Ordass's bishopric had negative financial consequences for his diocese. The church-state agreement stipulated a reduction in subsidy for the Lutheran Church in 1958. Knowing this, Mihályfi and Vető asked the party-state to provide "extraordinary" financial assistance for the church's pastors. The request was granted, but because Bishop Ordass was not working to solve the current church-state crises, his diocese was excluded from the "extraordinary" assistance until Ordass resolved the problems. This meant a pay cut for the Southern Diocese's clergy.[25]

On the day this news became public, János Horváth spoke to an assembly of all the pastors in the Southern Diocese, which he had convened. Addressing his audience in a long speech, Horváth explained how the state viewed the Lutheran Church's present crisis. The state had rehabilitated Ordass only of embezzlement charges; it had not rehabilitated his politics. But when Ordass returned as bishop, he started courting the opinion of Western church leaders. "It came about," said Horváth, "that church reaction elected Ordass as its flag-bearer and imagined that as long as he led the church, church reaction would not have any problems." The state was compelled to initiate negotiations. "We tried to convince the church leadership that the position it was representing was detrimental for the church," Horváth said, but "the stiff, stubborn standpoint of the church leadership, especially of Lajos Ordass, led us to the point where the negotiations became completely pointless, and we broke them off."[26] Still, Horváth wanted to see reconciliation and cooperation between the state and the Lutheran Church: "I am convinced that the overwhelming majority of Lutheran pastors are of the opinion that reactionaries in the church should move to the background and that progressive thinking persons should lead the church." The crisis could be resolved if the pastors came together with the government, Horváth said and then adjourned the meeting without discussion. The pastors stayed afterward and talked over what to do. The next day, sending a delegation both to Ordass and to the government, they set forth their position: they asked Ordass to do all he could to remain as bishop.

This, however, was an ambiguous position. Were the pastors saying that they would stand by Ordass even if he could not be bishop, or were they saying that Ordass should change his conduct so that he would be acceptable to the party-state? When the pastors delivered their message to Grnák, he told them that Ordass could remain as bishop only if he gave far-reaching guarantees that he would keep his promises.[27] At this point, the pastors started urging Ordass to meet with Horváth, in the hope that the bishop could repair his relationship with the party-state. A week later Ordass traveled to the appropriate government office to speak with János Horváth.

Horváth and Ordass talked about the freedom of the church. Ordass asked Horváth if he recognized the part of the agreement that guaranteed the church's right to regulate its internal life in accordance with church law. The state, said Horváth, approves church law, and the state can take that approval away. Horváth was offended that Ordass never considered the interests of the socialism-building state but talked only of the church's autonomy. Ordass said that when he assumed the office of bishop, he had sworn himself to defend the church's freedom. He could not throw aside the treasure of the church to suit his pleasure. The two men had reached an impasse. Horváth asked Ordass what he thought was going to happen next. Ordass supposed the state was going to start a new trial against him. Horváth replied, "The Rákosi group made a mistake when they initiated a dollar-trial against you, thereby making a world affair out of your case. They could have left you comfortably in your post, because they had the means to make moral carrion out of you." Then, as Ordass was leaving, Horváth added with a sense of proleptic triumph, "I can predict for you that, whether you want it or not, you will be listed among the fiercest enemies of people's democracy." Ordass replied, "I am not inspired by any sort of political ambition. What I do, I do from my duty to the Gospel."[28]

This exchange, in fact, has an impact that cannot be translated into English. In recording this encounter in his memoirs, Ordass reveals that he and Horváth spoke to each other in the informal address. English, of course, has no formal address, but any English speaker who has studied a foreign language will understand from this that Horváth and Ordass had once been on close terms.

Horváth now moved to implement the final stage of his "moral carrion" strategy. The party-state started pushing the clergy in the Southern Diocese to issue a statement of no-confidence in Ordass. Word got out that at the next meeting of the pastors association in Budapest the clergy would be expected to express their lack of confidence in Ordass's leadership. The meeting was held, a few speeches against Ordass were delivered, but no no-confidence statement came forth. A few weeks later, in another part of the country, another pastors meeting was held. Critics of Ordass spoke out, but the pastors failed to issue the no-confidence.[29] Meanwhile, in the Southern Diocese generally, the reduction in pastors' salaries was not producing the desired effect. Instead, members of the church were sending money to Ordass's office, which was being distributed among the clergy, and pastors in the Northern Diocese were sharing their salary supplement with the Southern Diocese's pastors.[30]

Officials in the government offices were getting frustrated, and so they decided to have the church papers print more aggressive criticisms of Bishop Ordass. At the end of March, Bishop Vető had an article published in *Lelkipásztor* entitled "It Concerns Our Church." In its invectives, Vető's piece surpassed previously published vituperations against Ordass. The essay endeavored to demonstrate, by means of a well-rehearsed historical account of "reaction," how Bishop Ordass, when he insisted that the church must be politically neutral, was covering up his own "reactionary" politics. The Ordass group did in fact politicize, said Vető, just not for socialism.[31]

Vető's article exploded in the church. A week later, on April 9, the pastors association of Pest met to discuss the article. The clergy passed a resolution responding to the piece, which they mailed to every pastors association in the country. The resolution called into question Bishop Vető's legitimacy, pointed out a few factual errors in his historical account, and proposed that the common clergy become more involved in solving the current church crises. The resolution suggested that representatives of the pastors unions in each church county meet with the church leaders and the party-state to discuss whether, "the pastors, taking into account the common opinion of the church, desire to see the current church leaders stay in their current positions, or not."[32] The proposal was clearly directed against Bishop Vető.

This April 9 meeting probably marks the first stirrings in the Lutheran Church of organized resistance to the regime. Ordass was considered a symbol of true Christian fidelity, and in 1956 and 1957 many pastors started linking his person to their vision of a suffering church. Now that the party-state had unmasked its intentions, these pastors must have reasoned, the path for the church was clear—martyrdom. Admittedly, scant historical record exists concerning the attitude among clergy at this juncture, but circumstantial evidence suggests something was afoot. For example, in his memoirs Ordass notes that as early as January 1958 some pastors wanted to compose a "confessing church" statement, and they hoped that Ordass would join up with it. Ordass says about the proposed statement only that, "I am fairly doubtful that such a thing will happen, that they would support it in large numbers, but I will attempt this path."[33] He never mentions the matter again, and history has left no record of a "confessing church" statement. On the other hand, some evidence exists of talk about a church split. In January 1958, a secret report by a rural party secretary on local conditions in the Lutheran Church noted that some churchmen believed that Ordass's removal would cause an open split in the church.[34] In early 1957, clergy had been talking about a "suffering church," and some of them may have believed that the time had now come to be true to that vision.

The evidence suggests, also, that in 1958 Ordass did not consider larger schemes of resistance. His one reference to the "confessing church" idea is coupled with skepticism. Later, in the thick of his confrontation with the party-state, Ordass repeatedly exhibited the desire to disassociate and protect others from the consequences of his actions. When he recognized that the government wanted to coerce the clergy into a no-confidence statement, Ordass attempted to initiate disciplinary proceedings against himself to spare the clergy from party-state threats and manipulations.[35] When, soon after negotiations deadlocked, Grnák demanded the resignation of Ordass's bishop surrogate—the person empowered to act in the bishop's stead if the bishop is removed—Ordass recommended to the bishop surrogate that he resign in order to spare his family the consequences of a refusal.[36] When the pastors of Pest church county challenged Bishop Vető's legitimacy, Ordass told them that it was enough if Ordass alone paid the price of confrontation with the regime, that there was no need to create a situation where congregations would be deprived of their pastors.[37] Such is not the reasoning of a man about to lead a martyr church.

Meanwhile in the government offices they were furious about the latest uprising from the clergy. Horváth summoned the senior of the church county and the author of the April 9 resolution, Vilmos Nagybocskai, to his office. Horváth informed Nagybocskai that he was through, adding, "As long as I fill this office you won't even be a bell-ringer in the church."[38] He ordered the senior to call the pastors to another meeting within the week to retract the resolution. If the pastors declined, all government subsidy for the church would be withdrawn. Then Horváth concluded, "I do not understand why the pastors of the Lutheran Church will not accept that in this country there is a dictatorship, a dictatorship of the proletariat, and whoever opposes it will be flattened."[39]

Nevertheless Horváth seemed aware that his "moral carrion" strategy was floundering. A government document written less than a week later acknowledged that "every progressive proposal in the Ordass-affair by the Vető group has been ineffective" and recommended a series of measures to resolve the crisis. First, József Darvas, with or without Ordass's cooperation, was to convene a session of the Southern Diocese's presbytery. Second, before the presbytery met, two professors of church law were to publish an article in *Evangélikus Élet* in which they stated that the Southern diocesan bishopric had not been vacated by Dezséry's resignation, that Ordass did not fill the post in accordance with church law, and that therefore the Southern Diocese had no legal bishop. Third, the faculty of the seminary was to issue a statement saying that the church enjoyed religious freedom and that church life proceeded unobstructed. Fourth, the pastors associations were to be convened, "progressive" churchmen were to inform the pastors of the legal situation, and the pastors were to acknowledge their mistakes. Fifth, the church press was to initiate a general attack against Ordass and urge a resolution of the crisis. Sixth, threats or "administrative measures" were to be employed to make sure reluctant pastors complied.[40]

And so it happened, more or less. The government squeezed out, or simply printed, statements from the pastors associations that conformed to the party line. The professors of church law declared Ordass's bishopric illegal, and the seminary faculty concurred.[41] On June 18, 1958, the party-state informed the church that it had not approved Dezséry's 1956 resignation and that the party-state considered Dezséry the Southern Diocese's legal bishop. In the end, Horváth had to remove Ordass the same way he had removed Túróczy.

On June 24, the presbytery of the Southern Diocese convened. The presbytery announced that Dezséry was the diocese's bishop. Bishop Dezséry was called into the room. He commenced to speak for several hours, recounting not only the history of his ministry and its battles with "reaction" but also naming individually virtually everyone in the church who had ever wronged him. When Dezséry finally finished, he resigned his bishopric. The government approved his resignation. Horváth announced that the government deputy was being withdrawn from the church, and the pastors would receive the party-state subsidy deprived them during Ordass's administration.

Dezséry, who now openly professed party membership and atheism, worked afterward as a representative in Parliament and as a radio commentator. His self-serving, collaborating leadership style had made him "moral carrion," and he could no longer plausibly be bishop. Bishop Ordass had been set aside for good, too.

THEOLOGICAL EXCURSUS THREE

The Witness Type

A Readiness for Martyrdom, a Challenge to Ahogy Lehet

> And a great and strong wind rent the mountains, and broke in pieces the rocks before the LORD, but the LORD was not in the wind; and after the wind an earthquake, but the LORD was not in the earthquake; and after the earthquake a fire, but the LORD was not in the fire; and after the fire a still small voice.
> —I KINGS 19:11–12

The witness type represented a moral challenge to the strategies for coping with socialism hitherto present in the church. Those earlier strategies were either compromising or collaborating, and in terms of theoretical structure, they both emerged from the framework of *ahogy lehet*. *Ahogy lehet* originally designated a framework of compromise that recognized the reality of socialism in Hungary and that was willing to bargain with the party-state in the interests of protecting at least part of the church's ministry. The difficulties inherent in such bargaining, however, quickly produced distortions in the *ahogy lehet* framework, resulting in a new, morally unacceptable type of strategy, collaboration. So putrescent was collaboration that in 1956 the church's pastors rejected it outright. Beyond that, many pastors rejected the entire *ahogy lehet* framework that undergirded both collaboration and compromise. They called for a radically different way of living in socialism, one that demanded of the church only that it witness to its ministry, even if the cost of witness was martyrdom.

As an ideal-typical response, therefore, witness defined a moral strategy for the church; however, as a strategy for the church it depended upon the personal witness of Bishop Ordass. Pastors saw lessons in Ordass's life about how to be faithful, and they transformed Ordass's witness into the symbol and foundation of a moral ecclesiology that was to be an alternative to the *ahogy lehet* strategies of before. Thus Lajos Ordass was essential to the witness type. Without him it would not have existed. This was not simply because Lajos Ordass was a courageous church leader who inspired a following—although he was that, nor was it because one could not conceive of the theological principles represented in the type independently of Bishop Ordass. Rather, the witness type depended on Lajos Ordass because he was a real man who lived out its principles with a real life. Lajos Ordass represented, many believed, an option for the church that was realistic and possible. Ordass was not just an ideal, he was a person, and because he was a person he pointed the church to a path. To understand the witness type, therefore, one must understand Lajos Ordass.

Ordass's Personal Witness: Order of Privilege to Duty

The contemporary historian or theologian, despite knowing a good deal about Lajos Ordass, still has trouble discerning clearly the unifying rationale in his thought and actions. What is known about Ordass comes primarily through his autobiographical writings, and in these writings, although Ordass recounts the sequence of events in detail, he does not often step back from the telling to provide a full theological exposition of his reasoning. Only by digging through the narrative and putting together its disparate pieces can one find Ordass's basic theological convictions. In doing this, of course, one runs the risk of misunderstanding him, but by attending carefully to the unfolding of the narrative, one discovers that Ordass's most basic moral conviction rested in an unfaltering commitment to his pastoral office as bishop. As bishop, Ordass's actions were guided by a commitment to duty so unflinching that he disregarded every consideration of consequence.

In short, Lajos Ordass was a deontologist. Deontology means a commitment to duty that excludes from moral consideration the effects, even the most negative ones, that result from adhering to duty. For a deontologist, duty has order of privilege over consequence. Often, and certainly in the case of Bishop Ordass, deontology depends on a sense of hidden providence. For a deontologist of this sort, disregarding consequences makes sense because one believes that God controls history even when his providential care cannot be seen and, therefore, that God is responsible for the consequences, both good and bad, that result from adhering to duty. Without faith in hidden providence, keeping duty at great cost can appear foolhardy or irresponsible.

In 1948 Ordass's deontological conviction surfaced on two separate occasions, both times in response to state demands that a bishop resign. These occasions make clear that Ordass believed the bishop's office held inviolable pastoral duties. For example, when the state demanded Ordass's resignation, Ordass refused, reasoning as follows:

> I weighed over the thought of resignation carefully. At those times I always experienced a storm of conscience. The storm passed immediately, however, when I considered that prison awaited me. It was impossible for me to flee.... Not only fear of naked force would weaken Lutherans—mainly the pastors—in their loyalty to the church. Even more, the cowardice of men fleeing when they were required to set an example would disillusion them. I did not want to be the source of such disillusionment. I did not dare to place that on my conscience.[1]

Ordass believed that to resign his office because of threats would be the same as fleeing from it, and fleeing would betray those who had entrusted the office to him. Therefore Ordass refused to resign out of fidelity to his office. The obligations of the bishopric overrode considerations of personal risk.

In the case of Túróczy's resignation, Ordass argued against it before the other bishops as follows:

> We, and the church in general, believe that Túróczy has been unjustly imprisoned. It is impossible, therefore, that he admit the truth of those charges by resigning. It was not the state that made Túróczy bishop, but the common will of the church's members. These people are hoping that Túróczy will stand firm. Even more important, God may have need, in the interests of the church, for Túróczy to die in prison. Do we have the freedom to advice him to ask to be released when the price is his resignation?[2]

This was quick and dense and not altogether clear. One might understand Ordass to be asserting a principle of church autonomy, arguing that the government has no right to dictate who will hold church offices. Ordass, however, did not quite make that argument. More likely he was advancing the same argument he would make against his own resignation. Because church members had made Túróczy bishop, Ordass reasoned, they were hoping he would "stand firm." Túróczy would betray those hopes, and his obligation to those who held them, if he resigned under fear of imprisonment. Ordass reasoned that a bishop has duties to his office that he cannot relinquish for the sake of personal safety.

Coupled with this strong deontological principle was a strong sense of providence. Only because Ordass believed that his fate rested in God's hands did adhering to duty even at the cost of personal misfortune make sense to him. Importantly for Ordass God's providence was invisible, unlike for the Túróczy group. Ordass did not see God's plan in the course of events, but he believed, or trusted, that what was happening had meaning, and therefore he was willing to shoulder the misfortunes of duty without understanding why.

Consider, for example, what Ordass says in the passage below. Ordass, for part of his imprisonment, resided with fifteen Catholic priests, and in 1949, in prison together they celebrated Christmas. Ordass delivered a short sermon on the text of Luke 2:1–20, saying the following:

> We are spending our second Christmas Eve here. Why? Because of arbitrary human despotism. We would deceive ourselves and lead others astray if we should maintain that we see and understand everything clearly. Because we cannot see more than poor Mary and the burden-laden Joseph. There are masses of insoluble riddles that

we cannot understand, but these cannot keep us from celebrating Christmas. We are able to confess that first truth: It is not what Augustus wills for us that is realized, but what God wills. I speak now simply but pointedly: If a power opposed to God and thus the church seizes power in a country with Christian inhabitants, then what can be the will of God for those who hold their Christian faith precious? Is it not that they defend that faith without compromise? If the godless power is so blind that it even employs the instrument of violence, then what can be the will of God for the faithful? Is it not that they accept shackles in prison or a martyr's death on the gallows? And if this is the will of God, then is not this will directed most of all to us, who have been invested with the pastoral office in our congregations? What kind of infinitely great Christmas peace can fill our spirits if here, even behind the prison walls, we know that no human despotism overcomes us, but rather even here the blessed will of God guides us.[3]

The passage captures both Ordass's deontology and its intimate link to his faith in hidden providence. In these times of persecution, Ordass says, Christians must defend the faith without compromise. This is yet truer for Christians who hold the church's pastoral offices. The price of Christian conviction may be imprisonment or death, misfortunes that the believer cannot understand. But the Christian knows that God controls history, and knowing that, if not seeing it, he places his fate in God's hidden hands.

This core faith and its attendant conviction informed all the public actions of Bishop Ordass.

Pastoral Duty and Church Autonomy

Frequently Ordass has been interpreted as if his central theological conviction concerned the freedom of the church. For example, the Lutheran theologian Vilmos Vajta, who was himself of Hungarian origin, discusses the nationalization of Hungary's schools in 1948 in a way that makes the primary theological issue one of church-state relations. Vajta understands school nationalization to have been an attack on the church's autonomy, and working from this interpretation he identifies the freedom of the church as Ordass's central theological concern.[4] This view, although not entirely incorrect, nevertheless fails to place the issue of church autonomy within the overall contours of Ordass's thinking. Ordass cannot be understood correctly if his actions are seen as emerging first from a commitment to church autonomy (nor does Ordass appear to have been much of a church-state theorist). Rather one must understand Ordass's actions as emerging from a more existentially immediate conviction, namely, his commitment to the pastoral duties of his office.

To be sure, Ordass did consider the autonomy of the church important. In 1957 especially, in the church-state negotiations with János Horváth, the issue of the church's autonomy came to the fore. Horváth demanded extensive changes in church officeholders; Ordass countered that such demands violated the church's autonomy, and the negotiations deadlocked on the issue of personnel changes. At the same time, however, Ordass also exhibited some flexibility on the question of church autonomy. He accepted, as part of his second administration, party-state supervision of the church. He accepted that the party-state had nationalized the church schools. He consented to party-state demands to form a Lutheran Peace Committee. He took part himself in party-state sponsored organizations, such as the Patriotic People's Front—although, admittedly, only to a limited degree. Finally, in the church-state negotiations with Horváth, Ordass exhibited a willingness to discuss individual personnel changes dictated by the party-state, despite the fact that he did not like it. In short, if church autonomy was the issue on which Ordass stood or fell, he was not consistent.

Ordass in 1957 was concerned more with the freedom of the church than with the church's autonomy. The difference between the two is as follows: The principle of the church's autonomy concerns the church's ecclesiastical structures. It asserts that administratively, that is, in the selection of bishops, pastors, and other offices, the church must be independent from external, particularly state, coercion or interference. The principle of the freedom of the church is narrower than that. It asserts that the church must be free in the definition and exercise of its ministry, that external, non-church forces cannot dictate the content of the Gospel. This latter view, however, does not necessarily proscribe external influence on the selection of church administrators.

It should be noted that the Lutheran theological tradition does not assign great significance to church autonomy. Luther himself asked German princes to intervene in the resolution of church conflicts. Later the Lutheran Churches in Germany and Scandinavia assumed the features of a state church, subordinate in various ways to the political power. The Lutheran confessions do not mention administrative autonomy as a mark of the church. To the contrary, they seem to treat church order as *adiaphora*, that is, as something indifferent. From a Lutheran perspective, therefore, to assert an absolute right to church autonomy or to state that autonomy is an issue on which the true church stands or falls, is an extreme view.

One must also remember that by 1957 party-state supervision of the church, and hence encroachment on the church's autonomy, was a given. Ordass recognized this and was still willing to function as bishop. Even while tolerating a degree of external intervention into church affairs, however, Ordass was uncompromising in his commitment to his pastoral duties as bishop. Among those duties, as Ordass understood them, was the obligation to defend the true ministry of the Gospel. Ordass insisted that the church be free to define the shape and content of its ministry. That meant the party-state could not coerce from the church partisan and propagandistic affirmations of socialism or Soviet foreign policy. Such partisanship, Ordass believed, distorted the church's ministry.

Therefore even when the 1957 negotiations with Horváth turned to the question of personnel changes, the underlying issue remained the shape of the church's ministry. The party-state demanded change in ecclesiastical offices because it wanted to place "progressives" into those offices, persons willing to be partisans for socialism. Likewise the church delegation opposed the changes because it feared "progressives" would once again distort the church's ministry. Thus at stake in the personnel changes was more than the church's autonomy. At stake was the true ministry of the Gospel.

Admittedly, when protesting the party-state's demands, Ordass appealed to the principle of church autonomy. Such an appeal, in fact, was his best legal counter, because church autonomy had been guaranteed in the 1948 agreement. However, Ordass did not oppose the demanded personnel changes simply because they represented a violation of church autonomy, as if autonomy per se were the issue on which the true church stood or fell. He opposed the personnel changes because through them the party-state was attempting to define the ministry of the church. Similarly when earlier in 1957 Ordass had accepted party-state supervision over the church, he did so because he believed it would not encroach upon the church's freedom to define the Gospel.

However, as Ordass became convinced that the ministry of the Gospel was threatened, he became inflexible. His duty as bishop prevented him from compromising on what he understood as the church's ministry, and thus rather than be unfaithful to the office, he would accept any consequence. Ordass's deontological sensibility became evident late in the third day of negotiations with Horváth. Discussions had snagged; Horváth, who perhaps had never heard of deontology, attempted to move things forward with the following argument:

> This is about political interests. In this regard, neither in the negotiations, nor in the Lutheran Church, can political interests be realized other than our political interests. One needs to see this side of the question clearly. . . . But political interests now coincide with the interests of the church. Those who do not see that they coincide cannot lead well. It is not possible to defy historical progress, especially in Hungary, because the balance of power has changed worldwide.

Those who recognize the historical situation, I maintain, can play a historic role as church leaders in relation to Hungary.[5]

Ordass's response was predictable and, also, a resounding affirmation of deontological principle:

> In light of the words spoken by Mr. President, the question now stands before us perfectly clear. We need to recognize that the question . . . is one of unalterable will. My own opinion is as follows: I see and sense clearly that the state has the strength and power of which Mr. President spoke, and which it can bring to bear in respect to the church's life, if necessary even against the will of the church. On my part, I sat at this table with the conviction not that political caviling would guide me, but rather those church interests which I believe I have recognized. It is possible that to the state my position is mistaken. It is possible to produce arguments to the effect that I do not represent the church's interest best understood. This, however, does not change the fact that my position is formed according to my best conscience. The negotiations have reached an impasse. I sense they have reached an impasse to the greatest degree.[6]

As bishop, Ordass's responsibility to represent what he understood as the interests of the church was nonnegotiable. Practical considerations about the balance of power, or about the consequences to himself or to the church of failing to agree with the party-state, would not change his position. Thus fully aware of the consequences of his inflexibility, but not taking them into account, Ordass allowed himself to be removed. He could do no other.

Pastoral Duty and Church Resistance

Ordass's deontological commitment to the duties of the bishop's office also determined his conduct on the matter of school nationalization. Because Ordass opposed the nationalization of the schools so unflinchingly, some observers have suggested that in 1948 Ordass was contemplating organized resistance against the communist state. They suggest that Ordass wanted to model a church struggle in Hungary after the example of the Norwegian Church struggle against the Nazi-supported Quisling government.[7] This view, again, is not entirely incorrect, but again it fails to understand the issue as related to the core conviction that shaped Ordass's thinking and actions.

Indisputably Ordass was deeply influenced by his contact with the Lutheran Churches of Scandinavia. In 1927, shortly after his ordination, Ordass studied for a year in Sweden. This had a tremendous impact on him. He met famous theologians and prominent churchmen such as Anders Nygren, Gustaf Aulen, and Nathan Söderblom. He formed personal friendships with individuals, such as Martin Lindström and Bo Giertz, who would later rise to prominence in the Swedish Church.[8] Ordass's experiences in Sweden also helped to familiarize him with church life in the other Scandinavian countries. Thus once Ordass returned to Hungary, he managed always to stay informed about Scandinavian church life.

During the Second World War, in 1943, Ordass obtained a lecture delivered by the Swedish bishop, Gustaf Aulen, on the ongoing church struggle with the Nazis in Norway. Norway, which is 99 percent Lutheran, had been occupied by the Germans, who established a puppet government under the leadership of Vidkun Quisling. The Quisling government, however, confronted serious opposition in the Norwegian population, led by the Norwegian Lutheran Church and, in particular, by the Lutheran Bishop Eivind Berggrav.[9] Upon reading Aulen's account of the Norwegian church struggle, Ordass was so affected that he translated the lecture into Hungarian and sent copies to the four bishops of the Lutheran Church in Hungary, the central church office, and the dean of the Lutheran theological academy. Shortly afterward, Ordass spoke on the Norwegian struggle to an assembly of pastors and teachers because, as he explained it, "I considered it absolutely necessary that I open up a crack for at least one minute, through which the workers in our church, who, in general, naively believed the words of German propaganda, could get a glance of the real situation."[10]

Such actions in Hungary in 1943 evinced not only clear conviction but also notable courage. Ordass certainly intended some kind of theological statement. Perhaps he wanted no more than to goad the Lutheran Church in Hungary into a firmer stance against the German-friendly elements within it. However, he may also have intended to make a statement about how his church should be prepared to act if it ever faced Nazism directly. If that were the case, then this episode is early evidence of Ordass's readiness to consider organized church resistance as a response to dictatorship.

In 1947 Ordass traveled abroad extensively, meeting with Western church leaders. During his travels Ordass visited Eivind Berggrav, with whom he discussed the Norwegian church struggle as well as the developing situation in Hungary. Ordass later recalled their conversations as follows:

> Already then both of us saw clearly the kinds of difficulties which the Lutheran Church in Hungary could get caught up in, in its own dictatorship; and so [Berggrav] gave a few words of advice on the basis of his experiences in the Norwegian church struggle. They were of this sort: "Don't rush things, but don't be a minute late!"—"Sharply distinguish between little and big things!"—"Carry out your struggle

standing clearly on the basis of the Bible and the Confessions."—"If possible don't write down anything! It is better to rely on memory than to give a basis for accusations with notes!"[11]

Clearly this is the kind of advice one gives to a person preparing to enter a major church struggle, and the discussion suggests Ordass was considering such possibility. Furthermore one gets a clear sense from Ordass's memoirs that, in 1948, he was anticipating some form of church resistance. For example, when explaining his decision not to resign, Ordass adds:

> I am prepared to admit that I was full of a good dose of dreamful hope that the people of our church would not let themselves be brought to their knees so easily. I believed that the Lutheran Church could not be brought down without arresting countless Lutherans. I see clearly now that this expectation of mine was unfounded. In this respect, reality proved me quite wrong.[12]

Thus by Ordass's own admission, he expected his arrest to mark the beginning of a church struggle in Hungary in the Lutheran Church.

However, despite the evidence that Ordass was willing and ready for a major confrontation with the regime, there is the strange, utter absence of any indication that Ordass was taking even minute steps to prepare or organize the anticipated resistance. In his memoirs, although he mentions expectations of confrontation, Ordass never mentions any plans or preparations for it. Importantly, after Parliament nationalized the schools, Ordass did nothing to try to bring about resistance in the congregations. Thus the evidence also indicates that in terms of actual, concrete resistance, Ordass had no plans. His intentions seem incongruous with his expectations. To understand this, one needs to view Ordass's position on the church schools within the larger context of his conception of his duties as bishop.

As explained earlier in the narrative, Ordass expected the school question to be decided locally. In Ordass's view the congregations were the ones who cared for the schools; they might want to fight for them, and, in that case, the bishops had no right to give the schools to the state over the heads of the congregations. Ordass believed that as bishop his duty was to defend the right of congregations to maintain schools. Additionally he seemed to believe that nationalizing the schools could lead to some sort of Kulturkampf, and he did not shrink from such a prospect—but neither did he plan for it. That is to say, Ordass was willing to accept a Kulturkampf as the consequence of his position on the schools, but he formed his position independently of such considerations. Ordass's position unfolded from an understanding of his duty to the congregations as bishop. What might follow from adherence to duty did not impinge on his moral judgment. That is why Ordass never devoted attention to planning resistance. Orchestrating a struggle was not his responsibility. Although he was willing to fight if necessary, Ordass did not think of himself as a revolutionary or freedom fighter. He was only a bishop.[13]

Ecclesiological Deontology and a Suffering Church

Having grasped the deontological sentiment at the core of Ordass's conduct, one is then able to understand the nature of the witness type as a collective moral strategy. The blood of martyrs, it has been said, is the seed of the church. Lajos Ordass was one of socialism's martyrs, and many saw in his martyrdom theological significance for the church in socialism. Pastors seized hold of the deontological principles embodied in Ordass's personal witness and made them into a moral model for the church. Thus, as an ideal-typical response, witness can be understood as ecclesiological deontology. It called the church to adhere to its ministry without compromise, expecting that in socialism uncompromising commitment to that ministry would mean suffering.

The ecclesiological transformation of Ordass's personal witness emerged in the vision of a suffering church articulated in 1956. Pastors rightly discerned the deontological conviction at the core of Ordass's conduct, and they saw it as a guide for the church. A pastor named László Scholz, for example, speaking before his colleagues in December 1956, defined the significance of Ordass's witness as follows:

> In my heart I asked myself why I have faith in him [Ordass] and why so many of us ostensibly have faith in him. Firstly, because with his life he provided an example of how one must take up the cross of Jesus Christ. Thus I could even say that we have faith in him because he had faith in God. He had faith even when he was left to himself. . . . Secondly, I believe we have faith in our bishop because he has given many signs of how purely the issue, the struggle, the defense, and the life of the church burns in his heart. . . . Nor did he resort to other instruments even when—as it is often said—the "interest" of the church would have required this. But the interest of the church can never be to step out of its character as a church. . . . We have faith in Lajos Ordass because we see that he unwaveringly endeavored to remain completely a man of the church.[14]

Pastor Scholz identified two features in Ordass's witness that he set before the church as a model. One feature was Ordass's uncalculating commitment to his pastoral office. Ordass committed himself fully to the cause of the church. Therefore even when the so-called interests of the church seemed to dictate otherwise, Ordass never faltered in his adherence to the church's true mission. Secondly, Ordass was willing to accept the consequences of his unfaltering commitment to duty. He was not afraid to take up the cross. Finally—although this was not explicit—Scholz understood the two features of Ordass's witness to be integrally related. Those who were unwilling to compromise on the church's true ministry were destined to suffer; the cross was the consequence of faithfulness.

Thus Ordass's witness pointed well beyond his person; it revealed something about how to be a church. To be a church meant adhering to the church's ministry regardless of the consequences. It meant resting the church's foundation on deontological principle. Consider the following, written for the *Lutheran Yearbook* in 1957:

> Whereas God is so much greater than we believed or thought, it is exactly for this reason that the church can do nothing against God's will. When it must speak or act, then it can weigh neither individual nor so-called church interests, but must obey. It must obey even if the road is narrow and difficult. It must obey with the faith that its things are God's things. In October 1956 God showed us clearly that he knows the meaning of meaningless roads, he sees the purpose of purposeless stumblings, and he shapes the fate of his servants, the life of his congregations, and the history of his church.[15]

The author sets up an explicit contrast between duty and interest, giving order of privilege to duty. According to the passage, obeying God is different from, and more important than, weighing interests. Obeying God is what faithfulness to the church's ministry requires. The passage also links the concept of duty to an understanding of God's hidden providence. It affirms that God knows the "meaning of meaningless roads" and therefore that the church's only task is to obey God. The church is not responsible for the consequences of adhering to duty, because God is in control of history.

Moreover, because the church must disregard consequences, it must be prepared to suffer. For the pastors who advocated witness, the readiness to suffer was concomitant with an uncompromising commitment to the church's true ministry. This was because the party-state was hostile to the church, and the church, when confronted with such hostility, must not compromise its ministry. It must witness to the truth and suffer persecution. Of course, that pastors understood suffering as a concomitant to faithfulness did not mean they were propounding political resistance or some kind of opposition church. Rather, they understood suffering as a consequence of faithfulness, a consequence from which the church must not shrink. That was something less than planning resistance.

Even more important, disregarding consequences meant disregarding questions about the church's survival. The church's task was not to ensure its continued existence. This point was argued eloquently by Pastor István Botta at the 1956 pastors conferences:

> We also profess about the future of the church that it will "remain forever." We heard in this morning's sermon that our faith in the future should determine our present as well; yet there were tremendous differences in our present conduct. There were those who said that the church will only remain if the pastors profess a theology of unconditional obedience toward the political authorities and church authorities. . . . There was also a group that said. . . . we must drive out error from the church. And they believed that the church will remain even if they must march into prison, and even if they must go to internment camps.[16]

Pastor Botta was reflecting on the moral significance for the church of survival. He argued that the confession "the church will remain" can have different meanings. It might be taken as a statement of responsibility, thereby obligating the church to act in ways that would ensure its survival. However, it might also be understood as a promise, a truth that remains even if church members go to their deaths. Indeed to confess as promise that the "church will remain" is to place ecclesiology within a deontological framework. It is to place the future in God's hands, thereby freeing the church from responsibility for its future. The duty of the church, Botta was saying, was to be true to its ministry, disregarding the consequences such faithfulness might bring or, perhaps more accurately, trusting that God would take care of the consequences.

Thus the witness type, by declining to worry about survival, rejected as a legitimate focus of theological concern the central concern for *ahogy lehet*. The church's task was to devote itself uncompromisingly to the ministry of the Gospel. If by ministering faithfully the church came into conflict with the political power, it should not modify its ministry in the interest of surviving. Rather, it should be prepared to suffer, witnessing to the truth, accepting martyrdom, entrusting its future to God's hands.

The disparity between the witness type and *ahogy lehet* on the issue of survival was related to different understandings of providence. For the proponents of *ahogy lehet*, God's providence was visible. Accordingly one task for the Christian was to read the "signs of the times." Both compromisers and collaborators were committed to a project of reading history, and they believed they had discerned God's providential will for Hungary in recent events. Having read "the times," they considered themselves in a better position to strike bargains. For the proponents of witness, however,

God's providence was invisible. They did not believe reading God's design in the course of events was possible, and rather than try to do the impossible, they committed themselves to duty, which could be known.

This fundamental difference can be seen clearly in the confrontation between Túróczy and Ordass in prison in 1949. Recall that Túróczy had asked Ordass to resign and became outraged when he refused, even accusing Ordass of wanting to place a halo around his own head. In Túróczy's eyes, Ordass's stubbornness was irresponsible because it could only bring the church harm. For Ordass, however, the question was one of duty. Because he was unwilling to compromise his duty as bishop, Ordass opted to stay in prison, trusting that God would take care of the consequences.

Thus, as a type, witness rejected the project of calculating consequences through the reading of history, a project essential to any strategy of compromise. The proponents of witness saw, or believed they saw, that such calculations always slid into collaboration and hence into a betrayal of the church's ministry. Rather than playing a game of wits with the communists, they called the church simply to witness.

The Possibilities and Limits of the Witness Type

Ahogy lehet is a strategy deeply rooted in Hungarian history, tracing its ancestry to the efforts of "labanc" armies to regain Hungarian independence by cooperating with the German Habsburgs. Equally rooted in Hungarian history, however, is the rejection of *ahogy lehet*, a rejection that goes back to the efforts of Transylvanian "kuruc" armies to win Hungarian freedom forcefully and quickly. Indeed the "labanc-kuruc" argument, that is, the argument between cautious, patient compromisers and uncompromising, unyielding radicals, constitutes a major dynamic in Hungarian history.

Strikingly, the miniature history of the Lutheran Church in communist Hungary has reproduced much of that "labanc-kuruc" dynamic. The question facing the Lutheran Church in Hungary in socialism is one that Hungarians have faced throughout their history, namely, "how can we survive?" In the Lutheran Church that question was answered in one of two ways, either with a pragmatic, compromising approach represented in the trope *ahogy lehet* or by a non-pragmatic, uncompromising approach represented in the person of Bishop Ordass. The representatives of *ahogy lehet*, both compromisers and collaborators, in answering the question of survival as they did, were repeating an answer given throughout Hungarian history, an answer of the sort called "labanc." Similarly, the witness type, in its rejection of *ahogy lehet* and in its uncompromising commitment to the church's free ministry, echoed from Hungarian history the theme of "kuruc."

However, if partly reprising a historical theme, the witness type also reconfigured the "kuruc" motif. As a strategy, "kuruc," like "labanc," is concerned with the issue of survival. It differs from "labanc" in that it sees the solution to survival through radical, uncompromising resistance. The witness type, however, removed survival from the arena of moral consideration altogether. Like "kuruc," witness was radical and uncompromising, but its radicalness came through rejecting the very premise of the *ahogy lehet* strategy, that is, the need to survive itself. In this sense the witness type deviated from the Hungarian historical pattern.

The deviation, in turn, emerged from the nature of the questions the protagonists in this story were asking. Hungarian Lutherans, to be sure, were asking the question "how can we survive?" That question, however, was implicitly linked to another one, namely, "how can we be church?" The witness type placed these two questions in diametrical opposition. It saw being church as a project fundamentally different from surviving. Being church meant obeying God despite all and thus accepting the suffering that is the consequence of obedience. Historical strategies for surviving, proponents of witness argued, offered no guidance for how to be church. Thus, in important respects, the proponents of witness answered their question without drawing on the "labanc-kuruc" dynamic at all. Here an essentially theological idea—an idea about a suffering church—started to impact the contours of the narrative.

But how much impact did this theological idea really have? The witness type, in fact, relates to this history only ambiguously, because as an ecclesial model, it never actually appeared in the history. Witness articulated an ideal about how the church should be church in socialism. The ideal, however, never assumed sociological form; that is to say, no community of believers in the Lutheran Church in Hungary ever concretely embodied the vision of a suffering church. That is not to say that individual believers in Hungary never suffered on account of their faith. Rather, the ecclesiological vision of a suffering church, inspired by the witness of Bishop Ordass and articulated by Lutheran pastors in 1956, never assumed historical, sociological form. As ecclesia, the Lutheran Church in Hungary traveled a different path.

This historical reality points to a critical question: was the ideal of a martyr church a realistic historical option for the Lutheran Church in Hungary in socialism? When Lutheran pastors summoned their church to collective witness, they were rejecting its past and calling it to a different future. The legitimacy of their criticism and call, however, depended upon whether or not they had pointed to a real alternative. If what they described was not a real choice then by not choosing it, the church—and the church leadership—could not have failed morally. Since the vision of a suffering church never took on historical form, can it really be considered a viable historical option?

The answer to this question can only be uncertain. Certainly many in the Lutheran Church believed the suffering church was a real historical possibility. They believed it possible because the ideals held up by the vision were embodied in the real man Lajos Ordass. If Bishop Ordass could live up to the ideal, they reasoned, so could others. Moreover the suffering church was perceived as a real possibility by its greatest enemies, the church leaders who came after Ordass. Indeed Ordass's figure haunted the Lutheran Church through the remainder of the socialist period, and fearing that legacy always, the post-Ordass church leadership was constantly reacting. In this sense therefore one can speak of a witness type affecting the contours of the history, even if the type consisted of a single man, one who spoke with the clarity of a still small voice.

CHAPTER FOUR

Service to Dictators

The Church for the Building of Socialism, 1958–87

> Do not listen to the words of the prophets who are saying to you, "You shall not serve the king of Babylon," for it is a lie which they are prophesying to you. . . . Serve the king of Babylon and live. Why should this city become a desolation?
> —JEREMIAH 27:14, 17

The American wanting to understand Hungarian politics and history stumbles quickly over a word for which there is no English equivalent: *mozgástér*. It is a compound of *mozgás*, meaning movement, and *tér*, meaning space. Thus it can be rendered into English as "space to maneuver," or perhaps better, "freedom of action." *Mozgástér* names a central feature of Hungarian history and a key challenge for every Hungarian politician. A small country in the proximity of big countries, sitting in a hardly defensible geologic basin, with restricted economic possibilities, Hungary has had in its history limited freedom of action. Its maneuvering space, its integrity as a sovereign state, has been constrained by external forces, and Hungarian political leaders have struggled always to increase their country's array of social and political options. They have succeeded or failed to different degrees, but in every case the issue of *mozgástér* for Hungary has been central.

When János Kádár grabbed power in November 1956, he confronted a knot of scabrous social and political problems that severely limited his freedom of action. Looking over his shoulder were unhappy Russians, distrustful of Hungary and dissatisfied with its communist leadership. Pressed under his feet were unhappy Hungarians, who saw Kádár for the Soviet toady that he was and who considered his Hungarian Workers-Peasant government thoroughly illegitimate. Thus, on the one hand, Kádár needed to demonstrate to the Soviets that Hungary was a reliable member of the socialist camp, and, on the other hand, Kádár needed to acquire legitimacy from, or at least win the acceptance of, the Hungarian people. On top of that, he faced an enormous chore of political, economic, and social reconstruction bequeathed to him by years of Stalinism and the destruction caused by the Revolution.

But Kádár proved to be a wily quisling. He had a plain man's proletarian look, which was enhanced in public by his bumbling manner of speech. The image in turn concealed a shrewd and calculating but cautious dictator who was capable of maximizing on his *mozgástér*. Over the many decades of his rule (he was removed from office in 1988), Kádár was able to assure the Soviets that Hungary was solidly within the Eastern Bloc while also implementing a moderate form of socialist dictatorship, sometimes called "goulash communism," which made Hungary a leader among socialist countries in the level of freedom and prosperity granted its citizens.

Not unlike János Kádár, the successor to Bishop Ordass would confront problems of *mozgástér*. On the one hand, he would need to demonstrate for the party his reliability. On the other hand, he would need to win the loyalty of his diocese, and, if he were sincere, he would want to protect his church from the excessive and harmful state interference of the previous ten years. From the point of view of Ordass's successor, the vision of a church freely defining its public ministry rested on a point somewhere outside his field to maneuver; but that the new bishop would be forced into the role of ideological mouthpiece, as had, for example, László Dezséry, also seemed unlikely. Somewhere between Ordass and Dezséry, therefore, lay the hidden boundaries of the new bishop's *mozgástér*. His challenge would be to increase, and not diminish, that freedom of action. Certainly any figure who was willing to take on the responsibilities of bishop post-Ordass knew this, and knowing this, he was, by taking on the responsibilities of bishop, committing himself to a kind of realpolitik, a game of claim, concession, and compromise vis-à-vis the party-state, whereby he hoped to defend the church's interests.

The communists also knew this, and they were deliberate in making their choice. A government report summed up matters as follows:

> After Ordass it will not be easy to be bishop. . . . For this office we recommend the senior from Pécs, Zoltán Káldy, who stands near to us. He has been making increasingly progressive statements in the hopes of a future bishopric, and at the same time he enjoys unconditionally the confidence of the middle layers. Even the extreme right wing elements are not putting obstacles in the way of his election, because they hope that they will be able to win him over for themselves, and they expect from him a diminished version of Ordass' church-politics. In spite of this we recommend Zoltán Káldy to be the second Lutheran bishop, in the hope that, if he stands under good influence, our hopes will be realized and not those of reaction.[1]

Thus began a twenty-five-year battle for the soul of Bishop Zoltán Káldy.

Bishop Zoltán Káldy and the Challenge of *Mozgástér*

In the Lutheran Church in Hungary today, they remember Bishop Káldy as a charismatic figure. This common recollection is striking to one who never knew him, because in his photographs, Káldy is altogether not striking. Rather he seems to have had one of those elusive faces that never looks the same in any two pictures. Despite, or perhaps because of this, Káldy managed to dominate the life of the Lutheran Church in Hungary until his death in 1987. He is an ambiguous, partly tragic figure. According to some he was a collaborator; according to others he was a pragmatic defender of the church. In either case, Káldy managed to inflict countless and unnecessary psychic wounds on the faithful pastors and parishioners of his church, wounds that have left a kind of collective emotional dysfunction and paranoia that lingers to this day. Ironically one thing Káldy did not leave was a theological legacy.

Káldy was born in 1919 in southwestern Hungary, in the village of Iharosbéreny.[2] He attended seminary in Sopron and was graduated in 1941. Afterward Káldy worked as a minister in Pécs, an ancient Hungarian city that lies near the Croatian border, where he remained until he became bishop. Káldy, like a number of important figures in this history, had his roots in the evangelization movement. Like Bishop Túróczy, Káldy established a reputation for great preaching, and he was recognized in the Lutheran Church as a leading evangelist. Being from southern Hungary, however, Káldy probably did not associate intimately with Túróczy and the evangelization circle in Győr. Also, because he was in Pécs, Káldy was far removed from the big battles in Budapest of 1948 and removed also from the Budapest-based collaboration of the Dezséry years.

Káldy's career in higher ecclesiastical office began in 1954 with an appointment as senior of his church county. In the fall of 1956, when the majority of pastors were voicing sharp criticisms of the higher church leadership, Káldy seems to have adopted the strategy of hedging his bets, acknowledging legitimacy in points made by both the clergy and the leadership.[3] In 1958, however, he sided clearly with the small group working to oust Bishop Ordass, although his public speeches on the unresolved church "crisis" were far more measured than the rantings of collaborators like Bishop Vető and therefore much more convincing.[4] Thus, even in 1958 when he became bishop, Káldy was largely an outsider. Being from Pécs he was only vaguely associated with the leadership of the Rákosi years, and being a serious evangelizer he enjoyed a solid base of support in evangelization circles. In 1958 perhaps no one seemed more capable for the difficult task of replacing Lajos Ordass and rebuilding unity in the church than Zoltán Káldy.

Káldy was installed as bishop on November 4, 1958, in the Lutheran church at Deák tér. A massive, rectangularily shaped building, which from the inside resembles a huge nineteenth-century American revival hall, the Deák tér church can hold 2,000 people. It was full, perhaps not packed, that day, and one imagines that Zoltán Káldy, standing before the tremendous audience, listening to the many speeches putatively in his honor—József Darvas, unscrupulous collaborator, atheist, and high inspector of Káldy's diocese, saying, "Our Lutheran Church in Hungary was born in the spirit of progress and has accepted this ministry.... We all would like it if the Reverend Bishop would work in the spirit of progressive Protestantism"; Ernő Mihályfi, committed party member and highest authority in the Lutheran Church, saying, "The churches, and our church, too, are responsible for beautiful and great tasks in our socialism-building society"; and János Horváth, with mildly reassuring words, reporting, "With the rise to dominance of the progressive church forces, the relation between church and state has been successfully normalized"—looking out at the churchmen who were to become his colleagues, rivals, and enemies, Zoltán Káldy, one imagines, was thinking about his *mozgástér*.[5]

In fact Káldy had first considered the question of the church's *mozgástér* (not explicitly but obliquely) in a speech delivered before his fellow seniors and published afterward in an issue of *Evangélikus Élet* under the title "How Do We Move Forward?" There Káldy had attempted to provide a complete survey of the possible responses of the church to socialism. He started off by addressing the ecclesiological vision of a suffering church. The church, Káldy said, had been traveling like a car down a hill, speeding up and finally landing in a ditch. There were people, Káldy said, who thought this was how it should be, but he was not one of them. Káldy said:

> Certain kinds of people have sprung up in our church who consider this "ditch-situation" the normal condition for the Lutheran Church in Hungary living according to God. That is, they think that if the church truly dares to be a church it can only be broken to pieces, covered with blood in a ditch. According to them the church in the ditch, and not the church on the highway, is the church in socialism. Consequently they profess a "ditch-philosophy" which says we ought not only reconcile ourselves to the "ditch-situation," but we should expressly rejoice at it, because after the "serious mistakes" of the pre-1956 years, at last the church is straightened out. Anyone among the pastors and secular leaders of the congregations—this philosophy goes on to say— who is working at trying to help this car out of the ditch, and is trying to put it once again on that highway, the highway on which the life of our people thrives, that person harms the church; he is a "false prophet," because he will not allow the Lutheran Church in Hungary "to be a martyr's church," and he will not allow its "martyr" character to develop all the way to where perhaps it is compelled into complete silence, and, thus, with its silence it can "preach." According to this opinion, therefore, to the question, "How do we move forward?" the answer is: We should do nothing.[6]

Káldy's words were directed against those who thought they saw in Ordass a path for the church. Rejecting the "Ordass-position," Káldy mocked the idea that suffering as witness against an anti-Christian political regime has moral significance, and also, significantly, he rejected martyrdom as a legitimate moral option for the church in Hungarian socialism. Thus Káldy began defining the church's *mozgástér* in a way that took one significant theological and sociological option off the map completely. By rejecting the "ditch-philosophy," Káldy was saying in effect that to live in socialism the church had to work within the limits set by the regime. This did not necessarily mean collaboration, but it at least meant committing oneself and one's church to a long game of tug-of-war with a cheating bully, to the kind of pragmatic compromises with the party-state propounded in 1948 by the Túróczy group.

With his room to maneuver thus restricted, Káldy proceeded to set forth and interpret what he saw as the church's five possible responses to socialism. The first was simple opposition, a position that considered socialism "some kind of demonic thing" to be opposed with all the strength of a "confessing" church. Káldy, however, rejected this view, asking the pragmatic question, "Who would cross the threshold of our churches in such a case?" He then went on to reject the next three options before arriving at the right way, the "fifth way." Traveling on the fifth way, Káldy said, the "church should be church in socialism." Being church in socialism meant carrying out the true ministry of the Word, but it also meant recognizing that the church was carrying out its ministry in a communist state that expected contributions to the building of socialism.

In sketching out this so-called fifth way, Káldy was honestly searching for a new, tempered kind of partnership with the party-state. He wanted to formulate the relationship within the framework of a "both-and." On the one hand, he intended for the church that it carry out its central ministry of Word and Sacrament; on the other hand, he intended that the church assist in the project of building socialism. The church, however, would assist in those aspirations of socialism that were morally commendable, things like peace work; it would not contribute to every communist project. Thus Káldy insisted that partnership with the communists should be practical only, not ideological. The church's contribution to building socialism was to be grounded in its own social teachings and ministry, not in a hybrid of Christianity and Marxism. The church was to seek a practical partnership with the socialist state on its own theological terms.

As a normative description of the church's place in Hungarian socialism, Káldy's "fifth way" represented a genuine attempt to redefine the church's ministry in a manner that preserved its moral and theological integrity. Káldy's strategy was grounded partly in theological conviction and partly in realpolitik. From a theological point of view, Káldy believed the church could ally itself with those aspects of the socialist project that were morally estimable without compromising its commission to administer the Gospel. From a political point of view, he believed that if the public church cooperated with the party in building socialism, it would obtain the internal freedom necessary to carry out its true ministry. Stated differently, Káldy was willing to relinquish his external *mozgástér* in the hopes of obtaining greater room to maneuver internally. This was a reasonable strategy, and not without theological integrity.

At the same time, the long-term viability of this strategy had been undermined when Káldy excluded from the outset the possibility of suffering opposition to the regime. By excluding painful opposition a priori, Káldy excluded the possibility of any sort of friction between the church's mission and the work of socialism. Given the regime's totalitarian record, this was a discomforting a priori. Káldy's vision of a serving church ran the risk of sliding into sycophancy—unless the bishop were extraordinarily capable.

The Emergence of the Theology of Diaconia

One may assume that Káldy threw himself vigorously into the tasks of bishop. This meant not only building support among the clergy in his diocese but also earning the confidence of the party-state. Káldy was the junior member among the higher church leadership, and most of his colleagues were men with sound "left-wing" credentials. Lajos Vető functioned as senior ranking bishop, and many higher church offices were occupied by persons who had been second-tier collaborators under Bishop Dezséry. Káldy, too, worked to prove his political reliability. He swore to adhere to the constitution of the Hungarian People's Republic. He accepted party-state measures to return stricter supervision over the churches (in 1959, for example, the party-state reestablished the State Office of Church Affairs).[7] He joined the National Peace Council and the Patriotic People's Front, and said to the people the necessary falsehoods. Thus, in time, Káldy, too, won the confidence of the party-state.

However, it seems that Káldy also wanted to develop a theological vision for the church in socialism different from the ideological vacuities voiced by church leaders at conventions of the Hungarian Peace Council or the Patriotic People's Front. Káldy truly loved his church, and he must have felt the need for a more genuine social ethic. Early on he began devoting attention to what would in time become the official theology of the Lutheran Church in Hungary, namely, the Theology of Diaconia. *Diaconia* is the Greek word for service, and, as the word suggests, the Theology of Diaconia made service a central category for the church in socialism.

A thorough historical etiology of the Theology of Diaconia, tracing its origins and rise to dominance in the Lutheran Church in Hungary, has never been done. The Theology of Diaconia, however, may have drawn upon diverse sources. On one level, the concept of diaconia as social service had been present in Hungarian Protestantism for a long time. In the Horthy period, for example, diaconical associations, either affiliated with or supervised by the churches, carried out various forms of social work. Even after these were disbanded by the communists, the Lutheran Church continued to carry out what it called diaconical work, although this now designated a much narrower field of action. On another level, a Theology of Service was being developed in the Hungarian Reformed Church, and commentators often point to the Reformed Theology of Service when accounting for the emergence of the Hungarian Lutheran cousin.[8] At the same time, the language and concept of diaconia had also started to assume broad ecumenical currency. It was used, for example, by churches in other communist countries and by the World Council of Churches.

Thus, the Lutheran Church in Hungary could have drawn upon a variety of theological sources in developing its own Theology of Diaconia. What is odd, therefore, is how closely this theology became linked to the person of Bishop Káldy. Toward the end of his career, Káldy used to boast that the Theology of Diaconia was tied to his name.[9] He was probably right. On the basis of articles from the period in the Hungarian Lutheran press, one can say that the Theology of Diaconia does not assume a central place in the church's consciousness until relatively late, sometime after Káldy became senior bishop in 1967. To be sure, earlier mention of the "way of diaconia" can be found but not as synonymous with the "way of the church in socialism." Thus the Theology of Diaconia was in some sense Káldy's special creation, a product to which he had a peculiar personal relationship.

Káldy first unveiled his Theology of Diaconia in June 1964 in a speech entitled "The Life-form of the Church: Diaconia."[10] In the speech, Káldy attempted to draw the outlines of a theological system built around the biblical concept of diaconia. Using the biblical text from Matthew 20:28, "the Son of Man came not to be served, but to serve, and to give his life as ransom for many," Káldy argued that the concept of diaconia was central to the Christian message about Jesus Christ. Christ, Káldy said, was the Diakonos, the one who came to serve humanity. Diaconia, in turn, was Christian practice rooted in Christ's love for humanity. It was Christian love for the neighbor, an active, self-giving love that thought not of itself but only of the other. The radical other-regarding character of diaconia meant also that it was self-abnegating. Christ, the Diakonos, incarnated self-abnegating love on the cross and made it the model for all who would follow him. He who practices diaconia, Káldy said, "not only looks to the neighbor, but subordinates himself to him."[11]

Following the way of the Diakonos, the task for the church was to make its every action diaconia. Christ's church was a serving church, that is, a subordinating church. According to Káldy, "Christ's command to follow me announces the duty to the church that, while carrying out diaconia, it should subordinate itself to the one for whom and toward whom it conducts diaconia." The subordinating posture of Christian love stood in sharp contrast with a domineering, critical stance toward the world. According to Káldy, the serving church should not tell the world what to do but should rather support the good things the world is already doing:

> It is not part of the church's diaconia that it should issue some kind of "Christian program" for the solution of the world's "secular problems." Much differently, the church needs to conduct its diaconia so that it helps and supports those ambitions that already actually exist, and which are directed to the realization of the peace and happiness of humanity.[12]

In other words, the serving church should strive to link up with those morally worthy social projects already in place and not inject its own moral agenda into a society acting independently of the church.

This Theology of Diaconia represented Káldy's attempt to place his initial "both-and" strategy for dealing with the regime on sound theological footing. In understanding the Gospel as a message of God's selfless love for humankind, and in seeing the believing response to God's love as selfless love of neighbor, Káldy was concurring with a large body of Christian opinion throughout the ages. By further interpreting Christian love as the model for Christian behavior in society, Káldy was making an unforced extension of the Gospel into the realm of social ethics and a move for which one could find parallels elsewhere. In socialism, the argument went, love meant cooperating with the worthwhile projects of the party-state. Communism, like every political institution on earth, was not perfect, but like virtually every political institution, it sought to achieve worthwhile objectives. Thus the church expressed its love for a socialist society appropriately by assisting in the realization of socialism's worthwhile goals.

However, the Theology of Diaconia unveiled in 1964 was not merely a theological elaboration on Káldy's earlier "both-and" approach. It was also an adjustment of his original strategy. This became clear four months later when Káldy addressed students at the Lutheran seminary in Budapest in a speech entitled "The Fifth Way." In this speech, Káldy identified five possible paths for the church in socialism, just as he had done in 1958. However, Káldy's rendering of those five ways in 1964 did not simply repeat the rendition of his 1958 speech. By comparing the two speeches, submitting each to a kind of "form criticism," one can discover differences that point to meaningful changes in the "Sitz-im-Leben" of the 1964 speech, differences that indicate important ideological shifts in Káldy's thinking.[13]

The 1964 speech began with an unnuanced historiographical account of the church's life before World War II, an account that resonated with, although it was not as crass as, the tales of collective guilt offered in the Dezséry years. After Horthy's Hungary had collapsed, said Káldy, the church was forced to choose between five paths. The first of these was the path of "hierarchy." Proponents of "hierarchy" held that the church was "born to rule," to stand over "the world" and to instruct. This had clearly been the church's error in the Horthy period. Significantly, however, in 1958 Káldy never mentioned "hierarchy" as a potential way for the church; in 1958 the first temptation had been "opposition." Káldy's new designation of "hierarchy" as the first way set up an implicit contrast with the fifth way, namely, the way of diaconia or service in socialism. Káldy was constructing a crude dichotomy between the evil "hierarchy" of the Horthyite past and the good "diaconia" of the socialist present, thereby intimating a familial relationship between diaconia and socialism.

Káldy's 1964 depiction of the other "false" ways indicated further change in his relationship to the regime. The second church way, Káldy said, had been "conformism," a stance that required the church to relinquish its principles and conform to the world in which it lived. Káldy had also identified conformism as the second wrong way in 1958, but his presentation of this option in 1964 was different. Káldy now explicitly identified conformism as the church's error under Horthy, adding that in the socialist present, "conformism did not represent a special danger for the Lutheran Church in Hungary." A much greater threat, Káldy now believed, was represented by the third way, what Káldy called "withdrawal into the ghetto." Withdrawal had also been the third option in 1958, but in 1964 Káldy conflated withdrawal from the world with neutrality in politics, as if these two attitudes were the same. Being neutral toward political and social changes, and barricading oneself from the world were, according to Káldy, equivalent moral postures. By conflating these attitudes, Káldy was in effect eliminating neutrality as a legitimate moral stance toward socialism. Considering that he had just dismissed the moral danger of conformism, Káldy's 1964 descriptions of the second and third ways marked a clear movement toward the regime.

Thus a comparison of the 1958 and 1964 speeches suggests that Káldy was no longer the same man who had assumed the bishopric in 1958. He was less wary and more willing to work with the communists, a man shaped by the necessary compromises he had at first reluctantly accepted.

His ambition that the church travel on a middle way through socialism, standing both on the true ministry of the Gospel and on partnership in the building of socialism, had driven Káldy, like a soldier with a bum leg, to favor the latter of his two supports. In this respect, the Theology of Diaconia was not merely the unfolding of a decision-in-faith Káldy had made in 1958, although it was a consequence of that decision. Rather, the Theology of Diaconia marked a turning point in the campaign for Káldy's soul, and a noticeable stumble to the left. Although, at least conceptually, diaconia was a workable framework by which to steer the church through socialism, Káldy could never overcome his weaknesses, and in time he degenerated into a clerical tyrant and communist lackey.

From Service to Sycophancy: Káldy's Decline

When evaluating the actions of church leaders in communist countries, one must always be conscious of the distinction between the regime's intentions and those of the churchmen. True, the regime placed bishops in power and expected them to fulfill certain public roles that served its own interests. However, the bishops understood this, and their intentions were not necessarily the same as the party's. Bishops, like Káldy, were playing a deliberate political game in which by satisfying the party in some things they hoped to reap benefits for their church in others. Thus to assess Káldy's bishopric fairly and rightly, one must look not just at his public activities and official theology, but also at what he did for the church internally.

In fairness, Káldy did obtain things for his church, such as the renovation of church buildings, the construction in the 1980s of a new building for the Lutheran seminary, and the publication of a new hymnal. These things might be listed under the title of accomplishments in infrastructure, and the truth is, Káldy helped to preserve the infrastructure of his church. At the same time, one must remember that the church is not merely an infrastructure but also a spiritual community with higher purposes. And the truth is that Bishop Káldy inflicted serious spiritual wounds on his church and its ministry, wounds that were not even required by the communists. Early in his bishopric Káldy started exhibiting symptoms of serious defects in character. He had a predisposition toward megalomania and a capacity for extraordinary pettiness. These traits first appeared publicly in 1962, in an incident so full of Káldy's vindictiveness that it remains a living memory in the church to this day.

In August 1962, Pál Zászkaliczky, one of Ordass's most loyal supporters, died. In 1948 Zászkaliczky had sided with Ordass in opposing school nationalization, and in 1950, as Ordass's prison sentence drew to an end, he had signed the petition protesting the formation of the church court that would deprive Ordass of his bishop's office. During Ordass's second administration, Zászkaliczky was elected Ordass's bishop-surrogate. Interestingly, Zászkaliczky was also part of the evangelization movement. He traveled throughout the country holding evangelization weeks and in this way became one of the church's public figures, both respected and loved. Zászkaliczky was also the pastor in Fót, a small village about thirty kilometers north of Budapest. Under Zászkaliczky's stewardship, Fót became the home of a vibrant congregation.[14]

Zászkaliczky died, as it happened, shortly after a meeting of the Moscow Peace Conference. Thus, on the day of his funeral, pastors from all over the country had assembled in Budapest to hear reports about the conference. In the afternoon, after the Budapest meeting was over, more than eighty pastors traveled to Fót for Zászkaliczky's funeral, making it one of the largest in the church in memory. Unfortunately Káldy saw in this display of affection the agitation of "clerical reaction," and in his anger, he began a vendetta.

Normally congregations voted for their own pastors and then had their choice approved by the bishop. In Fót the congregation wanted one of Zászkaliczky's sons (two of them were pastors) to take the place left by their father. The leaders of the congregation traveled to Budapest to meet Káldy in person, and requested that the eldest son, Pál Zászkaliczky Jr., be their new pastor. Káldy made clear he was not going to allow it.[15] The congregation's leaders, having failed to persuade the bishop, went home. Next the women from the congregation came down to Pest, telling Káldy they would stand in the street outside his office praying, until he had a change of heart. Káldy warned them, "Here inside I have the power to protect you, but on Puskin street I am not lord."[16]

Sensing, after this, opposition in the congregation, Káldy decided to speak personally to the Zászkaliczky boys (both of whom Káldy had ordained), telling them first, "I don't want to paint myself large, but you owe your collars (Luther-kabátjuk) to me." Then he asked the eldest son to tell them in Fót that he was not interested in being their pastor. The son refused. Having received two petitions, one from the congregation and one from the bishop, the son said, he was honoring that from the congregation. Temporarily set back, Káldy searched for another pastor to replace the deceased Zászkaliczky, finally sending a candidate to Fót to deliver a trial sermon. The congregation, unflinching, explained to the candidate that they wanted Zászkaliczky's son to be their pastor. Rebuffed again, Káldy decided to have another chat with the congregational leadership, but, in his words, "once again they only stubbornly rejected my well-intentioned explanations."[17]

When the time came for the presbytery in Fót to elect a new pastor, they voted unanimously for Pál Zászkaliczky Jr. Káldy did not approve the choice. He announced he was sending another pastor to work in the congregation, but the following Sunday no one showed up in church. Three weeks later, Káldy himself traveled to Fót to install his pastor. The congregation, gathering around the church, refused to let the bishop into the building. Eventually Káldy turned back to Budapest without having installed the new pastor. The matter dragged on for a year. Every Sunday for a year Káldy sent a pastor to Fót to conduct the Sunday services, and the congregation was left without a regular pastor.[18] Finally a compromise was reached. The congregation listed five pastors it considered acceptable, and from that list Káldy selected the pastor of Fót.[19] Naturally that pastor was not a Zászkaliczky.

Why Káldy reacted to the Zászkaliczky funeral as he did remains a mystery. Perhaps the party was behind it from the beginning, insisting that no more Zászkaliczkys work in Fót. Just as likely, however, Káldy himself initiated the confrontation, and only later, after the situation had escalated, did the matter attract the party's attention. In either case, Káldy had, from the beginning, personalized the Zászkaliczky affair in a way that went beyond political necessity and made a personal vendetta out of it. In a meeting of pastors in January 1963, Káldy lectured the assembled about the "Fót-affair" in a tone that was bitter and personal. First labeling the deceased Zászkaliczky a "reactionary," then labeling the funeral an "organized demonstration," he next slandered Zászkaliczky's sons, saying:

> When it came time to ordain Pál Zászkaliczky Jr., many people warned me and asked if I was even free to ordain the son of a family with such tendencies. I ordained him nevertheless. The question was frequently posed to me about the younger one, too, Péter Zászkaliczky, whether this boy should be allowed to stay in seminary. He was among those six that both the church and the state thought should be removed from the seminary. I had to intercede with the full weight of my bishop's office to protect him, so that he could still complete seminary. Indeed, I even ordained him. As I did all these things there were constant predictions that I would regret my behavior, because I would have even more problems with these two boys. Those predictions have come true.[20]

Káldy went on, maligning Zászkaliczky's widow, then the entire Fót congregation, including a few of its members by name. In short, whatever the party's initial attitude to the Zászkaliczky funeral may have been, Káldy quickly interpreted the affair as a personal affront to his authority. Somehow he felt threatened by the affection shown a dead man. True, Zászkaliczky had been a loyal supporter of Ordass—and Ordass was still alive—but nothing that happened in Fót ever threatened Káldy's bishopric. Rather, Káldy, feeling threatened, determined to prove he was lord in his own house, manhandling the entire congregation, and wrecking what had been a vibrant church life there.

Here was Káldy's weakness: he felt threatened by signs of spontaneity or independence in his church, and, therefore, instead of working to protect those few forms of religious vitality that could exist in socialism, he tried to stamp them out. Renovated church buildings posed no threat to Káldy; congregations who loved their pastors did. Thus his actions as bishop frequently went beyond partisanship for socialism at conferences for peace and sessions of the Patriotic People's Front; they often extended to attacks on the internal life of his own church. In 1962 when Káldy behaved in ways outside his original intentions, the communists, no doubt, relished their choice of Ordass's successor.

Over the years Káldy's power in the church increased. In 1967 he was elevated to senior bishop, and from that position he wielded more power in the Lutheran Church in Hungary than had any one individual in its history. In his own kingdom, the internal life of the Lutheran church, Káldy enjoyed nearly unbridled power, although the power he enjoyed was dependent always on the party. This latter fact surely bothered Káldy. Perhaps partly because he was anxious for the party's good pleasure, Káldy feared a freer church life. He liked being bishop, and it must have irritated him knowing that his position depended on satisfying the party-state. Maybe knowing this drove him to demonstrate his independence within the church through mean-spirited tyranny. There was in Káldy's petty histrionics always a taint of insecurity.

Around 1970 the forgotten Bishop Ordass gave a copy of his memoirs to an interested foreign visitor, who took it out of the country. When they learned about it, the church leadership decided to take up the issue at a meeting with pastors in Budapest. First, the bishops spoke out on the "Ordass-affair" then forced every pastor to comment on the leadership's position. To conclude the meeting, the pastors unanimously passed a resolution affirming the present church leadership, distancing themselves from Bishop Ordass, and condemning the action by which Ordass had illegally sent his memoirs abroad.[21]

The church leadership's actions on this occasion were no doubt dictated by the party. Nevertheless, Káldy's conduct at the meeting belied external compulsion. It was clear that for Káldy the "Ordass-affair" was an affair of the heart:

Gentlemen! I see that some of you are taking notes. You can feel free to write down everything and you can set it down on Ordass' table. In fact, I send all this as a message to him. Let him hear! We are talking about the Ordass-question. One must recognize that this is only an episode-question, just as Ordass is only an episode figure. . . . I have a right to speak and to speak this way! Because I am Ordass' direct successor! The one in the past years from whom they asked an account abroad at every step. At every step they posed the question, "You are Ordass successor?" I answer, "Yes! Sir!" They say, "Oh my, what's up with Lajos Ordass?" This, only, was the main question. . . . I am not bothered that Lajos Ordass' memoirs have appeared abroad! I am not bothered for a moment! Because of this I am not put out! The house is not burning! Something else! It is about something totally else! What happened is just a symbol. A symbol of the slander, vilification, denigration of honor (the honor of the church leaders; bishops and seniors, my colleagues) that up to now existed abroad and which at home I have yet to experience from atheists. . . . This is such a thing, that I am forced to take back a sentence said long ago. I do it here. In 1958 in Szekszárd I sat eye to eye opposite Ordass. Then I said to him, I respect you, I love you, I honor you. Then I spoke well. But today I cannot say this. Now I take it back! . . . The episode figures will disappear! Lajos Ordass has done many things, caused many problems for us, for our church—but sending out this book tops it all![22]

By 1970 Bishop Ordass posed no concrete threat to Bishop Káldy nor to the "way of diaconia." Ordass threatened only Káldy's moral legitimacy.

That at some level the church leadership sensed a moral threat in Ordass was clear from the comments of Káldy's junior colleague, Bishop Ernő Ottlyk. Ottlyk, in summarizing the nature of the "Ordass-question," described Ordass's thinking as follows:

Once again martyrdom theology, the theology of suffering has moved to the foreground. This is what [Ordass] offers. Conflict and suffering has to be shouldered! According to him the prophetic ministry can only be negative in socialism. He sits again in the judge's seat. He uses negative and only negative criticism.[23]

Even in 1970 church leaders felt compelled to respond to the vision of a suffering church. Ordass's mere presence posed a moral question to the church leadership: were they not, by working together with the party-state, betraying the church's true ministry? And if they were not betraying that ministry, then where was the border between honorable compromise and faithless collaboration? Ordass's witness challenged the church leadership to establish a clear limit to their partnership with the party, to state the point at which suffering would be preferable to cooperation. This was a challenge the church leadership rejected. Over time, the cost of not stipulating those limits became clear. The church leadership slipped ever closer to collaboration.

Bishop Káldy's Triumph: The Presidency of the Lutheran World Federation

In 1980 the Lutheran World Federation decided to hold its 1984 Seventh World Assembly in Budapest. Of itself the decision marked a victory for the leadership of the Lutheran Church in Hungary. The church of Lajos Ordass, a man who had been twice vice president of the LWF and who had been set aside at least in part by the leadership of his church, was to host the gathering of world Lutheranism. The event also would be the first meeting of a major international Christian organization in a communist country. Moreover, the Lutheran World Federation elects its officeholders at its world assemblies, and by convention, the head of the church hosting the assembly is elected president. Thus Zoltán Káldy, direct successor to the illegally deposed Bishop Ordass, was, if convention held true, to become the head of the Lutheran World Federation. As a personal triumph, and as a legitimization of his career, for Káldy there could be no greater achievement.

However, opposition to Káldy's presidency gathered in advance. It was led primarily by Hungarian emigrants who, familiar with Káldy's dark side, were unsettled by the prospect of his apparent impending moral victory. In March 1983, the recognized Lutheran theologian of Hungarian origin, Vilmos Vajta, published an article in the journal *Lutherische Monatshefte* criticizing the Theology of Diaconia.[24] Vajta, although recognizing the general validity of diaconia as a theological concept, argued that in Hungary diaconia was given a one-sided emphasis that precluded criticism of socialism. In Norway another Hungarian pastor, László Terray, published an article questioning whether Lutherans in Hungary had the possibility of discussing the Theology of Diaconia at all.[25] In response to these criticisms, Káldy began lobbying on behalf of his candidacy, noting that the LWF president was supposed to come from the host country and stating that a failure to elect him would be an insult to the churches of Eastern Europe.[26]

Federation leaders wanted the world assembly in Budapest to serve as a bridge between East and West, and, in their commitment to bridge building, they reacted coolly to any criticism of Bishop Káldy. For example, General Secretary Carl Mau, of the American Lutheran Church, responding to Pastor Terray's suggestion that Hungarian Lutherans were not free to discuss the Theology of Diaconia, said that Terray's article "misleads an uniformed reader by playing up the significance of the events of the past and by reflecting inadequately the developments during the last decades."[27] In general, the LWF leadership was placing its weight in favor of Káldy's presidency.

In Hungary preparations continued for the task of hosting the world assembly, which involved not only working through organizational challenges but also putting on a good face for the visitors. Throughout 1984 members of the Lutheran Church in Hungary wrote informative articles about their church and country that were published in the LWF's news bulletin. Additionally the church leadership took steps to ensure that all the church's pastors would be on their best behavior. Bishops Káldy and Gyula Nagy (the successor to Bishop Ottlyk in the Northern Diocese) issued a circular letter to the pastors in early 1984 in which they said:

> Do not obstruct and burden the preparations [for the assembly] with individual, familial, and congregational scandals. The church leadership does not now have time for such matters, and we are not willing to be occupied with such problems. The one for whom this request does not find receptivity should not be surprised if we deal with him as soon as we have time, not with the words of the "Gospel" but, in accordance with Lutheran theology, with the words of the "Law." In a given case, the leadership will even take up short "administrative measures" with a good conscience.[28]

"Administrative measures" was the conventional communist euphemism for the application of force to resolve difficulties. Clearly the bishops were not sparing tact in their preparation for the world assembly.

With preparations in place, the Seventh World Assembly of the Lutheran World Federation was convened in Hungary from July 22 to August 5, 1984. The unifying theme was "In Christ—Hope for the World," no doubt selected as especially suited for the task of bridge building. The agenda of the assembly was ambitious, including seventeen platform addresses and more than fifteen working committees. Moreover, it was in Budapest that the Lutheran World Federation made the significant ecclesiological decision to suspend two South African churches for using apartheid as a criterion for admission to the Eucharist. However, discussion about the situation of Eastern European churches was absent from the agenda altogether.[29]

In retrospect, for the Lutheran World Federation to hold its world assembly in an Eastern Bloc country while simultaneously seeking to avoid any discussion of Eastern European church life was not only odd, it was ill planned. The issue became unavoidable when, shortly before the assembly began, a Hungarian pastor named Zoltán Dóka sent an open letter to the LWF's executive committee criticizing the Theology of Diaconia and Káldy's tyrannical style of leadership.

Zoltán Dóka was a Lutheran pastor in the village of Hévizgyörk, about one hundred kilometers northeast of Budapest. He was an able pastor, and he tended a healthy congregation. Dóka was also intelligent and proud and stubborn, which meant he had periodic run-ins with the church leadership. In 1962, for example, Dóka had spoken out publicly against Káldy's treatment of the Zászkaliczkys and the village of Fót. But Dóka also resented the petty humiliations he had received through the years from Káldy. When he was older, Dóka engaged in serious scholarly work, publishing an extensive commentary on the Gospel of Mark. In 1984, before the world assembly began, Dóka was engaged in theological study in West Germany, and it was from there that he sent his open letter to the LWF leadership.[30]

Much that Dóka said in the *Open Letter* was true, and he was putting into words the feelings of many pastors in Hungary; but almost all that Dóka said was poorly formulated.[31] His critique of the Theology of Diaconia was particularly unconvincing, starting with the assertion that "it is common knowledge that 'diaconia' is not the central theological concept of the New Testament" but only "one individual peripheral New Testament idea." Building on this initial assertion, Dóka rejected, or seemed to reject, diaconia as an ethical concept altogether. Moreover, when criticizing Káldy's leadership style, Dóka sloppily employed terminology often used to analyze totalitarian dictatorships. For example, Dóka accused Káldy of surrounding himself with a "cult of personality." "Cult of personality," however, is generally a technical phrase used to characterize totalitarian dictators such as Hitler and Stalin. Dóka also accused Káldy of using the Theology of Diaconia as an instrument of "theological terror," making associations with the totalitarian uses of "terror." Meanwhile, as Dóka made these severe criticisms, he was studying theology in West Germany by permission of the allegedly totalitarian bishop. This gaping incongruity seemed never to have occurred to Dóka, and his conspicuous oversight, coupled with his unnuanced formulations, robbed the *Open Letter* of a good deal of credibility.

Nevertheless, the *Open Letter* did contain truths. Káldy did threaten and intimidate his pastors into docility; the Theology of Diaconia did serve the ideological needs of Hungary's communist party; and religious freedom in Hungary did not exist in the Western democratic sense. Despite its many shortcomings, parts of the *Open Letter* were moving, particularly those parts that asked the Lutheran World Federation for help.[32] Finally, as Federation leaders should have known, dissent in a communist country always came with personal risk. For Dóka to write and post the *Open Letter*, with a wife and family in Hungary and himself returning to Hungary on August 20, was an act of considerable courage.

The bridge builders at the LWF offices in Geneva were less than courageous. Fearing a scandal, they apparently did everything possible to keep the *Open Letter* a secret. The executive committee neither responded to it nor made it public. When, nevertheless, copies of the letter appeared at the world assembly, attempts were made to obstruct its distribution. The LWF's European secretary reportedly helped Bishop Káldy draft a response.[33]

Káldy delivered the statement to the press, saying that it would "be helpful—even necessary—to discuss the theology of diaconia which has drawn interest here" but that now was not the best time to do it. Responding to criticisms of his leadership style, Káldy intimated that Dóka was motivated by personal vendetta. Dóka had been turned down for a teaching position in the church's seminary, and one of his daughters had recently defected to Sweden. The insinuation was that Dóka himself was about to defect, but Káldy added, "It is my interest and the interest of the church to do nothing which would make Pastor Dóka's return to Hungary more difficult, in case he would like to return."[34]

Káldy was generally being politic. On July 21, the day before the world assembly opened, he held a memorial service with LWF representatives at the grave of Bishop Ordass, who had died in 1978. Káldy spoke warmly of Ordass's ministry, although he added that the bishop was burdened with one-sided judgment. The next day Káldy greeted arriving participants and used the occasion to deflect criticisms tactfully. The Lutheran Church in Hungary and its leadership, Káldy said, had been charged in the past with excessively accommodating the state; the Theology of Diaconia, it was said, was contrived to support socialism. Such criticisms misled many, but, said Káldy, "God has accomplished that now you should come to us and be convinced yourself about . . . the truth."[35] Káldy also preached at the opening worship service. There he mentioned the great "cloud of witnesses" who had preceded the work of the present assembly, including in that list Bishop Ordass.[36]

Káldy's politicking notwithstanding, his election as LWF president was a close call. The victorious candidate needed to secure an absolute majority, and after the first round of voting, Káldy was in a tight race with Bodil Sølling, the first woman candidate for the post. After the second round of voting, however, Káldy emerged the winner.[37]

Thus Káldy became president of the Lutheran World Federation. It was a great personal triumph, a legitimation of his bishopric. Even more, it was—or seemed to be—a validation of the strategy Káldy first adopted in 1958 for steering his church through socialism. In 1958 Káldy's *mozgástér* had been restricted, but he had hoped, by conceding to the regime in certain things, to increase his freedom of action. Now he had done it. As president of the Lutheran World Federation, a major international ecumenical body, Káldy enjoyed independence from the party that had placed him in power. If the communists tried to remove him now, it would cause an international incident. This, of course, did not mean Káldy was free to start a revolution, but he had the independence to resist the party now and again on behalf of his church. For the Lutheran Church in Hungary in 1984, religious renewal was a political possibility.

But Káldy was discontented in his success. Zoltán Dóka had embarrassed him, and he could not be allowed to get away with it. When Dóka returned home, Káldy immediately suspended him from his pastorate. Preparations were made for a disciplinary church trial. *Evangélikus Élet* published an article harshly attacking Dóka, entitled "Theologized Treason," which was bolstered with false statements.[38] The article also contained confusing and grammatically incorrect sentences, suggesting that someone had tampered with the original text before publication. Dóka submitted a response to the accusations that *Evangélikus Élet* refused to publish. On this occasion, however, the world was watching. Newspapers in West Germany and Scandinavia covered the story in detail.[39] Bishop Káldy, after all, was a leader of world Lutheranism. The "Dóka-affair" attracted too much international attention; Káldy was forced to back off, and the charges against Dóka were dropped. Káldy could not punish an uppity pastor in his own church without causing an international scandal. Once again, he lacked *mozgástér*.

Thus, in the end, Zoltán Dóka, not as theologian but as spoiler, successfully exposed Zoltán Káldy for what he had become: a petty, vindictive tyrant who was used to lording over his church rather than defending it against the communist regime. In his moment of triumph, Káldy did not need to settle accounts with those who had crossed him, but he had grown accustomed to his ways. Káldy was too petty to sense his victory, and in victory, he revealed defeat. By 1984 Káldy was a lost man, preoccupied only with his own prestige—by habit, if not by heart, a sycophant to Hungary's communist party.

Káldy never enjoyed the benefits of being LWF president. In December 1985, on the way home from Geneva, Káldy suffered a serious stroke in the Zurich airport. He died in 1987 after a protracted illness, a man who never achieved his greatest ambition.

THEOLOGICAL EXCURSUS FOUR

The Diaconia Type

Between Service and Subordination (or Ahogy Lehet *Revisited)*

So they made the people of Israel serve with rigor,
and made their lives bitter with hard service.
—EXODUS 1:13–14

Diaconia was a considered correction and response to the two basic moral strategies that had appeared in the Lutheran Church prior to Káldy's bishopric. First, diaconia aimed to improve upon the *ahogy lehet* framework introduced in 1948 by giving compromise greater theological content and justification. Káldy recognized that with the Dezséry clique compromise had become collaboration, and he wanted to forge a strategy for cooperating with the communists that was theologically sound. Second, diaconia was an answer—for the Lutheran Church *the* answer—to Bishop Ordass's witness. That witness posed a persistent moral threat to Bishop Káldy, and consequently he needed to demonstrate that the path he had chosen, and to which he had committed his church, was morally legitimate. Therefore, as an ideal-typical response, diaconia was largely about legitimizing cooperation with the party-state. The diaconia type, given theological expression in the Theology of Diaconia, was more considered than the previous ideal strategies, but it nonetheless glossed over certain central theological issues—a fact which suggests that Káldy and the architects of the Theology of Diaconia, in their need for legitimation, needed also to avoid difficult questions.

The Theology of Diaconia: Love without Limits

Because the Theology of Diaconia was embedded within a larger framework of compromise, it was in certain respects a permutation of *ahogy lehet*. Admittedly, unlike *ahogy lehet*, diaconia was not up front about the hostility of the regime nor about the fact that it cooperated with the regime from compulsion; but those were the undeniable givens of the situation, realities demonstrated by the contours of the historical narrative considered here. The Theology of Diaconia, therefore, was partly theological justification for, and partly theological exposition of, Káldy's "both-and" strategy for coping with the regime. Accordingly the test for diaconia as a framework for compromise was how and whether it identified limits, because without limits, diaconia could easily slip into collaboration. On the question of limits, however, the Theology of Diaconia was consistently fuzzy. It emphasized so heavily the importance of service to, and cooperation with, society's already existing moral ambitions that it consistently obscured, rather than identified, the boundaries to cooperation, few though they were.

In its articulation of diaconia as Christian love, the Theology of Diaconia tended to equate love as subordination with love as submission. Because Christian love seeks the neighbor's good, the argument went, love subordinates the self to the other. Likewise, because the church seeks the good of humanity, it subordinates itself to humanity. Importantly, however, subordination here was a fuzzy concept. It might only mean subordinating one's interest to the interests of the neighbor, and thus fostering the neighbor's good, or it might mean subordinating oneself to the neighbor himself. If the latter were the case, then diaconia would require submission to the other regardless of what the other demanded. That is, diaconia would entail not only self-giving subordination to the other's good but also unquestioning submission to the other's demands. The Theology of Diaconia fudged this issue over, making it difficult for the church to establish critical distance between itself and the demands of a communist state building socialism.

The Theology of Diaconia was further hampered in setting limits by a defect, congenital in the near literal sense. Káldy felt morally threatened by Bishop Ordass. He had rejected at the beginning of his bishopric the possibility for the church of a suffering witness. If Káldy had recognized, even in part, a place for suffering ministry, he would have moved toward recognizing validity in Ordass's witness, and in doing so, he would have called into question his own moral legitimacy as bishop. The issue of suffering, however, was linked to the issue of limits, because in socialism, setting limits always came with the risk of suffering. Thus when Káldy eliminated for himself and his church the possibility of suffering witness, he also eliminated the possibility of setting limits.

This defect concerning limits, and the origins of this defect in the Ordass-question, surfaced in an intriguing interpretation of suffering that Káldy offered in a 1972 speech to Lutheran pastors. His argument merits extensive examination. It begins:

> Diaconical theology is identical with the theology of the cross. When individual Christians and congregations, as well as the church in its entirety, conduct diaconical service, they live and act the theology of the cross. That is to say, the basis of diaconical service . . . is renunciation of rulership, of special status, of one's own interest, and of one's own advantage for the good of the other person or an entire community. The most conspicuous example of this was given exactly by the great Diakonos, Jesus, on the Golgotha cross. Those who were jeering

around the cross shouted at Him, "If you are the Son of God, come down from the cross!" In this request was voiced the expectation that the Son of God, the Messiah, was coming to rule. Jesus, in fact, could have come down from the cross, and thus fulfilled the messianic expectations of the times. Instead, He stayed on the cross, and in this status He completed His messianic service. "He was obedient unto death, and to death on the cross." This was the diaconical service which took place "for many," that is, for human beings. This diaconical service of Jesus—which was not an avoidance of the cross, but exactly the acceptance of it—became the source, the animator and the determiner for the diaconical service of individual Christians and of the entire church.[1]

In simplest terms, Káldy reasons here as follows: Diaconia is the giving of the self to the other. Because on the cross Christ perfectly embodied self-renunciation for the good of others, Christ on the cross is the perfect embodiment of diaconia. Thus diaconia and the theology of the cross are essentially the same.

However, there are three distinct elements in Káldy's argument that should be kept conceptually distinct but that Káldy blurs. First, there is the good of the other to which diaconia directs its attention. Second, there is self-giving, by which the self subordinates its good to the good of the other. Third, there is the cross, that is, the suffering that attends self-giving, or in other words, the suffering that is attendant upon subordinating the self's good to the good of the other. The first two elements, other-regard and self-giving, are intrinsically linked. From the moral agent's point of view, they are two parts of the same activity. The agent places the other's good before herself and seeks to foster that good. Coupled with that is the subordination of her own good to the good of the other. If the two goods should conflict, the moral agent will sacrifice her good for the sake of the other's, and presumably for that reason will suffer.

Here, though, is a disjunction. Why should the two goods conflict? Why would the self suffer by seeking the other's good? One could, for example, imagine an ideal world where everyone loved everyone, that is, where everyone was a diakonos. In such a world, although nobody would seek his or her own good, everyone's good would be provided for, because each self would seek and foster the good of each other. The suffering—that is, the suppression in a conflict situation of the self's good for the sake of the other's—only takes place in an imperfect world, where the self-giving of the diakonos is unreciprocated or abused. Thus the cross—the third element in Káldy's argument—is contingently related to diaconia. The giving of the self to the other only leads to suffering in a world where diaconia is unappreciated.[2]

What Káldy does in his argument is to elide diaconia, or other-regarding self-giving, into suffering. He treats suffering as an inherent feature of diaconia. Consider the passage below, which continues where the previously quoted passage left off:

> Not only Jesus' great diaconical deed, but also His words call his disciples, and the church as a whole, to complete diaconia in the church and the world, traveling on the *via crucis*. . . . At Mt. 16:24 we read, "If someone wants to come after me, he must deny himself and take up his cross and follow me." In this connection the "renunciation of the self" and the "taking up of the cross" are two sides of the same thing. The consequence of "self-renunciation" is the "taking up of the cross;" and vice versa, the consequence of taking up the cross is self-renunciation. The two are a unity. Jesus' life-form, which the disciples must take up, is self-renunciation, which means disregarding one's own believed interests, renouncing self-realization and self-assertion.[3]

In this passage self-renunciation has been elided into suffering, which Káldy designates with the phrase "via crucis." According to Káldy, self-renunciation is identical with the "via crucis." But why should this be so? If self-renunciation entails subordinating the self's good to the good of the other, then indeed it might lead to suffering in certain cases. However, it could only be identical with suffering if one assumed that the renouncing self, or the diakonos, lived in a world where others would try to take advantage of its giving.

With these reflections on suffering in mind, one can properly consider the issue of limits. Diaconia subordinates the good of the self to that of the other. Such subordination raises a question: what should be done if the other attempts to exploit the self, demanding from her things that are illegitimate? There are at least two possible answers to this question. One answer (answer A) might be that, in the face of exploitative demands, diaconia simply submits. It submits because Christian love is inherently self-giving, and to resist the exploiter would be to assert the self over against the other. According to this answer, the diakonos issues to the other a kind of "blank check," agreeing to pay whatever the other asks.[4] Here the emphasis is not on seeking the other's good but on submitting to the other's will.

Within a Christian framework, the "blank check" answer to the question of limits (answer A) is often related to the argument whereby self-giving is elided into suffering. This is because in the case of elision, suffering assumes a centrality in the definition of Christian love that, conceptually speaking, it does not deserve. Either the act of self-suppression is taken as the central feature of Christian love, or self-suppression and self-subordination are taken to be equally central. In either case, suffering assumes an independent moral value. That is to say, suffering, or self-renunciation per se, without reference to the other's good, is taken as a noncontingent, essential element of Christian love (or diaconia). However, when self-renunciation per se is essential, then the self has no resources to limit its self-giving. Because self-suppression is taken to be the inseparable counterpart of self-giving love, that self-giving, when confronted with an exploiter, simply submits. In other words, it issues to the exploiter a "blank check."

However, the "blank check" answer to exploitation is not the only possibility. If what defines diaconia is fostering the other's good and not merely the other's wants, then self-giving love can refuse an illegitimate request without relinquishing its self-giving character (answer B). The self declines the other's exploitative demands not from concern for the self but from concern for the other's good. Diaconia, therefore, does not issue a "blank check" but rebuffs exploitation.

Answer B, perhaps, sounds like specious casuistry, as if the self-interested diakonos were inventing reasons not to give. However resisting exploitation may also lead to suffering, especially in political settings. If, for example, a Christian community rejects the unjust and exploitative demands of a state, then the state is likely to see in that community an enemy and persecute it. In such cases, rejecting unjust demands is not self-serving, because it comes with a cost. Answer B can produce a diaconia that suffers, too, although its suffering has a different quality than the suffering associated with answer A. For answer B, suffering is not an internal feature of Christian love, as if self-renunciation per se were a great value. Rather, suffering is the potential, contingent consequence of a love that is prepared to resist injustice for the sake of the other's good.

Not surprisingly, Káldy seems to have tended toward answer A and the "blank check" version of suffering. To be sure, he never argued this explicitly, but "blank check" self-giving was the necessary endpoint on his interpretation of diaconia. That endpoint was dictated by Káldy's elision of self-giving into suffering, and by Káldy's need to reject the Ordass legacy. The interplay of these two factors is evident in the way Káldy concludes the argument presented in the previously quoted passages:

> At this point I would like to say very clearly that "self-renunciation" is not yet diaconia in the true sense of the word. It is connected, but it is only the negative, the back side, the reverse of diaconia. I repeat, self-renunciation is only a negative picture of diaconia. Essentially, it is turning away from one's own interests, one's own selfish life-goals. This negative diaconia appears before us when individual Christians, or the church itself, renounce special status, deny the desire to rule,

and do not desire to realize their believed interests. It may also take such form where Christians as individuals, and the congregation and the church as a collective, "suffer" the world or the society in which they live. They "suffer" those who are ruling, and "suffer" that world order which it judges, from its own point of view, to be not advantageous, but rather disadvantageous for the church.

Unfortunately, in the Lutheran Church in Hungary, in the past two decades, numerous pastors and congregation members—those who did not find their place among the new historical surroundings in the socialist society—took up the behavior of "suffering" in the illusion that with this they were traveling on the path of "cross-carrying" that is desired by Jesus. They thought that if they humiliated themselves, accepted that they should be "little," if they withdrew back to the "final place," then they traveled on the right path. However, this conduct, even in the best sense, reflects only "resignation," resignation from ourselves. Even if we do not entirely belittle this behavior on the part of individuals and congregations, nevertheless it is a passive voice. . . .

If someone, or the entire church, wants to remain in discipleship with Jesus, then it is necessary to step beyond "self-renunciation," beyond "suffering." Jesus defines the step-beyond as follows: "If someone wants to be first let him be the last among everyone and the servant of everyone." . . . As long as the disciple endeavors only to disregard himself, to place himself in the back, to humiliate himself, to make himself little, then he still circles only around himself. . . . Diaconia means not only that a person steps back concerning his own person, turns away from himself; but also that he turns toward and steps toward the other, and serves him. Moving beyond the individual, the turning of the church away from itself is only the condition of its then turning to others, turning to human beings, to the world, and thus serving them. . . .

Individual Christians and the whole church need to travel on the path of the cross in such a way that, on the one hand, they deny themselves, renounce the path of glory, turn away from themselves; but in the second beat they immediately turn toward the individual, toward the neighbor, and with the commitment and sacrifice of their lives, and with actual and concrete acts of love received from God, serve them. More immediately: if among many pastors in our country the demand appears that our church travel on the "via crucis," then naturally this means that our church turns in greater measure to human beings, to our society, to our people, and that it serve them and help them.[5]

In the passage, Káldy draws a conceptual distinction between self-renunciation and giving to others. His distinction differs from the ones offered earlier in these pages between other-regard, self-giving, and suffering. It was argued earlier that other-regard and self-giving are inherently linked, constituting two aspects of the same activity, but suffering is related to self-giving only as a potential, contingent consequence. The other-regarding, self-giving agent subordinates her good to the good of the other, but only in cases of conflict does the subordination of the self's good to the other's good result in suffering. Káldy is working with a slightly different category, self-renunciation. Self-renunciation for Káldy is constituted of self-giving plus suffering, but it is distinct from other-regard. Thus Káldy, under the rubric of self-renunciation, has elided self-giving into suffering and separated self-giving from other-regard. Self-renunciation is only a first step toward other-regard. It is a mere suppression of the self, which must be supplemented by a second step, the giving of the self to an other.

However, Káldy's separation of self-renunciation and other-regard is unintelligible.[6] First, it is unintelligible because self-giving to the other necessarily implies subordinating the self's good to the good of the other, and self-subordination implies some kind of self-renunciation. Second, and more importantly, Káldy's distinction is unintelligible because it defines self-renunciation nonreferentially. That is to say, self-renunciation for Káldy means renunciation of the self without reference to some other good; it is self-renunciation per se. However, nonreferential self-renunciation would be activity that is not directed to an end; it would be nonrational unintelligible action, that is, such action would have no purpose or goal. Thus when in the passage cited above Káldy understands self-renunciation to be conceptually distinct from other-regard, and also equates self-renunciation with suffering, he has described a kind of suffering vis-à-vis the world that makes no sense. That is to say, he has described a submissiveness to the world that does not arise from, and is not linked to, any sort of commitment to any other good. One simply suffers because suffering is an independent moral value.

That Káldy considers suffering an independent value, however, does not mean he considers it a morally sufficient value. As the previous passage makes clear, suffering for Káldy is independent only in the sense that it is independent of any good, not in the sense that it encompasses the whole of diaconia. For Káldy suffering (of a "blank check" sort) is only the first step toward diaconia. Thus Káldy's equation of self-renunciation with suffering sets up a polemic against, and a feeble appropriation of, the Ordass legacy.

Much of Káldy's argument in the previous passages is directed against the vision of a suffering church that many pastors claimed to have discerned in Ordass's witness. Káldy enters here into direct argument with the witness type. He begins by upbraiding unnamed Lutheran pastors who claimed they were traveling on the "way of the cross" merely by suffering.

This view is inadequate, Káldy says, because it celebrates only self-renunciation; in other words, it treats suffering as a value sufficient in itself. Diaconia, in contrast, moves beyond suffering to a commitment to the other. Diaconia incorporates the vision of suffering but also builds upon it to fashion a complete moral system. Thus diaconia is the answer to those who call the church to travel upon the "way of the cross." The challengers are right, Káldy says, that the church must suffer. Indeed the church does suffer by submitting to the world order around it. However, Káldy says, the challengers need to move beyond a celebration of suffering to serving the neighbor, to supporting the society in which the church lives.

But of course Káldy has answered the challenge of the witness type on his own terms. The proponents of Ordass's legacy did not claim suffering was a good per se. Rather, they understood suffering to be a potential, contingent consequence of an uncompromising commitment to the church's ministry. The call to witness was not a call for the church to suffer but a call for the church to witness even if witnessing brought suffering. In other words, the witness type spoke not of "blank check" suffering but of the sort of suffering associated with answer B. The real argument about suffering, the one that actually appeared in the history, is an argument Káldy never answers. Instead Káldy has answered his own challenge, and the vision of suffering he has refuted and appropriated is his own. Furthermore, in the process of refuting the straw man, Káldy has deprived diaconia of the theoretical resources necessary to set limits. He has produced a diaconia that can issue to the exploiter only a "blank check."

Having said this, one must add that unequivocally pinning Káldy down on the questions of limits is difficult. Káldy certainly understood that if he defined diaconia in a way that excluded limits, he would have done no more than find a fancy Greek word for collaboration. Wanting to avoid collaboration, Káldy blurred the question of limits. The logic of his arguments nevertheless pushed inevitably toward love without limits. As a result, the Theology of Diaconia ended up legitimating Hungarian socialism rather than defining a strategy for coping with it. Frequently, although not always, expositions of diaconia extended to explicit and unbalanced affirmations of socialism. Even when it became partisan, however, the Theology of Diaconia never affirmed socialism theologically; that is, it never equated socialism with a manifestation of God's providential will or made socialism itself an object of religious faith. Thus diaconia never entailed the kind of theological collaboration characteristic of the Dezséry years. Diaconia supported socialism without establishing critical distance between the church and Hungarian society, and in this way it provided ideological legitimation for Hungarian socialism. This legitimation, however, was still something less than theological affirmation.

Moreover, this legitimation was, in a certain sense, the unintended consequence of a failed strategy for compromise. To understand the transformation of diaconia from compromise to legitimation, therefore, one must consider once again, from a slightly different angle, *ahogy lehet*.

Compromise and Self-Legitimation: Another Form of *Ahogy Lehet*

In a well-known essay entitled "The Power of the Powerless," the onetime Czech dissident Václav Havel begins an examination of life in communism by considering the case of a common greengrocer.[7] This greengrocer puts a sign up in his shop window that says, "Workers of the World Unite!" Havel asks, why does he do it? Does he really desire that the workers of the world unite? No, answers Havel; the greengrocer puts the sign up because everyone puts up signs like this in their windows, and not putting the sign up could cause trouble. It is not that the greengrocer identifies with the message of the sign, nor is he interested in awakening others to the ideal it expresses; rather he puts the sign up in his window because he wants to be left alone.

That sign, despite the greengrocer's indifference to its explicit message, communicates a message nonetheless. The sign was delivered with the vegetables by the central office, and the greengrocer understands that the central office expects him to place it in the window. By putting up the sign, therefore, the greengrocer complies with expectations and communicates a message of the sort that "I, the greengrocer, know what is expected of me, and I am obedient. Therefore, I have the right to be left in peace." The sign, in fact, communicates a message related to the greengrocer's vital interests, and putting the sign in the window is part of the greengrocer's strategy for living day to day in a communist regime. It is part of his strategy for surviving in a context of oppression.

At the same time, by putting up the sign and protecting his vital interests, the greengrocer compromises his moral integrity and indirectly reinforces the regime that oppresses him. Havel explains this dynamic as follows:

> Let us take note: if the greengrocer had been instructed to display the slogan, "I am afraid and therefore unquestioningly obedient," he would not be nearly as indifferent to its semantics, even though the statement would reflect the truth. The greengrocer would be embarrassed and ashamed to put such an unequivocal statement of his own degradation in the shop window, and quite naturally so, for he is a human being and thus has a sense of his own dignity. To overcome this complication, his expression of loyalty must take the form of a sign which, at least on its textual surface, indicates a level of disinterested

conviction. It must allow the greengrocer to say, "What's wrong with the workers of the world uniting?" Thus the sign helps the greengrocer to conceal from himself the low foundations of his obedience, at the same time concealing the low foundations of power. It hides them behind the facade of something high. And that something is *ideology*.[8]

The greengrocer articulates his compromise in the language of ideology. In truth he is merely searching for a modus vivendi, which means he is ready to compromise, yet he accounts for his inglorious compromising in a language that is dignified. This way he hides from himself the fact that he is compromised. The ideological slogan on the sign provides the greengrocer with an excuse. It allows the greengrocer to convince himself that the system he is cooperating with is in harmony with the way things ought to be.

The way in which the greengrocer justifies his compromising also helps to reinforce the regime. By using the language of ideology to express his loyalty to the regime, the greengrocer accepts the rules for behaving that the regime has established. The greengrocer becomes a player in the regime's own game, and because he is willing to play the game, he makes it possible for the game to continue. Ideology, originally only part of an excuse for cooperating with the regime, becomes a component of the regime itself. Its language and logic become the means for communicating and operating within the system. Thus ideology assumes a life of its own and starts to define the terms for playing the game. Ideology becomes the rule maker, and as rule maker it traps those who enter its game, overdetermining their decisions and actions. This is true even when the game players do not believe, or do not believe completely, in the ideology. It is enough that they are playing by its rules.

So with the example of a greengrocer, Havel seeks to demonstrate the way, within a communist system, reluctant compromise is transformed into reluctant collaboration. Perhaps, though, Havel has been unfair to the greengrocer. If this particular greengrocer were more articulate, he might point out that the regime concerned here is not one of his own making, that its continued existence does not in fact depend on whether or not he hangs up silly signs in his window, that its existence depends only on how long Soviet troops are staying in his country. The greengrocer might also call attention to his wife and children, and emphasize that selling groceries is the only way he has to support them. So, the greengrocer would say, he puts up silly signs in his window not because he is too self-deceived to recognize that plans to unite the world's workers are a lot of baloney, but because giving lip service to those plans is what it takes to sell groceries in communism. The greengrocer might even, were he versed in history, round off his argument by pointing out that the peoples of Eastern Europe have always lived under some kind of foreign domination and that they have survived precisely by making the kind of pragmatic compromises Havel objects to. Should the greengrocer be Hungarian, he might call this historical strategy *ahogy lehet*.

Interestingly, Havel is aware of this sort of objection. He considers the counter-position under the heading "small-scale work." Proponents of "small-scale work," Havel says, argue that the nation's good is best served by persons committed to honest and responsible work within the existing system. These persons pay the necessary minimum to the system but also try constantly to do the best that they can. Admittedly they achieve good work only on a small scale, but every piece of good work indirectly criticizes the regime and thus contributes in a concrete way to bettering the system. Havel is skeptical, however, that, given the nature of the regime, this approach can be sustained over the long run. He argues that those attempting "small-scale work" will eventually be forced to make a choice: either to retreat from "small-scale work" and adapt to circumstances or to continue the work begun and accept conflict with the regime. This is because the success of "small-scale work" depends on the limits it can establish to cooperation with the regime. If "small-scale work" entails limits, then, given the nature of the regime, sooner or later it will encounter those limits. Upon reaching the limit, the "small-scale" worker must make a choice: either he must accept confrontation with the regime and thereby step out of the compromising framework, or he must adjust to his surroundings but push the limits of "small-scale work" out to where they do not entail conflict.

Havel illustrates his point with the case of a dedicated beer brewer. This beer brewer was Havel's direct superior during the time Havel worked in a beer factory. The brewer loved beer, was well versed in the art of making it, and wanted the beer factory to make good beer. The brewer spent most of his time at work devising new ways to improve the beer factory's operation. Unfortunately the manager of the beer factory, a member of the party's district committee, had no special interest in beer. Eventually the situation became so desperate that the dedicated brewer wrote a letter to the manager's superior, analyzing the factory's difficulties and detailing ways to improve quality and production.

Here was an instance of "small-scale work." The dedicated beer brewer was working to improve the beer factory. His supervisors, however, did not appreciate the initiative. The beer brewer's letter was described as a "defamatory document," and he himself was identified as a "political saboteur." He was removed from the beer factory and assigned a new job elsewhere that required no skill. The dedicated brewer's commitment to "small-scale work" had led to conflict with the regime. He could have remained silent and kept his job, but by doing so he would have abandoned "small-scale work" and ended up a mere cog in the system's inefficient beer production, a collaborator in the production of bad beer.

Havel's analysis of the dynamic of compromise in communism, of the way compromise leads to a catch-22 and then often traps the compromiser in an ever tighter circle of cooperation, casts light on the moral experience in the history of the Lutheran Church in Hungary. In this context, the Theology of Diaconia provided the ideological excuse for compromising with the regime, and Bishop Káldy was the church's greengrocer.

As was noted earlier, Káldy had a peculiar personal relationship with the Theology of Diaconia. The circumstantial evidence suggests that diaconia was a special theological interest for Káldy starting from the earliest days of his bishopric. In this sense, diaconia was an "organic" development in the church; that is to say, it was a theological development not hoisted upon the church by the party. Of course, all higher church leaders were expected to be partisans for socialism, and they expressed their partisanship in Parliament, at meetings of the National Peace Council, at assemblies of the Patriotic People's Front, and elsewhere. Káldy was indisputably such a partisan. However, the Theology of Diaconia appears to have emerged independently of that partisanship. It was fashioned initially not in the general church but in Káldy's diocese, and it assumed the status of official church orthodoxy only after Káldy became senior bishop in 1967. If the party had demanded from the church a comprehensive theological and ideological vision of the church's place in socialism, then the Theology of Diaconia would probably have developed differently.

Thus the etiology of the Theology of Diaconia—not to mention Káldy's defensive histrionics—suggests that Káldy had a personal need to legitimate his cooperative relationship with the party-state. On the one hand, legitimacy was always a special problem for Káldy because of the Ordass legacy. On the other hand, legitimacy was a general problem for any church leader who was willing to work with, and hence compromise with, the party-state. The Theology of Diaconia served as theological justification for Káldy's strategy of compromise. Káldy was willing to compromise with the regime, but if he had said simply, "I will cooperate with the party-state, because it is going to supervise church life anyway, and this is what one must do if one is to be bishop and if the church is to survive," he would have been ashamed of his own moral degradation, and, importantly, he would have been left speechless before the Ordass legacy. Thus Káldy constructed a theological system that called cooperation diaconia.

As with every good excuse, the Theology of Diaconia was plausible. Its central concept, Christian love, or diaconia, was biblically and theologically sound. Moreover at some level Káldy probably intended diaconia to be a genuine bridge between the church and the regime. No doubt Káldy wanted to compromise within limits. But the Theology of Diaconia was not intellectually rigorous. It was foggy when it needed to be foggy, and in the fog, conveniently, were lost the moorings necessary to keep the church from drifting into collaboration.

Consequently the Theology of Diaconia, originally only a theological excuse for compromising with the regime, became in time one more way of ideologically legitimating socialism. And Bishop Káldy, despite his original intentions, became a mere player in the communist game, one more gear in a sociopolitical machine that oppressed Hungarian Lutherans. Although Káldy loved his church and wanted to protect it, he was not big enough for the game of moral tug-of-war he was playing. The inherent disparities of the game pulled at him unrelentingly, until in time Káldy was no more than a communist lackey—an unwitting quisling to be sure but a quisling nonetheless.

CONCLUSION

The End of an Unresolved Argument

As it is, we do not yet see everything in subjection to him. But we see Jesus.
—HEBREWS 2:8-9.

The Kádár regime had purchased legitimacy from the people largely by providing them with material comforts and consumer goods. Hungary became an oasis of relative prosperity in a socialist desert, and Hungarians grew accustomed to living well. Socialism itself, however, could not produce economically what it needed to meet the consumer demands of a comfortable and expectant population. When in the 1970s a worldwide oil shortage increased energy costs in Hungary, Kádár, in order to deliver on his implicit promises to the people, absorbed energy costs by borrowing money from the West. By 1987 Hungary's foreign debt was approximately $12.3 billion, and its economy showed signs of approaching crisis.

In the 1980s, also, the Kádár regime was forced to deal with growing and organized political dissent. In 1977 a significant group of Marxist intellectual reformers signed a letter in support of Charter 77, a Czechoslovakian document of political dissent. Soon afterward in Hungary, an organized group of intellectuals came together in dissent, forming what is often called the Democratic Opposition. In 1981 the Democratic Opposition launched a samizdat journal, *Beszélő (Speaker)*, which became an influential forum for criticizing "Kádárism" and presenting proposals for policy reform. The Democratic Opposition soon joined with a group of populist intellectuals, who together began to forge united opposition to the Kádár regime.

Meanwhile from within the party itself, a group of reform communists started pushing for fundamental changes. This was important. In Hungary communism was ended not by mass demonstrations but by negotiated agreement between the communist party and the new opposition parties. In May 1988, reform communists removed Kádár and a number of his associates from the Politburo. Kádár's removal helped to precipitate a shift of political power in Hungary from the party to the state, which in turn precipitated the end of the one-party system. On February 11, 1989, the party's Central Committee announced the end of the one-party system in Hungary.

Rarely in history do those who have power voluntarily relinquish it. In Hungary, however, in June 1989, the party entered into "National

Roundtable" discussions with opposition parties to negotiate the shape of a new democratic government. An agreement was reached on September 18, 1989, and with a wink of an eye and a handshake, communism in Hungary was over.[1]

The Legacy of Communism for the Lutheran Church

The end of socialism naturally brought opportunities for reform to the Lutheran Church in Hungary. However, it did not bring a negotiated resolution of competing interests and points of view in the church, but only an end to an unresolved argument. Leaders and dissidents in the Lutheran Church displayed less courage and wisdom than their political counterparts, and moves toward renewal were hampered by fragmentation and polarization.

In May 1987, Bishop Káldy died, and by the latter half of 1988, the church leadership had started to issue moral rehabilitations of wronged pastors. In December 1988, the leadership announced a general moral rehabilitation, stating that the church granted "complete moral satisfaction to those pastors who, together with their families, suffered unjustly in our church because of disciplinary judgments, transfer, or other administrative procedures." The sentiment no doubt was sincere, but the claim to have "granted complete moral satisfaction" for past wrongs was somewhat self-justifying, as if simply acknowledging the wrongs made up for them. The leadership, still, was confident in its moral satisfaction, adding:

> We ask confidently that you accept the complete moral satisfaction, publicly confessed and expressed by the National Presbytery and the current church leadership, for such sins which we ourselves did not commit, but for which in the name of our church we ask forgiveness.[2]

Thus the church leadership in 1989, in granting moral satisfaction for past wrongs, was also claiming an important discontinuity between itself and the previous forty-five years.

Many pastors did not accept the moral satisfaction confidently rendered by the church leadership. They reasoned that general apologies were too facile a reparation for the church's sins in socialism. They believed that the church leadership had committed concrete sins that needed to be confronted explicitly before the church could move forward. General confessions, apologies, and rehabilitations did not confront the past but glossed it over.

Disgruntlement with the leadership notwithstanding, real changes were taking place. On June 30, 1989, the State Office of Church Affairs dissolved itself, bringing an end to state supervision of the church. In September 1989, the Lutheran Church reopened one of its old nationalized high schools. In March 1990, the 1948 church-state was nullified, thereby removing the last tangible link to the communist past. Moreover, pluralism was returning to the church.

In mid-1989, a group of Lutherans formed an association that they named the Lajos Ordass Circle of Friends (Ordass Lajos Baráti Kör). According to its self-definition, the Lajos Ordass Circle of Friends was committed to the renewal of the church and to the preservation of Ordass's legacy.[3] Thus the name of the group reflected its belief that Bishop Ordass had bequeathed a moral legacy to his church that was a necessary part of its renewal. The group intended to represent the Ordass legacy before the church on behalf of the church's renewal. Unfortunately it would soon prove to be a shrill and ineffective instrument of reform.

After thirty years of Káldy's tyranny, clergy and common members of the church viewed the church leadership with deep suspicion. In 1989 one of the most important tasks facing the leadership was to reestablish confidence and trust between themselves and the broader church. The best step toward this end would probably have been an orderly arrangement of new elections for all church offices. Given that in socialism the church had not been free, and all church leaders had been selected with state approval, those who held leadership positions at the beginning of 1989 could not convincingly claim to have the confidence of the church. Members of the Ordass Circle called for general elections, but no plan for elections was forthcoming. Within the Ordass Circle, a radical faction began to emerge, which, frustrated by the lack of serious reform, began to deny the legitimacy of even new church leaders. On the basis of private and poorly articulated criteria, they disqualified certain persons from holding church office regardless of whether they were freely elected or not.

On November 10, 1989, Róbert Frenkl was elected the church's general inspector. At this point the State Office of Church Affairs no longer existed, and the state did not interfere in Frenkl's election. Frenkl had competed against two other candidates and won by only a narrow majority. Thus Róbert Frenkl was the first national leader to be elected freely in the Lutheran Church in Hungary since Bishop József Szabó in 1948. However, intransigents in the Ordass Circle refused to accept the election. Zoltán Dóka, for example, called into question Frenkl's legitimacy on the grounds that Frenkl had also held church office prior to the fall of communism.[4]

At the time of Frenkl's election, the bishop of the Northern Diocese, Gyula Nagy, announced his retirement. The church elected Imre Szebik to succeed him. Thus Szebik became the first Lutheran bishop to be freely elected after socialism, but, again, members of the Ordass Circle refused to accept it. Employing an absurd legal argument, they objected to Szebik's election on the grounds that church law stipulates that a bishop holds his position for life, without mentioning provisions for retirement. Therefore, according to the argument, Bishop Nagy could not retire without a special dispensation from the church's retirement council; since Nagy had failed to obtain this dispensation, he was still legally bishop, and no one could replace him. Members of the Ordass Circle even submitted a petition with the church court.[5] The petition was rejected, which the petitioners took to be evidence of continuing dictatorship in the church. Appealing the decision, the self-designated reformers insisted the issue implicated the rule of law in the church and held decisive import for the future.[6]

Their argument was ridiculous, and many other criticisms voiced by members of the Ordass Circle were unfair. Nevertheless, behind all the antics was a genuine effort to work through the serious moral issues embedded in the history of the previous forty-five years. Insofar as this book has been an extended effort to sort through those very issues, its argument should also bear relevance for the Lutheran Church in Hungary today.

A Moral Interpretation of the History of the Lutheran Church in Hungary in Communism

The key moral arguments in this history rotate around a central question-complex dealing with issues of survival and church. Placed in a context of oppression, Hungarian Lutherans asked, first, "how can we survive?" and, second, "how can we be church?" In actual experience these two questions were closely connected, and in fact most of the protagonists asked both questions simultaneously. When asking how to survive, Hungarian Lutherans were asking how to survive as church.

Outsiders, however, can distinguish the questions more clearly than the protagonists did and thereby identify an important dimension to the history. On the one hand, "how can we survive?" is a question that has been asked and answered repeatedly in Hungarian history. Thus, in thinking about how to survive, Hungarian Lutherans drew upon their national history and gave answers that mirrored answers given in Hungarian history. These Lutherans, when thinking about survival, thought like Hungarians. On the other hand, the question "how can we be church?" is explicitly theological. Thus, in asking this second question, the protagonists drew upon theological resources, sometimes identifiably Lutheran and sometimes more generally biblical. These Hungarians, when thinking about survival, thought like Lutherans. Their strategies for survival were theologically informed and articulated.

Four distinct ideal-typical responses to this question-complex appeared in the Lutheran Church in Hungary. The first of these was compromise, which answered the question of survival by drawing upon a typical Hungarian strategy called *ahogy lehet*. Rudimentarily, *ahogy lehet* meant both conceding to and resisting the regime. This rudimentary framework, however, was modified by theological reflections on how to be church. Proponents of compromise drew upon Article VII of the Augsburg Confession, which seems to say about the church that "it is sufficient if the gospel is rightly taught and the sacraments correctly administered." Understanding Augsburg this way, the compromisers argued that the church could concede to the regime those things that did not belong to its essence. Thus, while setting forth a Hungarian strategy of compromise, they also circumscribed compromise with theological considerations. For compromisers, issues of church set limits to what they could do in the interest of surviving.

However, in deliberating about specific compromise situations, compromisers also operated with a set of theological presuppositions about their historical setting. Specifically compromisers announced a sweeping judgment of general guilt against Hungary, and they claimed further to have discerned God's divine purposes in current events. These theological presuppositions coalesced in the concept of reaction and influenced the way compromisers decided when to concede and when to resist the regime. Moreover, theological presuppositions like these were related to the overall *ahogy lehet* framework. A successful strategy of compromise depends for its success on the capacity for discernment, and in advancing theological judgments about contemporary Hungary, compromisers were claiming to have discerned the deeper workings of contemporary history. Unfortunately compromisers did not discern matters as well as they thought. Further, despite efforts, compromisers never set clear limits to compromise. As an ideal-type, therefore, compromise was characterized by structural instabilities. If executed poorly, compromise would slip into collaboration. Not surprisingly, in this history compromise directly preceded collaboration.

Collaboration aimed at the survival of the church through unqualified cooperation with the regime. Collaborators also started out from *ahogy lehet*, but they understood this phrase differently from compromisers. For collaborators, *ahogy lehet* designated a category of necessity. It meant that the church could only survive by cooperating with the party-state. Treating survival as an unqualified good, collaborators chose to cooperate with the regime unconditionally. In doing this they acceded an autonomy to the question "how can we survive?" that it never had for the compromisers. In the collaboration type, "how can we survive?" subsumed the question "how can we be church?"

This subsumption was expressed via a particular theological vision for the church. Collaborators interpreted Hungarian socialism within the framework of a pseudo-salvation history, one that recounted the sin and bondage of the Hungarian past, the liberation from Hungarian sin by Russian occupation, and the beginning of a reborn future with the advent of Soviet-style socialism. On the terms of this salvation history, the destruction of "old Hungary" and the beginning of "socialism-building Hungary" were part of God's divine plan. Therefore the church, if it wanted to be faithful, must understand the building of socialism in Hungary as a religious project. The question "how can we be church?" was answered, "We are church by being for socialism." Socialism was treated as an object of faith.

The collaboration type, therefore, entailed not only unqualified cooperation with the regime but also a change in Christian teaching. The Lutheran confessions identify the marks of the church as true teaching and right sacraments. In Hungary between 1949 and 1956, however, collaborating Lutheran churchmen taught that "the church exists for socialism." This teaching is not rooted in Scripture nor is it found in the Lutheran confessions. It is false teaching. Thus, working within the framework of the Augsburg Confession, one must conclude that the Lutheran Church in Hungary, to the extent that it was represented and embodied by collaborating church leaders in the Rákosi period, ceased to be church.

In its feature as false church, the collaboration type is unique to this history. That is, in terms of what it said about the Christian faith, collaboration is qualitatively different from all the other types. However, in terms of the underlying *ahogy lehet* framework that led to theological collaboration, the collaboration type is structurally similar to the compromise type. Moreover, in terms of the *ahogy lehet* framework, collaboration and compromise are both similar to a third type, namely, diaconia.

The diaconia type, which was tightly linked to the person of Bishop Káldy, also started out from concern for survival. Káldy, like his typological progenitors, was prepared to work with the party-state. Unlike the collaborators, however, Káldy refused to subsume the question of church under the question of survival. More like the compromisers, Káldy wanted to preserve the church's true ministry while simultaneously working with the party-state. Where Káldy differed from the earlier compromisers was in the theological framework he developed for compromising. Káldy's framework was the Theology of Diaconia.

The Theology of Diaconia served to justify theologically Káldy's 1958 decision to work with the communists. This theological justification was achieved through elaborations on Christian love, which was described as diaconia. Diaconia designated the Christian obligation to serve the neighbor selflessly and also the church's obligation selflessly to serve society. Thus, for the diaconia type, the question "how can we be church?" was answered, "We are church by serving in love our socialist society." The problem was that diaconia never set limits to its love and therefore never set limits to its cooperation with the party-state. In time diaconia degenerated into sycophancy of socialism.

However, despite his real failures, Káldy and the church under Káldy never degenerated into the kind of theological collaboration characteristic of Iván Reök or László Dezséry. Thus the diaconia type differs in important ways from the collaboration type. Whereas collaboration affirmed socialism religiously, diaconia did no more than legitimate it. Affirmation subsumed the church under socialism so that the two were inseparable, but legitimation only failed to articulate critical distance between the church and socialism. By *only* failing to articulate critical distance, Káldy's church managed to preserve its self-definition, rather than being forced into redefinition. In other words, diaconia did not involve a change in Christian teaching. It taught a biblically inspired understanding of love but did such a sloppy teaching job that the limits to love were hard to discern. In this way the church became a partisan for socialism. Partisanship, however, is something less than identifying socialism as an object for Christian faith. Under Bishop Káldy, the Lutheran Church in Hungary remained church.

Therefore the diaconia, collaboration, and compromise types must be understood as distinct types of response to communism, although they bear structural similarities to one another. Each type started with a concern for survival and believed that the church, in order to survive, must cooperate with the regime. From this starting point, however, each type formulated a strategy for negotiating the church through communism that was distinct.

Against all three *ahogy lehet* strategies stands the witness type. The witness type is unique in that it separated the first question, "how can we survive?," from the second question, "how can we be church?" Witness denied the legitimacy of the first question altogether and answered the second question by saying, "We are church by suffering witness." The model for this suffering witness was Lajos Ordass. Ordass had acted from a deontological commitment to his pastoral duties, and because of his commitments, Ordass suffered. Inspired by Ordass's witness, some pastors argued that the church should adhere uncompromisingly to its ministry, even if the refusal to compromise brought martyrdom. The proponents of witness rejected survival as a legitimate moral concern and placed the church's survival exclusively in God's hands.

The history of the Lutheran Church in Hungary under communism, therefore, is also the story of a moral argument. The argument is about how much responsibility Christians have for the survival of the church. On one side were those who asserted that Christians are responsible for the church's remaining and therefore reasoned that the church in communism needed to make concessions to the regime in the interest of surviving. On the other side were those who denied that Christians have any such responsibility. They claimed that God alone is responsible for the church's remaining and therefore the question for the church was only how to fulfill its ministry. Because this was so, proponents of witness claimed, the church in communism should be a "suffering church."

This unresolved argument continues to overdetermine much of the discussion about the recent past in the Lutheran Church in Hungary today. Some believe they have found in Ordass's witness a definitive refutation of the slippery-sliding *ahogy lehet* strategy for being church. Others assert that ecclesial martyrdom was not a realistic possibility for the church in communism and see in Ordass a powerful but no more than individual witness. How can this disagreement be sorted out?

Those who claim that "suffering church" designated a genuine ecclesial option in communism must answer a number of difficult questions. The first of these concerns Ordass's own attitude toward the so-called suffering church. Namely, did Ordass think of himself as forging a path for the church? Taken as an ecclesial proposal, witness is a composite of three discrete historical moments. First, there was Ordass's witness in 1948 and 1949. Second, there were the 1956 pastors conferences, where pastors attempted to construct a model for the church on the basis of Ordass's witness. Third, there was Ordass's second active term as bishop, which ended with his removal in 1958. Those Hungarians who interpret Ordass's witness as an ecclesial model focus primarily on the first of these three historical moments. They see Ordass in 1948 as representing the true path for the church. Thus the split between Túróczy and Ordass and the quiet acceptance of Ordass's imprisonment were a betrayal by the church of its best bishop and a departure from the path of the "confessing church."

By focusing so exclusively on the "year of the turn," proponents of the "suffering church" find support for their interpretation of Ordass's legacy in his memoirs. At one point Ordass writes, "I came to the conclusion that God placed me in the bishop's ministry, so that through me He could speak those words which He believed needed to be spoken in the Lutheran Church."[7] What Ordass means by this exactly is not clear. He does not say his path was the path of the church. Nevertheless, he does claim to have represented God's cause in some special sense. Therefore later proponents of the suffering church have reason to read Ordass's comments as a criticism of the church that failed to follow him.

However, as indicated in earlier chapters, Ordass's attitude toward a resistance church changed. Significantly, Ordass wrote the previous lines before the Hungarian Revolution, and they refer only to his actions in 1948 and 1949. In his later memoirs, Ordass never repeats this kind of claim. In 1948 Ordass did consider (indirectly) the possibility of collective church resistance to the regime. However, in 1958, he seems to have rejected the possibility of a "confessing church." Thus present proponents of a "suffering church" may be advocating an ecclesial vision not shared by the man whose legacy it is putatively built on.

Moreover, proponents of the "suffering church" must reckon with the fact that their ecclesial vision never actually appeared in the history. This is an issue of historical realism: those who put forth the vision of a "suffering church" present it as a criticism of the actual path traveled by the Lutheran Church in Hungary in communism. They argue that Hungarian Lutherans failed to live up to the legacy of Bishop Ordass. For their criticism to be valid, however, the Ordass legacy must point not just to an ideal option for the church but to an option that was also historically realistic, that was a genuine possibility.

If, however, "suffering church" describes a real historical possibility, why do we find no ecclesiological traces of it? The historical fact is that no one in Hungary's Lutheran Church belonged to a "suffering church." This is not to say that no one in the Lutheran Church in Hungary suffered; indeed, virtually everyone suffered. But they suffered individually, not as a community, and therefore not in a way that was ecclesially significant. There was in communism no Hungarian Lutheran "suffering church," and the absence of a "suffering church" must make one hesitate to designate it a real moral option within the history.

However, if, on the one hand, one must pull back from the concept of "suffering church" as a historical possibility, one must, on the other hand, accept the reality of Ordass's witness as a human possibility. Lajos Ordass was part of this history, a real man who refused to compromise on his duties as bishop and who suffered for his witness. Ordass's example makes clear that martyrdom was a historical possibility for the members of Hungary's Lutheran Church. Thus Ordass's witness calls into question the path traveled in communism by the Lutheran Church in Hungary; it raises the question: were the members of the Lutheran Church in Hungary really faithful to their Lord?

Collectively, the Lutheran Church in Hungary asserted a responsibility for its survival, and in the interest of survival it compromised with the regime. Its compromises, however, were rarely good ones. Thus, by compromising for the sake of surviving, the church compromised also—to varying degrees—its ministry. It is precisely for this reason that Ordass's witness holds such power and calls the church to explain why it accepted responsibility for survival rather than accepting martyrdom. If everyone in the Lutheran Church in Hungary had been as brave and faithful as Lajos Ordass, the history recounted in this book would have been much different. Perhaps it would have been the history of a suffering church.

On the one hand, the three *ahogy lehet* strategies compromised on, and hence betrayed, the church's ministry—although admittedly they did this in different ways and to different degrees. Thus each *ahogy lehet* type is a specimen of moral failure. Lajos Ordass, as a part of this history, makes it impossible to deny or pass over those failures, because he calls into question the fundamental premise of the *ahogy lehet* framework, namely, the church's need to survive. On the other hand, Ordass exposes these moral failures only negatively, by calling into question the underlying strategy and not by providing a picture of a historically realistic ecclesial alternative. Because no traces of a "suffering church" ever appeared in this history, the notion cannot be treated confidently as a real moral option, and one's judgment of those who failed must be tempered by a recognition of what was historically possible. On the one hand, one must recognize a standard in Ordass's witness because that witness was a genuine individual possibility. On the other hand, one must temper the application of that standard because it may have been an ecclesial impossibility.

Some may sense in this "two-handed" approach to the Ordass-question a sneaky bi-dexterity. However, treating Ordass this way in fact assigns him tremendous theological significance. It is to present Ordass as a confessor, one who points the church to God's Word, which in turn is comprised of judgment and promise.

On the one hand, Ordass's witness stands over against this history as a sign of judgment, exposing the many moral failures of the Lutheran Church in Hungary. Hungarian Lutherans today are justified in leveling criticisms against the compromise, collaboration, and diaconia types, because the person of Lajos Ordass provides historical evidence that the protagonists in this history could have acted differently. They had choices. They were not mere victims of dictatorship but moral actors, and as moral actors, they often chose poorly. In this sense, Lajos Ordass is a permanent thorn in the flesh of Hungary's Lutheran Church, a concrete reminder that things could have, and should have, been different. On the other hand, Ordass's witness points beyond this history as a sign of promise. Ordass's faithfulness is testimony both to God's grace and to the importance of the Lutheran Church in Hungary. Only a great church could produce such a great man. Lajos Ordass, the confessor, precisely because he emerged from Hungary's little Lutheran Church, conveys to that church a special message: God is with the Lutheran Church in Hungary, and he promises it a future; the failures of the past do not forfeit the promise of the future.

Thus the way forward for the Lutheran Church in Hungary is in the promise of Ordass' witness. That promise is the assurance of things hoped for, which gives confidence in oneself and one's destination. For Hungarian Lutherans today, still determined by their past, the destination is yet unknown. Looking back at communism, many in the churches think of it as a kind of Babylonian captivity. Unlike the fall of Babylon, however, the end of communism opened no straight highways back to Jerusalem, but only an uncertain path through the desert. Moreover, Christians in communism, unlike the Jews in Babylon, never exerted influence in the king's court. Rather, they served with vigor; their lives became bitter, and they forgot what it was to be free. Sadly, slavery instills habits that are hard to unlearn. Hungarian Lutherans, if they are to move beyond their past, will need to unlearn bad habits. Their future depends much on whether they have the strength of will and the power of imagination to define new purposes. To do that they will need to believe they are free. Those in the Lutheran Church in Hungary who struggled and stumbled and persevered to keep the faith in communism will never see the promised land. But they see Jesus, and the future belongs to the next generation.

Notes

Chapter 1

1. Statistics are taken from Csaba Horváth, *Magyarország 1944-től napjainkig* (Hungary from 1944 until the present), 4th ed. (Pécs: PREZIDENT Betéti Társaság, 1993), 17–19; and Károly Szerencsés, *Magyarország története a II. világháború után, 1945–1975* (The history of Hungary after the Second World War, 1945–1975), 4th ed (Budapest: IKVA, 1990), 11–13.
2. A nuanced analysis of Horthy and the Horthy era can be found in Thomas Sakmyster, *Hungary's Admiral on Horseback: Miklós Horthy, 1918–1944* (Boulder, Colo.: East European Monographs, 1994).
3. Jenő Gergely et. al., *Az egyházak Magyarországon Szent Istvántól napjainkig* (The churches in Hungary from Saint Stephen until the present day) (Budapest: Korona kiadó, 1997), 172.
4. Ibid., 173.
5. Margit Balogh and Jenő Gergely, *Egyházak az újkori Magyarországon, 1790–1992: adattár* (Churches in modern Hungary, 1790–1992: Data collection) (Budapest: MTA Történettudományi Intézete, 1996), 165.
6. Gergely, *Az egyházak Magyarországon*, 174–5, 211.
7. Tibor Fabiny, *Az evangélikus egyház a magyar művelődés századaiban* (The Lutheran church in the centuries of Hungarian cultural development) (Budapest: n.p., 1994).
8. Gábor László Dobos, "Belmissziói és szociális irányzatok a protestáns egyházakban és vallásos szervezetekben" (Home mission and social trends in the Protestant churches and religious organizations), in *A magyar protestantizmus, 1918–1948* (Hungarian Protestantism, 1918–1948) (Budapest: Kossuth Könyvkiadó, 1986), 276–302.
9. In constructing the biographical sketch of Zoltán Túróczy, I have relied on the following sources: Géza Kovács, "Túróczy Zoltán (1893–1971)" *Diakónia* 15, no. 4 (1993): 32–39; *Evangélikus naptár az 1996 évre* (Lutheran calendar for the year 1996) (Budapest: A Magyarországi Evangélikus Egyház Sajtóosztálya, 1996), 56–58. I have also relied on the collective memory of the Lutheran Church in Hungary as it was accessible to me through personal conversations. A two-volume collection of documents, sermons, and various other writings by and about Bishop Túróczy has been published in Hungarian: *Isten embere: Túróczy Zoltán evangélikus püspök (1893–1971)* (Man of God: Zoltán Túróczy, Lutheran bishop, 1893–1971), 2 vols., ed. Péter Cserháti et. al. (Budapest: Magyarországi Evangélikus Ifjúsági Szövetség, 2002).
10. Lajos Ordass's autobiographical writings have been published in two edited volumes: Lajos Ordass, *Önéletrajzi írások* (Autobiographical writings), 2 vols., ed. István Szépfalusi (Bern: EPMSZ, 1985–87). In addition, there are two edited volumes of selected writings related to Bishop Ordass: Lajos Ordass, *Válogatott*

írások (Selected writings), vol. 1, ed. István Szépfalusi (Bern: EPMSZ, 1982) and *Válogatott írások*, vol. 2 (Lakitelek: Magyarországi Evangélikus Egyház Sajtóosztálya, 1998). A biography of Lajos Ordass, translated into English, is: László Terray, *He Could Not Do Otherwise: Bishop Lajos Ordass, 1901–1978*, trans. Eric W. Gritsch (Grand Rapids, Mich.: William B. Eerdmans Publishing Co., 1997).

11. See Ordass, *Önéletrajzi*, 1:31.
12. Ibid., 129–34. Ordass's refutation of the memorandum is printed in Ordass, *Válogatott*, 1:58–69.
13. Ordass himself mentions his Scandinavian connections as one reason behind his election. Ordass, *Önéletrajzi*, 1:165.
14. Szerencsés, *Magyarország története*, 26.
15. The history surrounding Túróczy's trial has not been thoroughly researched. According to the collective memory of the Lutheran Church in Hungary, Bishop Túróczy was unjustly convicted. Thus, for example, István Rőzse notes simply, "About Zoltán Túróczy everybody knows that he was sent to prison as an innocent man, as even Lajos Ordass recalls." István Rőzse, *A halál árnyékának völgyében* (In the valley of the shadow of death) (Budapest: Az Ordass Lajos Baráti Kör, 1997), 128n35. Jenő Gergely, writing a general historical survey of the churches in the communist period, notes simply in connection with the Túróczy trial, "The charges were fabricated and based on deliberate distortions of his earlier sermons." Gergely, *Az egyházak Magyarországon*, 232. As the people's courts were little more than kangaroo courts, these historians are almost certainly correct. Nevertheless, basic historical questions, such as why Túróczy was selected by the court at all, have yet to be explored and answered.
16. Ordass, *Önéletrajzi*, 1:181.
17. Evangélikus Országos Levéltár (National Lutheran Archives, hereafter EOL) Püspöki konferenciai doboz, 1945. október 29–1 püspöki konferencia jegyzőkönyve (Minutes for the October 29, 1945, bishops conference).
18. For recollections of Mihályfi's speech see, Gábor Vladár, *Visszaemlékezéseim* (My recollections) (Budapest: Püski kiadó, n.d.), 318–19; Ordass, *Önéletrajzi*, 1:244–48; István Herényi, *Az Evangélikus Egyház az egyházjogtörténet tükrében* (The Lutheran Church in the mirror of church law) (Velem: privately published, 1991), 62–63; and Terray, *He Could Not Do Otherwise*, 68–70.
19. Ordass, *Önéletrajzi*, 1:248–49.
20. My biographical sketch of Iván Reök relies on Rőzse, *A halál*, 30–31. For more on Reök's background and evangelical disposition, see Iván Reök, *A sebész találkozik Istennel Budapesten* (A surgeon meets God in Budapest), Budapest, Evangéliumi Könyvkiadó, n.d.. The compilation of lectures by Túróczy, Reök, and others is *Isten ismerete: Az Országos Luther Szövetség által Máriabesnyőn 1942 nagyhéten a férfiintelligencia részére rendezett evangelizáció előadásai és áhítatai* (Knowledge of God: Lectures and devotions from an evangelization for male intellectuals, held by the National Luther Alliance in Máriabesnyő during Holy Week) (Győr: Baross-nyomda, n.d.).
21. The bishops' letter was printed in *Lelkipásztor* (April 1948): 162–64 and reprinted in Ordass, *Válogatott*, 1:175–76.
22. Ordass, *Önéletrajzi*, 1:266–67.
23. Ibid., 268–69.
24. Ibid., 283–84.
25. Ibid., 288–90.
26. Ibid., 294.
27. My sketch of Imre Veöreös relies on the biographical information supplied in Imre Veöreös, *A középpont felől* (From the center point) (Budapest: A Magyarországi Evangélikus Egyház Sajtóosztálya, 1988), 351–56 and on personal conversations with Veöreös. See also the interview with Veöroes in

Nem voltam egyedül: Beszélgetések az evangélikus közelmúltról (I was not alone: conversations about the recent Lutheran past), ed. Katalin Mirák (Budapest: Magyarországi Evangélikus Ifjúsági Szövetség, 1999) 2:321–50.

28. For more about Mindszenty, see Jozsef Cardinal Mindszenty, *Memoirs*, trans. Richard and Clara Winston (New York: Macmillan Publishing Co., 1974). A recent Hungarian biography of Mindszenty is Margit Balogh, *Mindszenty József* (Budapest: Elektra Kiadóház, 2002).
29. Ordass, *Önéletrajzi*, 1:308.
30. EOL, Magyar Evangélikus Lelkészek Egyesülete (Association of Hungarian Lutheran Pastors, or MELE) 1948. június 14-én tartott rendkívüli közgyűlés jegyzőkönyve (Minutes of the exceptional assembly of MELE, held on June 14, 1948).
31. On Ordass's 1947 travels, see Terray, *He Could Not Do Otherwise*, 49–54 and Ordass, *Önéletrajzi*, 1:199–224.
32. Ordass, *Önéletrajzi*, 1:320, 326; Vladár, *Visszaemlékezéseim*, 322; Terray, *He Could Not Do Otherwise*, 76–77.
33. See Ordass, *Önéletrajzi*, 1:325, 329.
34. Ibid., 358–60.

Excursus 1

1. A small lexical problem exists concerning the terms *socialism* and *communism*. In English usage *communism* usually designates the political and social systems that existed in Eastern Europe from the end of World War II until 1989, and *socialism* connotes the kind of broadly ranging state programs of social care found in places like northern Europe. In the usage of communist ideology, however, *socialism* referred to the social-political systems actually existing in Eastern Europe, and *communism* referred to the ideal society toward which communists were striving. Following the usage of the period, therefore, I often use the term *socialism* to refer to what English speakers would more likely call *communism*. Readers should understand that, within the framework of this book, *communism* and *socialism* are interchangeable. In this book *socialism* never refers to the kind of thing that exists, say, in Sweden.
2. Imre Veöreös, "Mit szólunk az iskolák államosításához?" (What do we say to the nationalization of the schools?), *Új Harangszó*, June 6, 1948.
3. Imre Veöreös, "Álláspontunk a fakultatív hitoktatás kérdésében" (Our position on the question of optional religious education), *Lelkipásztor* (April 1947): 121. See also the article in the same volume by a certain T. S. [Tibor Schulek?], "Javaslat a fakultatív hitoktatással kapcsolatban" (Proposition in connection with optional religious instruction), *Lelkipásztor* (April 1947): 122.
4. "Augsburg Confession," in *The Book of Concord: The Confessions of the Evangelical Lutheran Church*, trans. and ed. Theodore G. Tappert (Philadelphia: Fortress Press, 1959), 32. For Veöreös's discussion, see Imre Veöreös, *A harmadik egyházi út, 1948–1950* (The third church way, 1948–1950) (Budapest: Evangélikus Sajtóosztály, 1990), 7–11.
5. Imre Veöreös, "Missziói egyházzá kell válnunk!" (We must become a missionary church!), *Lelkipásztor* (February 1950): 43–44.
6. On the so-called Decade of Revival, see Tibor Schulek, "A magyar evangélikus ébredés kezdeteiről" (The beginnings of the Hungarian Lutheran awakening), *Diakónia* 10, no. 2 (1988): 8–11; Béla Csepregi, "Adalékok a magyar evangélikus ébredéshez" (Facts about the Hungarian Lutheran awakening), *Diakónia* 11, no. 1 (1989): 39–42; Béla Csepregi, "Az evangelizáció évtizede, 1940–1950" (The decade of evangelization, 1940–1950), *Diakónia* 11, no. 2 (1989): 42–46; Imre Veöreös, "Kétarcú évek, 1945–48" (Two-faced years, 1945–48), *Credo*, vols. 1–2 (1996): 57–65.

7. Csepregi, "Az evangelizáció évtizede," 42.
8. László Scholz, "Számsorok tanúsága" (The testimony of numbers), *Új Harangszó*, May 1, 1949. A discrepancy exists between the numbers provided by Scholz and those provided by Csepregi concerning the number of evangelizations in the late 1940s. According to Csepregi there were 78 "evangelizations" in 1947–48, and 117 in 1948–49. Csepregi, "Az evangelizáció évtizede," 42. These numbers are lower than Scholz's, which are the ones I have cited. In any case, the point remains valid, namely, that a marked increase in Lutheran evangelizations occurred in the late 1940s.
9. See Veöreös, *A harmadik egyházi út*, 9.
10. Sándor Reményik, *Összes versei* (Collected verses) (Budapest: Evangélikus Sajtóosztály, 1997), 400.
11. Statistical information in Margit Balogh and Jenő Gergely, *Egyházak az újkori Magyarországon, 1790–1992: adattár* (Churches in modern Hungary, 1790–1992: Data collection) (Budapest: MTA Történettudományi Intézete, 1996), 154–61. Admittedly, the number of 1.3 million Lutherans includes members of the Transylvanian Saxon Lutheran Church, an independent church of ethnic Germans that existed in "Greater Hungary." According to 1870 statistics, the Saxon Lutheran Church accounted for about 20 percent of all Lutherans in "Greater Hungary." See Balogh and Gergely, *Egyházak az újkori Magyarországon*, 179–78. Thus we can infer that in 1910 the membership of the Lutheran Church in Hungary was approximately 1 million.
12. Balogh and Gergely, *Egyházak az újkori Magyarországon*, 165, 170. On the decrease in Hungary's Lutheran population, see also Zsolt Giczi, "Rögös úton: A Magyarországi Evangélikus Egyház és az államhatalom viszonyáról, 1948–1950" (On a bumpy road: The relation between the Lutheran Church in Hungary and the state, 1948–1950), *Valóság* 15, no. 2 (February 1997): 74.
13. Not everyone agrees about the etymology of *kuruc*. Some people, lacking poetic sensibility, insist the word derives not from "crux" but from some other term. Even if not literally true, however, the view that *kuruc* comes from cross ought to be true, so aptly does the word convey the suffering that attends an uncompromising commitment to Hungarian freedom.
14. Zoltán Túróczy, "Megegyezés az állam és egyház között" (Agreement between the state and the church), *Evangélikus Élet*, December 4, 1948.

Chapter 2
1. Csaba Horváth, *Magyarország 1944-től napjainkig* (Hungary from 1944 until the present), 4th ed. (Pécs: PREZIDENT Betéti Társaság, 1993), 61.
2. *Magyarország története, 1918–1990* (The history of Hungary, 1918–1990), eds. Ferenc Pölöskei, Jenő Gergely, and Lajos Izsák (Budapest: Korona Kiadó, n.d.), 212.
3. László Dezséry undoubtedly wrote more political essays in the pre-communist era, but I have uncovered the following in *Evangélikus Élet:* "Jó emlékezet kedvéért" (For the sake of good memory), October 30, 1943; a series of articles entitled "Levelek a kibontakozás elé" (Letters toward the way out), December 4, 11, 25, 1943; "Evangélikus, aki szocialista" (Lutheran, who is socialist), January 1, 1944; "A mi szocializmusunk" (Our socialism), June 17, 1944; and "A mi nacionalizmusunk" (Our nationalism), July 15, 1944.
4. László Dezséry, "A mi szocializmusunk" (Our socialism), *Evangélikus Élet*, June 17, 1944.
5. László Dezséry, *Templomozó káté* (Little church catechism), 2nd ed. (Kecskemét: n.p., 1942), 114.
6. This is suggested by Pastor Vilmos Nagybocskai, who says, "Most of all [Dezséry] was burdened by the fact that in the beginning of the 1940's he published articles

in the columns of *Evangélikus Élet* friendly to National Socialist ideals. . . . One can easily imagine a conversation where Rákosi once said to Dezséry: Two paths stand before you; either we bring out your articles and on this basis you go to prison, or you take on the bishopric, but in a mode suitable to us." Interview with Vilmos Nagybocskai in *Nem voltam egyedül: Beszélgetések az evangélikus közelmúltról* (I was not alone: Conversations about the recent Lutheran past), ed. Katalin Mirák (Budapest: Magyarországi Evangélikus Ifjúsági Szövetség, 1995), 1:200. A similar suggestion is made by István Szépfalusi in his annotation of Ordass's memoirs. See Lajos Ordass, *Önéletrajzi írások* (Autobiographical writings), ed. István Szépfalusi (Bern: EPMSZ, 1985) 1:139n41.

7. Interview with István Botta in Mirák, *Nem voltam egyedül*, 1:72–74.
8. See "Dezséry László," *Evangélikus Élet*, January 15, 1949.
9. The biographical information I have provided on Lajos Vető relies heavily on personal conversations with members of the Lutheran Church in Hungary.
10. The events surrounding Lajos Vető's election as bishop have never been fully researched. The existing evidence suggests, however, that Vető's election resulted from political manipulation. For an attempt to piece together the fragmentary archival evidence, see István Rőzse, "A tiszai evangélikus egyházkerület utolsó püspökválasztásáról" (About the Tisza diocese's final bishop election), *Keresztyén Igazság* 16 (Winter 1992): 25–42. See also the comments of Bishop Ordass in Ordass, *Önéletrajzi írások*, 1:358; also, László Terray, *He Could Not Do Otherwise: Bishop Lajos Ordass, 1901–1978*, trans. Eric W. Gritsch (Grand Rapids, Mich.: William B. Eerdmans Publishing Company, 1997), 104.
11. "Két püspökavatás" (Two bishop ordinations), *Evangélikus Élet*, January 1, 1949.
12. "Reök Iván főorvos, országgyűlés képviselőt választották egyetemes felügyelőnek" (Iván Reök, head doctor, parliamentary representative, is elected General Inspector), *Evangélikus Élet*, March 19, 1949.
13. Lóránd Boleratzky, "Az Ordass-per (Jogi szempontból)" (The Ordass-trial [from a legal perspective]), *Keresztyén Igazság* 27 (Fall 1995): 20.
14. "Beiktatták Darvas Józsefet, az új egyházkerületi felügyelőt" (József Darvas, new diocesan inspector, installed), *Evangélikus Élet*, February 26, 1950.
15. This, anyway, is the collective memory of the Lutheran Church in Hungary. For example, Ordass makes reference to Darvas's atheism in Ordass, *Önéletrajzi*, 1:380. See also István Herényi, *Az Evangélikus Egyház az egyházjogtörténet tükrében, 1945–1990* (The Lutheran church in the light of church law, 1945–1990) (Velem: privately published, 1991), 59; cf. Terray, *He Could Not Do Otherwise*, 68.
16. Terray, *He Could Not Do Otherwise*, 103–4.
17. So recalls Ordass in Lajos Ordass, *Önéletrajzi írások* (Autobiographical writings), ed. István Szépfalusi (Bern: EPMSZ, 1985–87), 2:474. István Botta believes the petition was delivered to Rákosi, who decided which pastors would be suspended. Interview with István Botta in Mirák, *Nem voltam egyedül*, 1:76. Others believe simply that certain names from the beginning of the list were selected for suspension. See István Rőzse, *A halál árnyékának völgyében* (In the valley of the shadow of death) (Budapest: Az Ordass Lajos Baráti Kör, 1997), 34 and 151n205.
18. See Tamás Fabiny, *Keken András életregénye* (The life-story of András Keken) (n.p.: PLANTIN Kiadó, n.d.), 209.
19. This is Ordass's guess. He writes, "One can conjecture that Dr. Reök felt obviously uncertain concerning the judgment of the church court and it could have been he who advised arresting Keken and Kendeh in order to guarantee a suitable atmosphere for the trial. This is suggested by the statement of József Szabó, made after the leader of the State Office of Church Affairs forced Reök, Túróczy, himself [Szabó] and Gyula Groó to resign. At that time Szabó stated literally, 'Iván Reök's conscience would have been much more at ease if he had

not delivered over Keken and Kendeh.'" Ordass, *Önéletrajzi*, 2:497–98n26. Rőzse also conjectures that Reök was responsible for the arrest of Keken and Kendeh in Rőzse, *A halál*, 35.

20. There are a couple of recollections about the proceedings of the trial that differ slightly from one another. According to the diary of Ottó Koritsánsky, a member of the court, Reök conveyed to Koritsánsky in personal conversation Rákosi's threat that "if the church does not convict Ordass, [the government] will initiate a treason and spy trial against him which comes with a sentence of 15 years to death. Furthermore, proceedings will be brought first against 8 pastors, then more." This is supplied in Szépfalusi's annotation of Ordass, *Önéletrajzi*, 2:498–99, n27. Another member of the court recalled that directly before the proceedings, Túróczy announced to the court that he had just been informed by a messenger from Rákosi that if the court did not deliver a guilty verdict, then Ordass would be tried by the state for treason and receive the death penalty. After this, "Túróczy posed the question: who will accept responsibility for this? It was a dramatic moment. We could not accept it!" Recollection supplied by Szépfalusi in Ordass, *Önéletrajzi*, 1:393n180. Cf. Rőzse's speculations on the trial proceedings in Rőzse, *A halál*, 58. A general account of the events surrounding Ordass's church trial is supplied in Terray, *He Could Not Do Otherwise*, 104–6. Various archival documents in connection with the trial are reprinted in Ordass, *Válogatott írások* (Selected writings), ed. István Szépfalusi (Lakitelek: Magyarországi Evangélikus Egyház Sajtóosztalya, 1998), 2:679–94.
21. Supplied by Szépfalusi in Ordass, *Önéletrajzi*, 2:499n27.
22. EOL, Bánya egyházkerületi jegyzőkönyve 310/1950 (Minutes of the Bánya diocese).
23. EOL, Bánya egyházkerületi jegyzőkönyve 316/1950 (Minutes of the Bánya diocese).
24. Cited in Rőzse, *A halál*, 112.
25. Politikatörténeti Intézet Levéltár (Archives of the Institute of Political History), 276 f. 65/364. ő. e. 70. 1. Citation here taken from the reprint in Ordass, *Válogatott*, 2:812.
26. "Dezséry Lászlót választották meg bányakerületi püspöknek" (László Dezséry is elected Bánya diocesan bishop), *Evangélikus Élet*, June 18, 1950.
27. "Az egyetemes presbitérium elfogadta Túróczy Zoltán püspök lemondását püspöki tisztéről" (The general presbytery accepted Zoltán Túróczy's resignation of his bishop's office) and "A Dunáninneni Egyházkerület Presbitériuma elfogadta Szabó József püspök lemondását" (The presbytery of the Dunáninnen diocese accepted Bishop József Szabó's resignation), *Evangélikus Élet*, February 24, 1952.
28. See Reök's speech found in EOL, Zsinati anyag (Synod material) 1952 II. 5. II. ülésszak 3. sz. ülés.
29. Ordass, *Önéletrajzi*, 2:475n1; see also Rőzse, *A halál*, 150n198. The explanation for Reök's forced resignation may also be that he had started to crack under the pressure of his position. His complicity in the ruin of others and his responsibility for the arrests of Keken and Kendeh began to weigh on him, and he could no longer be relied upon. After 1952 Reök more or less disappeared from church life and on his deathbed asked Keken for forgiveness. His funeral was attended by the pastor, the cantor, and three mourners.
30. "Megállapodás a Bányai Evangélikus Egyházkerület által felajánlott és az Állami Egyházügyi Hivatal Elnökéhez felterjesztett gimnáziumok átadásáról, illetőleg átvételéről" (Agreement concerning the relinquishment and acceptance of gymnasia offered by the Bánya Lutheran diocese to the President of the State Office of Church Affairs). Found in the National Lutheran Archives in a box of unorganized material.

31. See Fabiny, *Keken András életregénye*, 205–8, and Rőzse, *A halál*, 29–30. It appears that not even all the bishops enjoyed attending these conferences. Commenting on the agenda for the pastors conferences of 1951 in a letter to László Dezséry, Bishop Szabó would say, "although for my own part I am a believer in more healthily organized and theologically weighty programs, I accept the planned program." EOL, Bánya 278/1951.

Excursus 2

1. See István Rőzse, *A halál árnyékának völgyében* (In the valley of the shadow of death) (Budapest: Az Ordass Lajos Baráti Kör, 1997), 29.
2. Ibid., 33.
3. Lajos Ordass, *Önéletrajzi írások* (Autobiographical writings), ed. István Szépfalusi (Bern: EPMSZ, 1985), 1:267.
4. Ibid., 272, 273.
5. István Bibó, "A kelet-európai kisállamok nyomorúsága" (The misery of the small states of eastern Europe), in *Válogatott tanulmányok, 1945–1949* (Selected studies, 1945–1949), ed. István Vida (Budapest: Magvető Könyvkiadó, 1986) 2:216–17.
6. Historical accounts of the rise of this reform movement and the Reformed Free Council are offered in János Bolyki and Sándor Ladányi, "A református egyház" (The Reformed church), in *A magyar protestantizmus, 1918–1948* (Hungarian Protestantism, 1918–1948), ed. Ferenc L. Lendvai (Budapest: Kossuth Könyvkiadó, 1987); and in István Kónya, *A "keskeny úton" a "szolgáló egyház" felé* (On the "narrow path" toward the "serving church") (Budapest: Akadémiai Kiadó, 1988), esp. 50–72. The proceedings of the Reformed Free Council were published as *Országos Református Szabad Tanács, Nyíregyháza, 1946. augusztus 14.-17., határozatai, deklaráció, kérelmei, és az ott elhangzott közérdekű beszédek* (The National Reformed Free Council, its resolutions, declarations, requests, and the speeches of common interest given there, Nyíregyháza, August 14–17, 1946), comp. Standing Committee (Budapest: n.p., 1946). The quotation is taken from these proceedings, *Szabad Tanács*, 17.
7. For this position, see especially "Az egyház és a magyar jelen" (The church and the Hungarian present), in *Szabad Tanács*, 67–71.
8. Similar criticisms of the theological premises articulated at the Reformed Free Council have been voiced before. See Gyula Gombos, *The Lean Years: A Study of Hungarian Calvinism in Crisis* (New York: The Kossuth Foundation Inc., 1960), esp. chap. 3; and István Bogárdi Szabó, *Egyházvezetés és teológia a Magyarországi Református Egyházban 1948 és 1989 között* (Church leadership and theology in the Hungarian Reformed Church between 1948 and 1989) *Societas et Ecclesia* 3 (Debrecen: A magyar Protestáns Közművelődési Egyesület, 1995), esp. 85–89.
9. Imre Veöreös, "Reform-tanácskozás elé" (Before a reform-conference), *Lelkipásztor* (March 1947): 86–90. The document itself was signed on November 19, 1946.
10. Imre Veöreös, "Egyházunk 1948-ban: Történelmi helyzet" (Our church in 1948: the historical situation), *Lelkipásztor* (January 1948): 14–18.
11. Imre Veöreös, "Egyházunk politikai állásfoglalása" (The political position of our church), *Új Harangszó*, April 25, 1948.
12. Zoltán Túróczy, "Megegyezés az állam és egyház között" (Agreement between the state and the church), *Evangélikus Élet*, December 4, 1948.
13. László Dezséry, *Nyílt levél a Magyarországi Evangélikus Egyház ügyében* (Open letter in the matter of the Lutheran Church in Hungary) (Budapest: privately published, 1948).
14. Ibid., 21.
15. "Reök Iván egyetemes felügyelő: A Felszabadulás Ünnepe" (General Inspector Iván Reök: The holiday of liberation), *Evangélikus Élet*, April 2, 1950.

16. See the account of the peace movement offered in Ernő Ottlyk, *Az evangélikus egyház útja a szocializmusban* (The path of the Lutheran Church in socialism) (Budapest: A Magyarországi Evangélikus Egyház Sajtóosztálya, 1976), 83. In Hungary today, so low is the esteem for the peace movement that in everyday conversation when one wants to refer to a clergyman who collaborated with the communists, one simply designates him a "peace priest" (in Hungarian, *priest* can be used for both Catholic and Protestant clergy).
17. "Egyházunk üzenete a nyugati lutheránusokhoz" (The message of our church to Western Lutherans), *Evangélikus Élet*, March 12, 1950.
18. "Dezséry László evangélikus püspök a protestáns egyházak feladatairól" (Lutheran bishop László Dezséry on the tasks for the Protestant churches), *Evangélikus Élet*, November 4, 1951.

Chapter 3

1. See Lajos Ordass, *Önéletrajzi írások* (Autobiographical writings), ed. István Szépfalusi (Bern: EPMSZ, 1987) 2:471–514, quotation on 514.
2. Ibid., 530–36.
3. Ibid., 536–39. The agreement with the LWF was reported in *Lutheran World Information*. See "Bishop Ordass (Hungary) to be rehabilitated," *Lutheran World Information*, release no. 25/56, August 10, 1956.
4. Untitled paper by András Keken, formerly in the Ordass Archives, Oslo, Norway (hereafter referred to as the Ordass collection), now in possession of the Magyar Országos Levéltár (Hungarian National Archives) in Budapest. Also reprinted in Ordass, *Válogatott írások* (Selected writings), ed. István Szépfalusi (Lakitelek: Magyarországi Evangélikus Egyház Sajtóosztálya, 1998), 2:695–707.
5. "Észrevételek" (Observations), in the Ordass collection. Later published in the church press in *Lelkipásztor* (October 1956): 618–20 and reprinted also in Szépfalusi's annotation of Lajos Ordass, *Önéletrajzi írások* (Autobiographical writings), ed. István Szépfalusi (Bern: EPMSZ, 1985), 1:407–409, n188.
6. The 1956 pastors conferences were a significant theological event in this history. Their significance is not diminished by the unfortunate fact that only sparse records of these meetings are available for the historian's perusal. My discussion relies on the detailed footnotes provided in Szépfalusi's annotation of Ordass's autobiography (Ordass, *Önéletrajzi*, 2:541–48) and helpful but fragmentary accounts of the meetings found in the Ordass collection. Perhaps further accounts of these conferences exist in the private possession of pastors who attended them, and perhaps in time more information will come to light.
7. Ordass, *Önéletrajzi*, 2:557n44.
8. "Az állami és az egyházi bíróság rehabilitálta D. Ordass Lajos püspököt" (State and church courts rehabilitate Bishop D. Lajos Ordass), *Evangélikus Élet*, October 14, 1956. Archival documents in connection with Ordass's rehabilitation are reprinted in Ordass, *Válogatott*, 2:727–44.
9. Ordass, *Önéletrajzi*, 2:568n4.
10. Archivists at the National Lutheran Archive in Hungary could find no official record of the November 3 meeting when I requested it. For information about the meeting, see Ordass's recollections and the annotations provided by Szépfalusi in Ordass, *Önéletrajzi*, 2:579–90. See also the account in *Evangélikus naptár az 1957. évre* (Lutheran calendar for the year 1957) (Budapest: Az evangélikus egyetemes Sajtóosztály, 1957), 18–46.
11. Ordass, *Önéletrajzi*, 2:585n28.
12. Magyar Országos Levéltár (Hungarian National Archives, hereafter MOL), Állami Egyházügyi Hivatal (State Office of Church Affairs, hereafter ÁEH) Titkos Ügy Kezelés (Top Secret, hereafter TÜK) 1957 2d "Előterjesztés az egyházpolitikai

helyzet rendezésére" 0014/1957. (Proposal for setting in order the church-political situation).
13. See Ordass's recollections and Szépfalusi's annotations in Ordass, *Önéletrajzi*, 2:590–604, quotation on 595–6. On these events see also, "Visszatekintés az elmúlt hónapok egyházi eseményeire" (A look back at the events in our church of the last months), *Evangélikus Élet*, March 24, 1957.
14. "A forradalmi munkás-paraszt kormány nyilatkozata a legfontosabb feladatokról" (Statement of the Revolutionary Workers-Peasant Government concerning the most important tasks), *Népszabadság* (a daily newspaper), January 6, 1957.
15. "Az evangélium levegőjében—Részletek D. Ordass Lajos püspöknek az egyetemes közgyűlésen elhangzott jelentéséből" (In the air of the gospel—Excerpts from the report of Bishop D. Lajos Ordass to the general assembly), *Evangélikus Élet*, July 21, 1957.
16. MOL, ÁEH Elnöki (president's material) 1957 5d *Evangélikus Egyház I. 257.* "Feljegyzés: Elgondolásunk az Evangélikus egyházzal kapcsolatban" 257–1/1957. (Report: Thoughts in connection with the Lutheran church).
17. Ordass's original letter, together with extensive marginal remarks, can be found in the archival material of the State Office of Church Affairs [MOL, ÁEH Elnöki 1957 5d *Evangélikus Egyház I.* 257/14]. It is also reprinted in Ordass, *Önéletrajzi*, 2:683–701.
18. The government minutes for the negotiations can be found in the Hungarian National Archives, MOL, ÁEH Elnöki 1957 5d "Evangélikus egyházi tárgyalások. Jegyzőkönyv" 257–15/1957. (Lutheran church negotiations. Minutes). Detailed records of these negotiations, based on Ordass's notes, coupled with Ordass's own reflections, can also be found in Ordass, *Önéletrajzi*, 2:702–734.
19. MOL, ÁEH Elnöki 1957 5d "Evangélikus egyházi tárgyalások. Jegyzőkönyv" 257–15/1957. (Lutheran church negotiations. Minutes), 88.
20. MOL, ÁEH TÜK 1957 2d "Előterjesztés az egyházpolitikai helyzet rendezésére." 0014/1957. (Proposal for setting in order the church-political situation).
21. See Ordass, *Önéletrajzi*, 2:743–56; also "Vető püspök ismét átveszi hivatalát" (Bishop Vető once again takes over his office), *Evangélikus Élet*, December 25, 1957.
22. See "Az Egyetemes Presbitérium ülése" (Session of the General Presbytery), *Evangélikus Élet*, January 5, 1958; see also, Ordass, *Önéletrajzi*, 2:745, 747.
23. Pastor László Scholz, who accompanied Túróczy to visit Ordass in prison in 1949, says the following about the relationship between the bishops: "It was a serious conflict [i.e., the confrontation in prison]. Yet I know the following: After Lajos Ordass was freed, one of the first things he did was to resolve this conflict, in love and with a brotherly spirit. How and in what way this happened is a secret of the two men. Lajos Ordass did not say what happened, only that it happened. Then in 1956–57 they served together again as bishops." Interview with László Scholz in *Nem voltam egyedül: Beszélgetések az evangélikus közelmúltról* (I was not alone: Conversations about the recent Lutheran past), ed. Katalin Mirák (Budapest: Magyarországi Evangélikus Ifjúsági Szövetség, 1995), 1:227.
24. "Az Egyetemes Presbitérium ülése" (Session of the General Presbytery), *Evangélikus Élet*, January 5, 1958. See also Ordass, *Önéletrajzi*, 2:758–59.
25. "Hivatalos közlemények" (Official announcements), *Evangélikus Élet*, January 26, 1958. See also Ordass, *Önéletrajzi*, 2:782–83.
26. MOL, ÁEH Elnöki 1957 5d 257–15/1957/E. "A Művelődésügyi Minisztérium Egyházügyi Hivatalának elnöke által 1958. január 24.-re összehívott evangélikus lelkészi értekezleten elhangzott tájékoztató" (Informatory speech delivered by the President of the Office for Church Affairs of the Ministry of Culture on January 24, 1958). Horváth's "informatory speech" is also printed in Ordass,

        Önéletrajzi, 2:958–70 (part of the appendix). The pastors meeting and Horváth's speech were reported on in "Közegyházi hírek" (News of the church), *Evangélikus Élet*, February 2, 1958; see also, Ordass, *Önéletrajzi*, 2:786–87.
27. Ordass, *Önéletrajzi*, 2:787–88.
28. Ibid., 800.
29. Ibid., 801–3, 810–13.
30. Ibid., 794.
31. Lajos Vető, "Egyházunkról van szó" (It concerns our church), *Lelkipásztor* (February/March 1958): 145–58.
32. EOL, Déli Evangélikus Egyházkerület (Southern Lutheran Diocese, or DEEK) Lt. 85. doboz Országos Lelkészi Munkaközösség (National Pastors Worker-Association, or OMLK) 35/1958. In his memoirs Ordass describes this resolution as "truly mild in tone," a judgment that appears to be shared today by the collective memory of the Lutheran Church in Hungary. Far from being mild, however, the resolution was a direct attack on Bishop Vető and, in the context of the times, remarkably bold. See Ordass, *Önéletrajzi*, 2:842–46 and also the interview with Vilmos Nagybocskai in Mirák, *Nem voltam egyedül*, 1:201–3.
33. Ordass, *Önéletrajzi*, 2:766.
34. ÁEH TÜK 1957 2d "Összefoglaló jelentés." /Tolan m.Tan-0018–35/1957. (Summary report).
35. Ordass, *Önéletrajzi*, 2:803–9.
36. Ibid., 769–71, 777.
37. Ibid., 848–49.
38. Interview with Vilmos Nagybocskai in Mirák, *Nem voltam egyedül*, 1:203.
39. Ordass, *Önéletrajzi*, 2:847.
40. MOL, ÁEH Elnöki 1958 7d "Tervezet az Ordass-ügy megoldására" 58.9–18/a/1958. (Plan for the resolution of the Ordass-affair).
41. "A törvényesség megóvása egyházi közigazgatásunkban, írták Sólyom Jenő és Göttche Ervin egyetemes ügyész" (The defense of legality in our church-administration, written by Jenő Sólyom and Ervin Göttche), *Evangélikus Élet* May 11, 1958.

Excursus 3
1. Lajos Ordass, *Önéletrajzi írások* (Autobiographical writings), ed. István Szépfalusi (Bern: EPMSZ, 1985), 1:325, 329.
2. Ibid., 180.
3. Lajos Ordass, *Válogatott írások* (Selected writings), ed. István Szépfalusi (Bern: EPMSZ, 1982), 1:285.
4. Vilmos Vajta, *Die diakonische Theologie im Gesellschaftssystem Ungarns* (The theology of diaconia in the social system of Hungary) (Frankfurt am Main: Verlag Otto Lembeck, 1987), 19–34.
5. MOL, ÁEH Elnöki 1957 5d "Evangélikus egyházi tárgyalások. Jegyzőőkönyv" 257–15/1957. (Lutheran church negotiations. Minutes), 61.
6. Ibid., 62.
7. For more on this question, and for an argument that Ordass did not try to employ a "Norwegian model," see László Terray, "Lajos Ordass és Eivind Berggrav" (Lajos Ordass and Eivind Berggrav), *Keresztyén Igazság* (Fall 1995): 30–47. See also László Benczúr, *"et nos mutamur": Interjú önmagammal 1995 végén* ("Et nos mutamur:" Interview with myself at the end of 1995) (Privately published, 1995), 19.
8. On Ordass's travels to Sweden see Ordass, *Önéletrajzi*, 1:62–71; see also László G. Terray, *He Could Not Do Otherwise: Bishop Lajos Ordass, 1901–1978*, trans. Eric W. Gritsch (Grand Rapids, Mich.: William B. Eerdmans Publishing Company, 1997): 23–37.

9. An English language biography of Bishop Berggrav, which includes an account of the Norwegian church struggle, is Edwin Robertson, *Bishop of the Resistance: The Life of Eivind Berggrav, Bishop of Oslo, Norway* (St. Louis, Mo.: Concordia Publishing House, 2000).
10. Ordass, *Önéletrajzi,* 1:137. Ordass's translation of Aulen's lecture is published in Ordass, *Válogatott,* 1:40–57.
11. Lajos Ordass, *Akikkel az Úton találkoztam* (Those I met along the way) (Budapest: Ordass Lajos Baráti Kör, 1996), 41.
12. Ordass, *Önéletrajzi,* 1:321.
13. Here my interpretation of Ordass's position differs, at least in emphasis, from that of Vajta in *Die diakonische Theologie,* 19–77.
14. László Scholz, "Egyházunk mai helyzete és lelkészi feladataink. Előterjesztés a magyarországi evangélikus lelkészek értekezletén Budapesten, 1956. december hó 13-án" (The present situation of our church and our pastoral work. Proposal to the meeting of Hungarian Lutheran pastors in Budapest, December 13, 1956), in Ordass, *Önéletrajzi,* 1:932–33.
15. *Evangélikus naptár az 1957. évre* (Lutheran calendar for the year 1957) (Budapest: Az evangélikus egyetemes sajtóosztály, 1957), 43.
16. István Botta, "Az egyház mai helyzetéről szóló előadáshoz hozzászólás" (Response to the lecture on the church's present situation), in the Ordass collection. Also reprinted in Ordass, *Önéletrajzi,* 2:545n42.

Chapter 4
1. MOL, ÁEH Elnöki 1958 7d 58.9–36/1958. "Javaslat az evangélikus egyházban a két egyházkerületes rendszer fenntartására" (Recommendation for the preservation of the two diocesan system in the Lutheran church).
2. For biographical information on Bishop Káldy, see J. V. Eibner, "Zoltán Káldy: A New Way For The Church In Socialism?" *Religion in Communist Lands* 13 (1985): 33–46.
3. See Káldy's comments at a seniors meeting October 9, 1956, as reported in "Az Országos Esperesi Értekezlet" (National seniors meeting), *Evangélikus Élet,* October 14, 1956.
4. See, for example, Zoltán Káldy, "Beszámoló az országos egyházi helyzetről" (Report on the national church situation), *Lelkipásztor* (April 1958): 229–41.
5. See "A Déli Egyházkerület Tanács elrendelte a püspökválasztást" (Southern Diocese's Council arranges new elections), *Evangélikus Élet,* September 7, 1958; "Káldy Zoltán a Déli Egyházkerület püspöke" (Zoltán Káldy bishop of the Southern Diocese), *Evangélikus Élet,* October 19, 1958; and "A Déli Evangélikus Egyházkerülete rendkívüli közgyulésén beiktatták hivatalába Káldy Zoltán püspököt" (Bishop Zoltán Káldy installed into his office at an exceptional general assembly of the Southern Lutheran Diocese), *Evangélikus Élet,* November 9, 1958.
6. Zoltán Káldy, "Hogyan menjünk tovább?" (How do we move forward?), *Evangélikus Élet,* July 26, 1958.
7. Margit Balogh and Jenő Gergely, *Egyházak az újkori Magyarországon 1790–1992: kronológia* (Churches in modern Hungary, 1790–1992: chronology) (Budapest: MTA Történettudományi Intézete, 1993), 326.
8. See Vilmos Vajta, *Die diakonische Theologie im Gesellschaftssystem Ungarns* (The theology of diaconia in the social system of Hungary) (Frankfurt am Main: Verlag Otto Lembeck, 1987), 12–19.
9. See Zoltán Káldy, "Vallomás az elmúlt 25 évről" (Confession about the last 25 years), *Lelkipásztor* (January 1984): 3.
10. See "Káldy Zoltán püspököt díszdoktorra avatják Pozsonyban" (Bishop Zoltán Káldy to receive honorary doctorate in Bratislava), *Evangélikus Élet,* June 21, 1964; "Díszdoktorra avatták Káldy Zoltán püspököt" (Bishop Zoltán Káldy

receives honorary doctorate), *Evangélikus Élet*, June 28, 1964; "Doktoravatás Pozsonyban" (Doctorate given in Bratislava), *Evangélikus Élet*, July 5, 1964; and "D. Káldy Zoltán püspök, a teológia díszdoktora" (Bishop D. Zoltán Káldy, honorary doctor of theology), *Evangélikus Élet*, July 12, 1964.

11. See "Az egyház életformája: diakónia" (The life-form of the church: diaconia), in Zoltán Káldy, *A diakónia útján* (On the way of diaconia) (Budapest: A Magyarországi Evangélikus Egyház Sajtóosztálya, 1979), 43–53, quotation on 45.
12. Káldy, *A diakónia útján*, 48, 52.
13. See "Az ötödik út" (The fifth way), in Káldy, *A diakónia útján*, 35–42.
14. My biographical sketch of Pál Zászkaliczky relies largely on Lajos Ordass, *Akikkel az Úton találkoztam* (Those I met along the way) (Budapest: Ordass Lajos Baráti Kör, 1996), 85–95.
15. See EOL, Déli Evangélikus Egyházkerület 77/1963 for a letter from Bishop Zoltán Káldy to the Fót congregation council (*egyházközségi tanács*) dated December 5, 1962.
16. The story of the "Zászkaliczky-affair" is related in Lajos Ordass, *Önéletrajzi írások* (Autobiographical writings), ed. István Szépfalusi (Bern: EPMSZ, 1987), 2: 983–98 (part of the appendix), quotation from 987.
17. Ibid., 987.
18. In this connection see *Fóti evangélikus gyülekezet irattára* 1/1963 (Records of the Fót Lutheran congregation), letter from Bishop Zoltán Káldy to Inspector János Kurucz and Caretaker (*gondnok*) József Mike, dated February 6, 1963; also, letter from Káldy to Kurucz and Mike, dated February 12, 1963.
19. See *Fóti evangélikus gyülekezet irattára* 1/1963, letter from Bishop Zoltán Káldy to the Fót presbytery, dated April 17, 1963; also, minutes (*jegyzőkönyv*) of the Fót general assembly session, May 5, 1963, and minutes of the Fót presbytery session, May 19, 1963. For more on the "Fót affair" see also the interviews with Imre Bohus and Zoltán Dóka in Mirák, *Nem voltam egyedül: Beszélgetések az evangélikus közelmúltról* (I was not alone: conversations about the recent Lutheran past), ed. Katalin Mirák (Budapest: Magyarországi Evangélikus Ifjúsági Szövetség, 1999), 2:25–35, 111–13.
20. Ordass, *Önéletrajzi*, 2:986.
21. EOL, Északi evangélikus egyházkerület (Northern Lutheran diocese) 81. doboz LMK 1970.
22. Ordass, *Önéletrajzi*, 2:918–19.
23. Ibid., 915.
24. Vajta's article, originally published in German, was republished twice in English. See Vilmos Vajta, "Umstrittene Theologie der Diakonia" (Controversial Theology of Diaconia), *Lutherische Monatschefte* 3 (1983): 45–60; Vilmos Vajta, "The Hungarian Lutheran Church and the 'Theology of Diaconia': Dispute over the 'Theology of Diaconia,' the Hungarian version of 'the Church in Socialist Society,'" *Religion in Communist Lands* 12 (1984): 130–48; Vilmos Vajta, "Debatable 'Theology of Diaconia:' Hungarian Example of 'The Church in Socialist Society,'" *Occasional Papers on Religion in Eastern Europe* 4, no. 1 (1984): 45–60.
25. "Hungarian church, critics trade charges," *Lutheran World Information*, release no. 8/84, February 23, 1984.
26. On Bishop Káldy's aggressive campaign for election, see "Leaders of Church and State in Hungary Speak on Church-State Relations in Their Country," *Religion in Communist Lands* 12 (1984): 209; see also *From Federation to Communion: The History of the Lutheran World Federation*, ed. Jens Holger Schjørring et. al. (Minneapolis: Fortress Press, 1997): 468–69.
27. "Hungarian church, critics trade charges," *Lutheran World Information*, release no. 8/84, February 23, 1984.

28. EOL, Püspöki körlevél (Bishops letter) D 150–7/1984., and Püspöki körlevél É 36/1984.
29. For a summary of events at the LWF's Seventh World Assembly, see Schjørring, *From Federation*, 401–11.
30. My biographical sketch of Zoltán Dóka relies on the interview with him in Mirák, *Nem voltam egyedül*, 2:94–148, and on personal conversations with Zoltán Dóka.
31. Dóka wrote his *Open Letter* in German. It was later translated and published in English twice. See "Hungarian Lutheran Controversy," *Religion in Communist Lands* 13 (1985): 99–103; also "Open Letter," *Occasional Papers on Religion in Eastern Europe* 5, no. 6 (1985): 18–24.
32. At one point in the *Open Letter*, Dóka said, "The LWF could render a great service to the HLC [Hungarian Lutheran Church] if it were to help bring about as soon as possible a free and brotherly dialogue within the HLC. . . . I ask all who read this letter that they should not regard it as an attack on the person of Bishop Káldy. Please understand this letter to be a cry for help from the pastors of the HLC." Quoted from "Hungarian Lutheran Controversy," 102.
33. László Terray, "Was the Reality Cut Out? Lutheran Held World Assembly in Budapest," *Occasional Papers in Religion in Eastern Europe* 5, no. 6 (1985): 10.
34. Statement by Bishop Káldy on July 27, 1984. Published in *Occasional Papers on Religion in Eastern Europe* 5, no. 6 (1985): 29, 30.
35. "Welcome to the Participants of the VIIth Assembly of the Lutheran World Federation!" *Evangélikus Élet*, July 22, 1984 (title in English, article in Hungarian).
36. "Nekifeszülve a jövőnek. Dr. Káldy Zoltán püspök igehirdetése a LVSZ megnyitó istentiszteletén" (Preparing for the future. Bishop Dr. Zoltán Káldy's sermon at the LWF's opening worship service), *Evangélikus Élet*, July 29, 1984.
37. Pál Redey, "A világgyűlés legizgalmasabb napja" (The World Assembly's most exciting day), *Evangélikus Élet*, August 12, 1984; also, Schjørring, *From Federation*, 409–11.
38. László Keveházi, "Megteológizalt árulás," *Evangélikus Élet*, September 2, 1984. Translated and published twice in English as part of "Hungarian Lutheran Controversy," *Religion in Communist Lands* 13 (1985): 103–4, and as "Betrayal with a Theological Twist," *Occasional Papers on Religion in Eastern Europe* 5, no. 6 (1985): 33–36.
39. Later, after the incident had passed,"Theologized Treason" and Dóka's response were translated and published in English language journals. The English language journal *Occasional Papers on Religion in Eastern Europe* devoted an entire issue to the "Dóka-affair" (vol. 5, no. 6 [1985]). *Religion in Communist Lands* also devoted special coverage to the incident ("Hungarian Lutheran Controversy," 98–106).

Excursus 4
1. Zoltán Káldy, *A diakónia útján* (On the way of diaconia) (Budapest: A Magyarországi Evangélikus Egyház Sajtóosztálya, 1979): 63.
2. Some readers may notice that my critique of the Theology of Diaconia draws upon Anglo-American discussions of *agape*—a theological and philosophical discussion about the relationships between equal regard, preferential regard, self-regard, altruism, and so on. The essential issues for this discussion were set out by Gene Outka, *Agape: An Ethical Analysis* (New Haven, Conn.: Yale University Press, 1972). My own reflections on Hungarian Lutheran diaconia were very much informed by having read Outka's book. Certain aspects of my analysis were also shaped by the arguments in Paul Ramsey, *Basic Christian Ethics* (1950; repr., Chicago: University of Chicago Press, 1978).
3. Káldy, *A diakónia útján*, 63–64.

4. For discussion of the question of a "blank check," see Outka, *Agape*, 21–24.
5. Káldy, *A diakónia útján*, 64–66.
6. The argument in this paragraph is Aristotelian in inspiration.
7. The detailed summary that follows is from Václav Havel, "The Power of the Powerless," in *The Power of the Powerless: Citizens against the State in Central-Eastern Europe*, ed. John Keane (1985; repr., Armonk, N.Y.: M. E. Sharpe Inc., 1990): 23–96, esp. 27–64.
8. Ibid., 28. Emphasis in the original.

Conclusion

1. My brief sketch of the end of socialism in Hungary relies on Rudolf L. Tőkés, *Hungary's Negotiated Revolution: Economic Reform, Social Change, and Political Succession* (Cambridge, U.K.: Cambridge University Press, 1996). See also Csaba Horváth, *Magyarország 1944-től napjainkig* (Hungary from 1944 to the present), 4th ed. (Pécs: PREZIDENT Betéti Társaság, 1993); *Magyarország története 1918–1990* (History of Hungary, 1918–1990), eds. Ferenc Pölöskei, Jenő Gergely, and Lajos Izsák (Budapest: Korona Kiadó, n.d.).
2. EOL, Országos Egyház 173/1988. Letter of the Hungarian Lutheran Presidium to the pastors of the church.
3. "Az Ordass Lajos Baráti Kör alapszabálya" (Charter of the Lajos Ordass Circle of Friends), *Keresztyén Igazság* 1–2 (June 1989): 61.
4. Zoltán Dóka, "Zsinat elé" (Before the synod), *Keresztyén Igazság* (June 1990): 44.
5. See "Beadvány az Országos Egyházi Bírósághoz püspökválasztás ügyében—Bírósági ítélet" (Petition to the National Church Court in the matter of the bishop election—Court judgment), *Keresztyén Igazság* 6 (June 1990): 13–16.
6. "Beadvány az esperesi értekezlethez—és válaszok" (Petition to the seniors conference—and answers), *Keresztyén Igazság* 6 (June 1990): 17–20.
7. Lajos Ordass, *Önéletrajzi írások* (Autobiographical writings), ed. István Szépfalusi (Bern: EPMSZ, 1985), 1:330.

Lajos Ordass as a young man, undated photograph.
Courtesy of the National Museum of the Lutheran Church in Hungary.
Bishop László Dezséry, undated photograph.
Courtesy of the Evangelical-Lutheran Theological University, Hungary.

Bishop Zoltán Túróczy (center) prior to signing the church-state agreement on December 14, 1948. On the left is Zoltán Mády, general inspector-surrogate for the Lutheran Church; on the right is Gyula Ortutay, minister of culture.
Courtesy of the National Archives of the Lutheran Church in Hungary.

Pastor Imre Veöreös, undated photograph.
Courtesy of Péter Zászkaliczky.

Front row, left to right, Bishop Lajos Vető, Bishop Jozsef Szabó, General Inspector Iván Reök, Bishop Zoltán Túróczy, Bishop László Dezséry, 1952.
Courtesy of Péter Zászkaliczky.

Bishop Zoltán Káldy, undated photograph.
Courtesy of the National Museum of the Lutheran Church in Hungary.

The Lutheran church at Déak tér, Budapest, 2004.
Courtesy of Péter Zászkaliczky.

Bibliographic Essay

Hungarian is unrelated to almost every other language on earth. Most Europeans, even the Russians, speak in Indo-European tongues, but Hungarians speak Magyar, which is Finno-Ugric. Magyar is closely related to the language of a few tribal peoples east of the Ural Mountains and distantly related to Finnish and Estonian. It is difficult for foreigners to learn, and its uniqueness contributes to Hungary's relative obscurity even in Europe. If learning one Slavic language quickly leads to the next, and familiarity with one Romance language helps with another, Hungarian must be studied for its own sake—a fact that has tended to mean that good scholarly books on Hungary accessible to non-Hungarians are few and far between.

In writing the present book, I have relied almost exclusively on Hungarian sources. They are not listed in a separate bibliography, however, because I assume most of my readers cannot read Hungarian and would not benefit from such a bibliography. Those who are interested may consult the endnotes, where they will find full citations for all Hungarian sources. Here I intend only to describe the kinds of Hungarian material used in my research, as that information is both relevant to an academic evaluation of the book and accessible to English speakers.

Although I was working with historical material, my primary research objective was always to discern the kinds of theological responses to communism found in Hungary's Lutheran Church. The most straightforward way to do this, I believed, was to look for theological arguments in published materials. Those materials can be divided into three groups: newspaper and journal articles from the period, published memoirs and interviews by and with participants in the history, and secondary sources about the period.

The newspaper and journal I relied on most were *Evangélikus Élet*, the official weekly paper of the Lutheran Church in Hungary, and *Lelkipásztor*, a monthly journal intended primarily for ministers. In working with these sources, the greatest difficulty I encountered was that the articles in them have not been catalogued. This meant the only way to search for articles relevant to my theme was to flip through the pages one by one. Since the number of pages published in these periodicals between 1947 (when the Lutheran presses first started working after the war) and 1989 runs in the hundreds of thousands, I had to find a way to select which parts to read. For the early years, when events were happening very quickly, say between 1947 and 1953, I looked at nearly every page of *Evangélikus Élet*. After that I limited myself to key moments or key years. Thus I worked through most of *Evangélikus Élet* for 1956 through 1958 but was fairly selective for the years 1954 and 1955. Thankfully, each issue of *Lelkipásztor* comes with a table of contents, so although I have read a good many of the table of contents from that journal, I have been more selective with the articles. The period from 1958 through 1989 was the Káldy era, a time of relative stability. For that period I have relied more on books, collections of sermons and essays, and so on, and less on newspapers and journal articles, looking through the latter only at key moments when the Theology of Diaconia seemed to be undergoing development.

I also relied on memoirs, interviews, and published collections of archival documents. More and more of these have been appearing since the fall of communism. However, the most important among them remains Bishop Ordass's lengthy and detailed *Önéletrajzi írások* (Autobiographical writings). Ordass's memoirs are at times quite moving and can rightly be placed alongside twentieth-century Christian classics such as Bonhoeffer's *Letters and Papers from Prison*. They are valuable, also, because of the wealth of information found in Ordass's account and because the editor, István Szépfalusi, provided extensive annotation, which includes the texts of valuable newspaper articles, private recollections of events written by various pastors, and similar items. Regretfully, Ordass's memoirs have never been translated out of Hungarian.

I also conducted personal interviews with figures from the history who were alive at the time I was doing the research. These deepened my understanding of the history, although usually they did not exert a decisive influence on my interpretation of events. The one notable exception was my encounter with Imre Veöreös, with whom I had numerous conversations and extended correspondence before his death in 1999. Had Imre Veöreös not been alive, or had he been unwilling to talk to me, it is unlikely I would have come to appreciate the strategy of *ahogy lehet* the way that I have or recognize its deep continuities with Hungarian history.

As concerns secondary literature, the reader should be aware of two English language periodicals, *Religion, State, and Society* (formerly *Religion in Communist Lands*) and *Religion in Eastern Europe* (formerly *Occasional Papers on Religion in Eastern Europe*), which specialize in religion in Central and Eastern Europe and have sometimes published articles on Hungary. The truth is, however, that very few secondary studies exist on the Lutheran Church in Hungary under communism, even in Hungarian. Under communism this little Lutheran Church had trouble sustaining serious scholarship, and the effects of that legacy continue to be felt today. The only book, apart from the present one, to deal exclusively with the history of the Lutheran Church in Hungary under communism is Ernő Ottlyk's *Az evangélikus egyház útja a szocializmusban* (The path of the Lutheran church in socialism) (Budapest: A Magyarországi Evangélikus Egyház Sajtóosztálya, 1976), which can be found in both English and German editions. Published in the communist era, however, this book is so ideologically bloated that one suspects it must have been an embarrassment to its author already at the time it was written. Even taking into account the left-wing bias, its presentation of the facts is highly selective and inadequate.

Only now, since the fall of communism, has lively academic investigation in this Lutheran Church, once characterized by the disproportionate number of intellectuals in its membership, started to return. Only now, with the new possibilities that come with freedom, have serious and committed individuals, often lacking the kinds of educational credentials that ensure others will take them seriously, started to sift through the ruins to piece together exactly what happened. They are true pioneers in what is an imposing and unexplored wilderness, and they are a powerful lesson in the fact that scholarship is a collective enterprise. If every generation builds on the insights and accomplishments of the past, these individuals are starting mostly from scratch, and the significance of their work, even if at times it is imperfect, should not be underestimated. I have tried to acknowledge them in my endnotes when appropriate.

The general dearth of scholarship on my topic meant that I was driven at times to engage in historical research—something in which I have no special competence—merely to put together the foundation from which to launch my theological-ethical speculations. My justification for encroaching on the historian's terrain this way is simply that it had to be done. When confronted with relevant questions that could not be answered through my work in the published material, I turned to archives. Most frequently I went to the National Lutheran Archives (Evangélikus Országos Levéltár) in Budapest. On a couple of occasions I worked in the National Hungarian Archives (Magyar Országos Levéltár) also in Budapest, once to look through early documents of the Hungarian Communist Party and the Social Democratic Party, and once to look through material from the State Office of Church Affairs (Állami Egyházügyi Hivatal) from 1956 through 1958. In connection with 1956, I also used materials from the archives of the Ordass Foundation in Oslo, Norway. The material held by the Ordass Foundation has since been transferred to the National Hungarian Archives in Budapest. I never looked at archival material from the Ministry of the Interior (Belügyminisztérium), although since the writing of this book, others have begun that delicate work, and not surprisingly, if still sadly, they are making uncomfortable discoveries about the secret lives of people in the church.

Lastly, I should add that I spent nearly three years in Hungary conducting the research necessary to write this book. Indisputably, the experiences arising from that extended visit profoundly, although intangibly, shaped the contours of my work. Working at the seminary, attending church, talking to people, students, and teachers, simply getting a sense of life in Hungary, were all essential elements of my research. The student of the church in communism is forced to work primarily with a record left by the official church, that is, the statements of bishops and the points of view expressed in the church press. Those official stances, however, were always the counterpoint to everyday happenings in the church, happenings that, because there was not freedom, often went unrecorded. One cannot understand the official history of this period without understanding the unofficial subtext. My encounters with Hungarians, who lived through this past and are still struggling with its legacy, gave me a glimpse of that hidden terrain. Listening to them, getting a sense of their perceptions, their hopes and disappointments, helped me to acquire at least some sense of the reality behind the history I have considered.

Below I list a few sources that may interest readers who would like to pursue further the topics treated in this book.

Hungarian History

Lendvai, Paul. *The Hungarians: A Thousand Years of Victory in Defeat.* Translated by Ann Major. Princeton, N.J.: Princeton University Press, 2003. This is a recent and comprehensive survey of Hungarian history, written with humor and zest. It is the best source for English speakers who want to learn the basic contours of Hungarian history.

Macartney, C. A. *Hungary: A Short History.* Edinburgh: Edinburgh University Press, 1962. Macartney is an older, well-respected, and frequently cited English-speaking scholar of Hungarian history. A good resource, it is probably difficult to find.

Sakmyster, Thomas. *Hungary's Admiral on Horseback: Miklós Horthy, 1918–1944.* Boulder: East European Monographs, 1994. This is a well-balanced, nicely written account of Horthy and Horthy's Hungary.

Tőkés, Rudolf L. *Hungary's Negotiated Revolution: Economic Reform, Social Change, and Political Succession.* Cambridge, U.K.: Cambridge University

Press, 1996. This is a detailed discussion of the Kádár era (Hungary from 1956 until the end of communism) written from the perspective of a political scientist. This book is excellent but may offer more detail than readers with primary interests in religion will need.

Walters, E. Garrison. *The Other Europe: Eastern Europe to 1945*. Syracuse, N.Y.: 1988. New York: Dorset Press, 1990. A good general resource, it offers an overview of Central and Eastern European history including useful discussions of Hungary.

Religion and the Lutheran Church in Hungary

Fabiny, Tibor. *Hope Preserved: The Past and Present of Hungarian Lutheranism*. Translated by Miklós Uszkay. Budapest: n.p., 1984. Written in preparation for the 1984 World Assembly of the Lutheran World Federation held in Budapest, this book is intended for an audience unfamiliar with the Lutheran Church in Hungary and thus provides a helpful, if brief, overview of that church's history. Of course, the book was written in the communist period, during the height of Bishop Káldy's career, and these factors affect its content. The author's discussion of the communist period is quite delicate and not too useful anymore. The book also exists in a German edition (*Bewährte Hoffnung: Die Evangelisch-Lutherische Kirche Ungarns in vier Jahrhunderten*. Erlangen: Martin Luther Verlag, 1984).

Pungur, Joseph. *The Churches in Communist Hungary 1948–1990*. Lectures and Papers in Hungarian Studies, no. 9. Calgary: Hungarian Studies Association of Canada, 1994. Originally delivered as a conference paper and then published in booklet form, this lengthy essay provides a helpful overview of the religious landscape in Hungary.

Ramet, Sabrina P. *Protestantism and Politics in Eastern Europe and Russia: The Communist and Post-Communist Eras*. Christianity Under Stress Series, vol. 3. Durham: Duke University Press, 1992. Professor Ramet has compiled and edited numerous books that deal with religion in Central and Eastern Europe. This book contains a chapter by Joseph Pungur titled "Protestantism in Hungary: The Communist Era."

Ramet, Pedro, ed. *Religion and Nationalism in Soviet and East European Politics*. Duke Press Policy Studies. Durham: Duke University Press, 1989. This book contains a chapter on Hungary by Leslie László titled "Religion and Nationality in Hungary."

Schjørring, Jens Holger, Prasanna Kumari, and Norman A. Hjelm, eds. *From Federation to Communion: The History of the Lutheran World Federation*. Minneapolis: Fortress Press, 1997. As the title suggests, this book is about the Lutheran World Federation. However, it contains brief discussions of both Bishop Ordass and Bishop Káldy, as both these men were important figures in the LWF.

Terray, László G. *He Could Not Do Otherwise: Bishop Lajos Ordass, 1901–1978.* Translated from the German by Eric W. Gritsch. Grand Rapids, Mich.: William B. Eerdmans Publishing Co, 1997. This short, readable biography of Bishop Ordass is quite subtle. Anyone interested in learning more about the Lutheran Church in Hungary during communism should read it.

Vajta, Vilmos. *Die diakonische Theologie im Gesellschaftssystem Ungarns* (The "theology of diaconia" in the social system of Hungary). Frankfurt am Main: Verlag Otto Lembeck, 1987. Vajta was a Hungarian Lutheran pastor studying in Sweden in the late 1940s. After the communists seized power in Hungary, Vajta sought asylum abroad and later rose to prominence in Europe as a Lutheran theologian. This book contains an extended critique of the Theology of Diaconia. It was published, interestingly enough, two years after Dóka's *Open Letter*, and it develops criticisms of the Theology of Diaconia along lines similar to those suggested by Dóka (although Vajta's critique is more considered and careful). Dóka once told me in personal conversation that he had shown a draft of the *Open Letter* to someone in Western Europe, but for reasons of confidentiality he would not tell me who. One wonders if the person might not have been Vajta, and more generally, whether the content of the *Open Letter* was influenced by conversations Dóka had with Vajta while the former was studying in Western Europe. All of this, I hasten to add, is pure speculation on my part. Vajta died in 1998, Dóka in 2000.

Appendix: Karl Barth and Hungary

Readers with theological interests, if they know anything about Hungary, probably know something about Karl Barth's visit to Hungary in 1948. That visit did not significantly influence events in the Lutheran Church, but the episode is so well known that I include a few words about it here.

Karl Barth, the great Swiss theologian, had played an important role in the early stages of the church struggle in Nazi Germany. Later, Barth argued that the Third Reich represented a unique kind of anti-state, one that made theological claims Christians were obliged to reject. For this reason, Barth argued, Christians had a positive duty to support the war against Hitler. After the Second World War, however, Barth refused to view communism the same way he had viewed Nazism, arguing that Christians could live with integrity under a communist state.

In the early spring of 1948, toward the end of what Hungarians later came to call the "year of the turn," Barth traveled throughout Hungary as a guest of the Reformed Church. He had visited Hungary before, in the conservative Horthy period, and as a man of liberal sympathies, Barth must have been impressed with how liberal Hungary's Reformed Church had suddenly become. Shortly after returning to Switzerland, Barth was approached by a man named János Péter, who asked Barth to write a letter to the Hungarian Reformed Church expressing support for the candidacy of Albert Bereczky for bishop. Péter was a Reformed pastor who would later leave the church to join Hungary's Central Committee and serve as Hungary's foreign minister. Bereczky was a Reformed pastor with roots in the evangelical tradition who had played an important role at the National Hungarian Reformed Free Council held at Nyíregyháza, and the communists wanted him to be the next bishop. Barth obliged Péter's request, penning an open letter to his "friends in the Reformed Church in Hungary."

Barth's attitude toward Hungary elicited criticism from another Swiss theologian, Emil Brunner, who argued that Barth was wrong to view Nazism and communism differently. Both were forms of totalitarianism, Brunner argued, and therefore fundamentally unjust. Barth told Brunner, "You do not seem to understand"; communism did not represent the kind of godlessness that Nazism did, because communism at least responded to a genuine social problem. On one occasion Barth even managed to say, "It would be quite absurd to mention in the same breath the philosophy of Marxism and the 'ideology' of the Third Reich, to mention a man of the stature of Joseph Stalin in the same breath as such charlatans as Hitler, Göring, Hess, Goebbels, Himmler, Ribbentrop, Rosenberg, Streicher, etc." (Both quotations are from Barth's book *Against the Stream*, 113, 139).

Whether or not, within the framework of his own thought, Barth was inconsistent in distinguishing between Nazism and communism, I will not venture to say. I am confident in asserting, however, that Barth was egregiously ignorant of the situation in Hungary. In the Stalinist era, Hungarian communists demanded exactly the kind of far-reaching theological affirmations of the state that Barth had objected to in the Third Reich. Those kinds of affirmations were the essence of theological collaboration as I have described it. The Hungarian Reformed Church, after receiving an open endorsement from the great Karl Barth, enjoyed the dubious distinction of being the first church in Hungary to collaborate. Later, Barth himself seems to have had some reservations, which he expressed in a long letter to Bishop Albert Bereczky in 1951. That letter was published in 1984 as part of Barth's collected works. I do not know when it was first made public; I have found a reference to it as early as 1960. In any case, Barth's second letter never received the same level of attention as the 1948 letter, and Barth himself, to the best of my knowledge, never acknowledged serious mistakes in his early perceptions of the Hungarian situation.

Below I list a few works helpful for readers interested in Barth's relationship to Hungary.

Barth, Karl. *Against the Stream: Shorter Post-War Writings, 1946–52.* Translated by Mrs. E. M. Delacour and Stanley Godman. London: SCM Press Ltd., 1954. Barth's book contains a collection of documents connected with his 1948 visit to Hungary, including the open letter and important essays by Barth on the proper Christian attitude toward the state. It does not contain the second letter Barth wrote to Bishop Bereczky, although the book was published three years after Barth wrote that letter.

Barth, Karl. *Offene Briefe, 1945–1968.* Vol. 5, *Gesamtausgabe.* Edited by Diether Koch. Zürich: Theologischer Verlag, 1984. This book, in German, contains Barth's 1948 open letter to the Hungarian Reformed Church and his 1951 letter to Bishop Bereczky.

Gombos, Gyula. *The Lean Years: A Study of Hungarian Calvinism in Crisis.* New York: The Kossuth Foundation Inc., 1960. Written in English by a Hungarian émigré to the United States, this book is excellent. It provides information about the Reformed Church in Hungary in the early communist years not accessible in English anywhere else.

West, Charles C. *Communism and the Theologians: A Study of an Encounter.* New York: The Macmillan Company, 1958. An older book, once frequently cited, it is now mostly forgotten but very good. It includes an extensive discussion of Barth's attitude toward communism as well as some discussion of the situation in Hungary.

Index

ÁEH. *See* State Office of Church Affairs
ahogy lehet, 27, 33–38, 46–51, 61, 76, 87–89, 110, 118, 120, 126–32
Augsburg Confession, 30, 127–28

Barth, Karl, 156–57
Berggrav, Eivind. *See* Ordass, Lajos
Bibó, István, 49–50
Botta, István, 41, 87

Catholic Church. *See* Roman Catholic Church
church autonomy. *See* freedom of the church
church schools: in Horthy era, 11–12, 31; nationalization of, 19, 20–25, 28–30, 44, 50, 54, 79, 84, 100; reopening of, 124–25
church-state agreement with the Lutheran Church, 67, 69, 72, 81, 125; negotiation of, 18–20, 24, 37, 50–51
churchly movement, Lutheran, 12, 13, 64
confessionalism, Lutheran. *See* churchly movement, Lutheran

Darvas, József, 42–43, 66, 75, 94
Diaconia, Theology of, 96–100, 105–108, 110–11, 117, 121–22, 128
Dezséry, László, 40–47, 60, 63–66, 75, 92, 96, 129; open letter of, 40–41, 55–57
Dóka, Zoltán, 106–109, 125

evangelical movement: 101; and 1956 pastors' conferences, 64; and collaboration type, 50, 51, 53, 56; and compromise type, 32–33; and Horthy era, 12–13; and Káldy, 93
evangelization. *See* evangelical movement

fifth church way. *See* Káldy, Zoltán
Fót affair. *See* Káldy, Zoltán

Free Council. *See* Reformed Free Council
freedom of the church, 69–70, 72, 78, 79–81
Frenkl, Róbert, 125
Fry, Franklin Clark, 63

Grnák, Károly, 70, 72, 74

Havel, Václav, 118–21
Horthy era, 10–11: place of churches in, 11–14, 97; theological assessment of, 52–53, 56–57, 99
Horthy, Miklós. *See* Horthy era
Horváth, János, 63, 65–67, 69–75, 80–81, 94

ideal-types: as methodology, 5–6; as responses to communism, 27, 46, 76, 85, 110, 126–29

Kádár, János, 62, 91–92, 123
Káldy, Zoltán: 124–25; and diaconia type, 110–18, 121–22, 128–29; and Dóka's open letter, 108–109; early life, 92–94; and the fifth church way, 95–96, 98–99; and Fót affair, 100–103; and LWF presidency, 105–109; and Ordass, 92–93, 95, 103–104, 108, 110–11, 114, 116, 121; on a suffering church, 94–95, 116–17; and Theology of Diaconia, 96–100, 121–22
Kapi, Béla, 14, 17–18, 19, 21, 41
Keken, András, 23, 42–43, 64
Kemény, Lajos, 43
Kendeh, György, 42–43
Kun, Béla, 10
kuruc. *See* labanc-kuruc

labanc-kuruc, 36, 88–89
Lilje, Hanns, 63
Lund-Quist, Carl E., 63

Luther, Martin, 54, 80
Lutheran World Federation, 23, 60, 63, 69–70; Seventh World Assembly of, 105–108

martyr church. *See* suffering church
Mau, Carl, 105
Mihálfyi, Ernő, 17, 19, 20, 44, 66, 70–71, 94
Mindszenty, József, 22
mozgástér, 91–92, 94–96, 108–109

Nagy, Gyula, 106, 125
Nagy, Imre, 62–63
Nagybocskai, Vilmos, 74
Niebuhr, H. Richard, 4

open letter. *See* Dóka, Zoltán *and* Dezséry, László
Ordass, Lajos: 6, 40–41, 59, 105, 125; arrest and imprisonment, 23–26; and Berggrav, 83–84; and church-state negotiations (1948), 18–20; Circle of Friends ("Baráti Kör"), 125–26; conviction by church court, 42–43; deontology of, 77–79, 81–82; early life, 14–16; and freedom of the church, 79–81; and Káldy, 92–93, 95, 103–104, 108, 110–11, 114, 116, 121; memoirs, 103–104; on nationalization of schools, 20–22, 80, 84; rehabilitation of, 63–65; on Reök, 47–48; on resignation of bishops, 17, 24, 77–78; second bishopric, 65–75; on suffering church, 73–74, 130–31; and Túróczy, 20, 25–26, 50, 88 130; and witness type, 76, 85–86, 88–90, 129–32; and Zászkaliczky, 100–102
Ortutay, Gyula, 19
Ottlyk, Ernő, 104, 106

parochial education. *See* church schools
pastors' conferences (1956), 64–65, 68, 87, 130
peace work, 59–61, 69, 80, 95
pietism. *See* evangelical movement

Quisling, Vidkun, 83

Radvánszky, Albert, 14, 23, 24
Raffay, Sándor, 15
Rákosi, Mátyás, 16, 39, 62; and Dezséry, 41, 43; and Ordass, 25; with Reok and Turoczy, 18–20, 50, 58

reaction, 17, 20, 73, 75, 92, 101; as a theological concept, 51, 53–57, 127
Reformed Church, 11, 51–52, 66, 97
Reformed Free Council, 52–53, 56
Reményik, Sándor, 33
Reök, Iván, 18–19, 22, 42–43, 44–45, 129: role in collaboration type, 46–48, 50, 58
Roman Catholic Church, 11, 22, 66

Scholz, László, 85–86
State Office of Church Affairs, 44–45, 63, 65–67, 96, 124, 125
suffering church, 65, 68, 73–74, 85–90, 94, 104, 115–17, 130–32
synod, general church, 20, 23, 24, 43–44
Szabó, József, 17, 19, 20–21, 24, 32, 44, 125
Szebik, Imre, 125

Terray, László, 105
Túróczy, Zoltán: 78, 93; as bishop after the Revolution, 66–67, 69–71, 75; and collaboration type, 46, 48, 50–51, 53, 56; and compromise type, 27, 30–33, 37–38; and Dunántúl diocese, 41–42; early life of, 14–16; group, 20–21, 27–28, 30–31, 35, 37, 50, 55–56, 78, 95; and Ordass, 20, 25–26, 50, 88, 130; people's court conviction, 16–17, 19, 22; resignation of, 44; and Reök, 18–20, 50; and school nationalization, 20–21, 23–24, 54–55

Vajta, Vilmos, 79, 105
Vargha, Sándor, 23–24
Veöreös, Imre: in 1958, 70; and collaboration type, 46, 48, 50–51, 53–54, 56; and compromise type, 27–33, 37–38; and school nationalization, 21, 28–30
Vető, Lajos, 41–42, 44–46, 93; after the Revolution, 66, 69–71, 73–74, 96
Visser't Hooft, Willem A., 63

Wolf, Lajos. *See* Ordass, Lajos
World Council of Churches, 23, 63, 97

year of the turn, 16–17, 39, 47, 130

Zászkaliczky, Pál, Jr., 101–102
Zászkaliczky, Pál, Sr., 100–101
Zászkaliczky, Pétér, 102

www.ingramcontent.com/pod-product-compliance
Lightning Source LLC
Chambersburg PA
CBHW030325080526
44584CB00012B/714